WALKING INTO IT

WALKING INTO IT

A PILGRIMAGE THROUGH FOREIGN
LANDS TO INNER WORLDS

BORGHILD BØ

By the same author

Fire of Creation: Painting Visions of Energy

Walking Into It: A Pilgrimage through Foreign Lands to Inner Worlds
Copyright © 2015 Borghild Bø
Nordic Mandala Press
www.borghildbo.com

All rights reserved. No part of this book may be reproduced or transmitted in any form or by any means, electronic or mechanical, including photocopying, recording or by any information storage and retrieval system, without permission in writing from the author.

First Edition 2015
ISBN-13: 978-8293244011
ISBN-10: 8293244011

Photography © Borghild Bø
All artwork © Borghild Bø

Cover design: Mat Thorne
Cover & book photography: Borghild Bø
Author photography: Christin Eide
Art photography: Tor Helge Øygarden
Back cover photographs: Trolltunga, Norway, by author's friend
Peruvian Andes, Apu Salcantay, by author's guide
Introduction: Ulriken, Bergen, Norway, by author's sister

Foreword: George Burns

Editing: Penney Peirce
Proofreading: Perry Iles
Typesetting & Design: Damonza

TABLE OF CONTENTS

What People Are Saying ix

Acknowledgments. xv

Foreword xvii

A Message from the Author. xxi

Introduction. xxvii

Part 1: El Camino de Santiago de Compostela, Northern Spain 1

Part 2: Six Days in the Mountains and Valleys of Leh in Ladakh, Northern India. 19

Part 3: The 21-Day Sacred Walk: The Himalayan Kingdom of Ladakh and Zanskar 81

Afterword. 241

Ganesha 245

Appendix 1. 247

Appendix 2. 271

Appendix 3. 275

About the Author 277

Other Books and Offerings from Borghild Bø. 279

Sacred Journeys with Borghild Bø. 281

Speaking, Teaching, Counselling and Consulting 283

WHAT PEOPLE ARE SAYING

"Borghild's story inspires us to take a walk into discovering our mystical, true nature. Her poetic account of her external travels is a luminescent reflection of her inner adventurer. Her gift of 'seeing' the sacred in the ordinariness of life is beautifully expressed in her images, which take us on our own journey home. In this world of external success and strivings, Borghild acts as a guide to reconnect to the sacred feminine and the wisdom of Mother Earth."

B. RAVEN LEE, PhD, Transpersonal Psychotherapist, Meditation Teacher, and fellow in Clinical Hypnotherapy

"Borghild is a life adventurer. She loves to travel. She loves to photograph. She loves nature. But she is no ordinary traveller. On her journeys she brings her intuition and divine connection into her experiences. She allows herself to be led to those areas of the world that reveal the true nature of our lives. Her connection to nature and consciousness is truly unique.

So take a walk with Borghild and experience the world through her pictures and writings so that you may have a tremendous adventure and come to an expanded awareness of who you are, of what the universe is, and how you fit into this wonderful cosmic world."

RITA FEILD, LCSW

"Borghild's story is so interesting! Here is a professional person who began with a strong left-brain emphasis and used it to open a right-brain, intuitive, mystical vision. She found the courage to travel into the unknown, remaining loyal to the process in a moment-by-moment experience. You can do the same, using the methods she provides, whether you hike up mountains or live a regular life without dramatic adventure. This book is inspiring—it literally breathes spirit into ordinary physical life."

PENNEY PEIRCE, Intuition Expert and Author of *Leap of Perception, Frequency*, and *The Intuitive Way*

"Borghild's journey is an inspiration to all those seeking to reconnect with their inner selves through the exploration of their surroundings. A long walk through a natural landscape of mountains, mystical legends and ancient symbolism brings us to examine our own lives in a new and very different light."

PERRY ILES, Literary Consultant and Editor

"In the Himalayas, the souls of deities call yogis and yoginis to celebrate alongside them. In the modern world it is rare to find someone with enough wisdom and empathy to open themselves to nature's manifestations, but Borghild is such a person; she has the sort of personality that is intuitively attracted to natural phenomena. She has a special way of seeing nature, of listening to its melody, of feeling its divine touch on her skin and inhaling its unique fragrance. This book inspires us to explore nature; to go inside its world and discover our own supreme consciousness and divinity."

DR. VAGISH SHASTRI, Professor of Sanskrit & Tantric Kundalini Master

"We are all on a journey, a metaphorical or literal trip across this amazing world. Borghild's journey is profound; an experience that explores Mother Nature and uses it to produce a wonderfully introspective analysis of her most personal thoughts and emotions. She demonstrates amazing courage and fortitude as she scales steep mountains and reflects on the deepest questions we can ask ourselves. If you are curious about introspection or trekking across unique parts of our Earth, Borghild offers an eloquent and beautiful guide that will stimulate and reward you in many ways."

JOHN RYDER, Ph.D. Psychologist, Author of *Positive Directions*

To my

Mother — Else Margrethe
&
Father — Helge

To Silje and all beings on their journey of heart

ACKNOWLEDGMENTS

My infinite gratitude to Mother Nature and the mountains in the Himalayas of India and Nepal, the Andes of Peru and in my home country of Norway—which continue to inspire me.

With heartfelt thanks and love to my family: my mother, Else Margrethe; my brothers and sisters—Evelyn, Jarle, Signe, Ingvill, Magnar, Helge and Øystein; my nieces and nephews and all their children; and especially my father, Helge and grandmother, Borghild.

My deepest gratitude to venerable *Guruji*, Dr. Vagish Shastri, who taught me *kundalini* yoga meditation, which opened the doors of wisdom and allowed the poetic flow of my writing express itself freely, furthered the understanding of my connection with nature and my visionary experiences that became real in the Himalayan mountains.

I wish to express gratitude and appreciation to Penney Peirce for invaluable and expedient help with the overall structure and editing in the final stage of this book; Perry Iles for his excellent proofreading skills and final touches. My heartfelt thanks go to: Diana Collis who was my mentor during the process of rewriting; Melissa Breau for editing the initial draft; my dear friends Rita Feild and Elles Louis for reading and giving feedback on the initial draft; Cindie Cohagan for helping me understand the publishing process.

I'd like to thank Mat Thorne for helping with the cover and map design, and Alisha at Damonza for the interior layout, and design.

Also a big thank-you to friends, relatives and passers-by who took pictures of me in various far-flung and exotic locations!

FOREWORD

Borghild Bø takes you from the heights of the Himalayas to the depths of the soul.

When you step from your door to start a journey—whether it be to the shops, to work or to the furthest reaches of the planet, who knows where it may lead you or more importantly, what you may discover along the way? While addressing a group of colleagues about some of my travel experiences and volunteer work in so-called 'developing' countries, I was asked, 'Why do you go to these countries with their poverty, lack of hygiene, remoteness and different cultures?' I found myself replying, 'Because they *are* different.' We are raised according to the myopic views and attitudes of our own culture. We unquestioningly accept what we have been taught for generation upon generation about the world, about others—and about ourselves. Stepping out of those shackles to see the ways others view themselves and their environment forces us to question our own worldviews, beliefs, practices and self-image. Freed from outer familiarities, we are free to explore our own fertile imaginations.

In this age of readily available air transport, packaged tight-scheduled tours, and a greed to tick off must-see tourist destinations, many of us travel. Few, however, take the time—or even have the desire—to take the most important journey of all: The journey within. Even fewer have the ability to describe those inner journeys of self-discovery. And fewer still are able to do so with the clarity, insight, and perceptiveness of Borghild Bø. Generously, personally, and intimately she shares her experiences of journeys we may never engage in ourselves…but hopefully will.

George W Burns
Perth, Western Australia, November 2014
Adjunct Professor of Psychology, Cairnmillar Institute, Melbourne
Clinical Psychologist and Therapist Trainer
Author of seven books, including *Happiness, Healing, Enhancement*

Child of the stars, women of the earth—
Boundaries are not your burden to bear
But horizons are yours to kiss.

—Pepper Lewis

A MESSAGE FROM THE AUTHOR

Nature tells me that every moment is an opportunity to transform—for the better; that we ought to love, respect, honour and celebrate this life and also be willing to share our joy, love, insights and revelations. That way we can all be free to reach the summit of nirvana—the ultimate reality of an enlightened state of mind.

I wrote this book as a result of unforgettable and life-changing experiences while on a trekking adventure in the Himalayas. It is a deeply personal story about what can happen when a woman intuitively and courageously follows her spiritual calling and connects intimately with nature.

If you have been attracted to this book, you may feel that something is missing from your life. You know there is something more just around the corner, but you can't find it—and this may make you feel restless and unsatisfied. Both restlessness and dissatisfaction can catalyse the search for *that thing*.

The overall intention of sharing my sacred journey of transformation and revelation —which is at the heart of this book—has been to inspire others to make the 'journey of heart' and to connect more deeply with nature and reality in a new way.

Over the following pages I share visions and epiphanies that explain how the divine consciousness of Mother Nature subtly revealed itself in my life. You will see how I discovered a new reality through an intuitive process of self-reflection, which I encourage you to try as well. You will also witness how I walked from a physical reality into a non-physical energy dimension.

The beginning of my physical journey was not truly the start of my spiritual one. The longing of my inner self had been whispering in my ear long before I chose to listen. Starting in 2007 I made journeys across 13 countries. I was looking for something, even though I was not consciously aware of what that thing was. Although I had been given glimpses of the connection to my inner self, I remained unconvinced that it was truly real.

It was not until I followed the inner calling that led me to this particular three month long physical journey that I started to truly believe, by seeing and experiencing powerful visions mirrored by nature's outer landscape. I saw these visions most often in mountain rock formations and rivers, in the trees and the sky.

The beginning of this journey of revelation was marked by the Camino de Santiago pilgrimage and continues to northern India. This adventure is divided into three parts and covers the following journeys:

Part 1:

Twenty-nine days walking the Camino de Santiago de Compostela, from the Pyrenees in France through northern Spain to Santiago.

Part 2:

Six days in the mountains and valleys of Leh in Ladakh, the northern Indian state of Jammu & Kashmir.

Part 3:

The 21-day sacred walk across the Himalayan kingdom of Ladakh & Zanskar, from Lamayuru in Jammu & Kashmir to Darcha, in the northern Indian state of Himachal Pradesh.

As we prepare to begin, I offer the following alignment prayers.

A Prayer for Reaching a New Level of Consciousness

'With every breath, we create the space to walk—to connect, to focus, to see beyond—to trust the unknown and to just flow with the present and be who we are.

'With every breath of pure awareness, we smell the fragrance of nature's beauty and can receive every moment as clear, light and fresh.

'With the courage to walk the path of truth, we find new experiences in every moment.

'With every diligent step we take in gratitude and devotion for our divine will, we awaken, purify, heal and ultimately become free from the mind's obstacles and limitations.

'May we walk in unity of mind and heart and embrace everything we encounter in everyday life with the transformational power of universal love.

'May we all walk together, interconnected in our own way, on the path to freedom.'

A Prayer for Auspiciousness on Your Journey to the Heart of Nature

When there is something I don't know I pray, meditate, reflect and let it go. I whisper a prayer to the divine will of supreme consciousness.

'OM…you know everything beyond my limited mind.
Please show me that which is auspicious for myself and others—
And produce what is best for everyone's highest good.'

With this, whatever I want to know and whatever I need to learn comes my way. That is the perfection of nature—an inner intelligence that has guided me on my journey to the heart of nature.

With blessings and love on your journey,

Borghild Bø

INTRODUCTION

When we set the mind free to walk and follow our calling, we arrive at the greatest mountain peak—a natural and enlightened state of mind. The simplest and most fulfilling things that are the best for our well-being are often the hardest for the mind to accept and embrace, until the veil is lifted and we go beyond the worldly mind. Then, we understand the nature of Mind and know how to navigate to the summit of true joy and peace. And all along the way we keep the greatest company: our soul's awareness and the inner guide of our intuition.

Walking and Walking and Walking: An Intuitive Self-Reflection Process

As part of my unfolding journey through foreign lands in Europe and across the Himalayas in northern India, walking became the vehicle for a process of intuitive self-reflection and healing, one that enabled me to look deeply into my consciousness and purify it. It was a process of expansion and contraction, apparently moving forward and backward both mentally and emotionally. By walking up and downhill, through paths that narrowed dangerously and widened into safety, I was always moving toward my goal, even when it seemed I was not.

My trekking experiences made me question my identity. It happened step by step, and very gradually. Over a period of time the masks of illusion that were once so firmly held in place fell apart. What I thought was real became less real. The more intense experiences of my life became the catalysts that shook me to the core and made me understand that I am so much more than I thought I was.

In moments of epiphany I discovered the secret life force energy that reflected my own core internal vibrational rhythm connecting with the pulsating heartbeat of Mother Nature. I use capital letters to refer to Mother Nature because I view her as a deity.

I learned to move with the energy of nature's intelligence. With the intensity of a secret, passionate lover, Mother Nature pulled me towards her. I couldn't resist her natural power; I felt I had to go where she beckoned or I would wither. She played innocently and seriously with me. She is a force greater than I am; only years later did I realise that Mother Nature was the divine will calling me everywhere. And she is also my greater self, in me and around me, everywhere.

As I continued to cross one mountain pass after another, the sacred seals to the chamber of inner wisdom were unlocked. The secret patterns, codes and formulas of nature's untouched and pure natural energy vibration from the ancient land I traversed were awakened and activated. I was walking *inside* the land.

By gradually moving from the external world of the intellect to the subtle world of natural intelligence within, I opened myself to a deeper connection with the divine by paying close attention to my heart's desire and truth. And when I gave myself the space to enter the inner world, I discovered that it was essentially what nurtured my soul and connected me with Mother Nature and my own divinity.

I felt entirely nurtured and cradled by nature's powerful energy. It was as though I had become a little baby again; soft and vulnerable, yet feeling wonderfully held and protected by her arms and her unconditional love. Even so, learning to find the rhythm of harmony with Mother Nature was not a bed of roses. The obstacles of the intellectual mind were many, but the power of blissful moments of true joy always carried me forward into the deeper truth. And after a while I came to understand that the mighty mountains were gateways or portals to otherworldly realities where I was rewarded with the abundant spiritual gift of higher consciousness.

By practicing the freedom to just be and travel to spiritual and pure lands, a magnificent path of joy, beauty and truth opened. I repeatedly focused and re-centred my consciousness by asking these questions:

What is Mother Nature mirroring to me?

What is Mother Nature showing me in my life?

What is the message being shown to me?

What is my inner knowing saying to me about this?

Seeing the truth of reality, I found myself wondering:

Is it real or imagined?

What is reality anyway?

Maybe my reality—the way I see it—is not what I thought it was, is or will be. Nature continually mirrored a reality to me that I couldn't quite understand with my reasoning mind. I repeatedly asked myself: Who am I? I may think I know who I am, but do I?

I started to see the world from a place of wholeness and oneness. My perceptual vision changed from the external to the internal, so that what I saw outside mirrored or symbolised what my inner eternal eye was really seeing in the energy worlds. As a result, I discovered that I could see my innate natural state of mind.

What I felt to be my true inner self was revealed in the physical realms of nature around me, in which I observed Mother Nature as the seat of all creation; I came to believe that she reveals herself in the form of divine will.

As I wandered on, I wondered to myself: Who is Mother Nature, really? Will I meet her one day? What does she look like? I was aware of her reflection inside me as a voice—the voice of my own true nature. However, I also sensed that she might be a physical figure who I could meet and recognise. Was I being foolish? Was that too much to hope for?

I became aware that this wasn't something my mind could figure out or understand. Gradually I surrendered my questions and experiences to the divine will. Instead of expecting an answer, I whispered a prayer asking that revelations come for the highest good of all beings.

Who am I asking for truth?

Who are you, taking me from the unreal to the real?

The Inner and Outer Experience of Mother Nature

I call her Mother Nature because she feels like a real mother to me. Just like a loving mother could see me as I truly am rather than who she wants me to be, Mother Nature has shown me how to connect to my natural wisdom. I refer to her as 'she' because most of the time her energy feels feminine—although sometimes it also feels as if I can sense the masculine energy of a father coming through.

As I walked, I came to understand more and more why nature's energy sometimes differs in this way. This is the dance in which the feminine and masculine forces of nature get to know each other, fall in love and ultimately find pure love in the truth of oneness; the dance shows how they flow, like the yin-yang symbol, from white to black to white again.

Since I began to connect powerfully with Mother Nature and experience the intimacy of that connection, my commitment to teach and serve grew. I want to share her teachings so you too can connect, focus and flow with nature's divine will and drink the potent nectar from the source of your being.

As such I will show you how Mother Nature eloquently connects, heals and purifies. And she can—if you let her—nurture, empower and embrace you with her loving arms. She can restore harmony so you can find your natural rhythm.

When you listen to your inner knowing, Mother Nature expands your consciousness so that you can learn to be guided by your innate nature. She does this so you can discover, reveal and express more of who you really are. Finally, she helps you remember your core vibrational energy, which is reflected in the visionary, shifting perceptions that I reveal in this story.

Introduction

How to Use This Book

The book is really a teaching story. As you tune in to the situations I experienced on my pilgrimages and to the inner lessons I learned, you may find parallels in your own life or understand certain emotional states that you may wish to explore more fully.

So it is important to read each phase of each journey with a penetrating kind of attention, feeling into what unfolds. At the same time ask yourself:

> *What is this showing me about my own daily life?*
> *What is my inner knowing telling me about this?*

For each journey, I have created a variety of contemplations to help you deepen your understanding. These are called **Meditative Moments** and you will find them listed in Appendix 1 at the back of the book. As you read each of the three segments of the journey, pause and contemplate the Meditative Moments that go with that segment. In Parts 2 and 3, I recommend you do these in order for each day, but you can use your intuition as well and let yourself be drawn to whichever one feels right.

You can repeat the words inwardly or say them out loud. Then connect your inner experience to discover what's going on in your life. I suggest you take some time to write about your experiences, thoughts and feelings. Journaling can help you become more aware of what your inner knowing is trying to say. Over time, you might also want to write about how your perception is changing and how this is affecting the shape and form of your life.

The Meditative Moments guide you to experience intuitive insight spontaneously, available at any time. They encourage you to practice awareness and stay present in the flow, so that you can open more easily to new perspectives and possibilities. These exercises do not require any previous experience with meditation. Willingness to open to the new is the magic of transformation and creativity.

The practice requires patience and should be carried out with simplicity and peace. Just begin and let it unfold.

JUST BREATHE A MOMENT

Now is a beginning

J u s t b r e a t h e
And be present within yourself

B r e a t h e
The current of joy flowing in and out of you

B r e a t h e
The air that is full of who you are

B r e a t h e
The earth's essence of love

B r e a t h e
The co-creation of all beings

B r e a t h e
The nourishment in each moment

B r e a t h e
Your unity with Mother Nature

B r e a t h e
Into slow movement

Be Still
The end is a beginning
A vast emptiness is being filled with new consciousness

J u s t b r e a t h e

PART 1

El Camino de Santiago de Compostela, Northern Spain

I connected with Mother Nature through my longing to be with her. Suddenly, all I wanted was to be with her all the time. I also felt a tremendous thirst as if I needed to drink from the well of pure water nearby. I couldn't wait to be with her and when I listened in to her voice, she said: 'We have danced together before and found a natural rhythm.'

Ambivalence and the Beginning of a Pilgrimage

Although the search for something more had started long ago, walking the Camino de Santiago (the way of Saint James) in northern Spain was the beginning of a pilgrimage and a turning point, teaching me to look inward. It was also the start of something I could not predict. The nature of this particular pilgrimage had no personal resonance for me at the time, but I knew I was longing for something more that I could not explain.

I thought I was happy, but something deeper was missing. Despite a seemingly successful life on the outside, I was not fulfilled on the inside. I was facing the reality that I was not truly happy. After a failed marriage and other relationships, I was still yearning for *that thing* or *that place* where I could feel truly loved, free and at peace.

The idea of moving into a whole new phase of life was nothing more than a dream at this stage; I wanted it but it seemed out of reach, as though it could never really happen. I was trying to make life-changing decisions but I was too exhausted from overwork to settle on any clear plan of action. But all the time I was aware of a deep longing inside—and strangely enough I could sense something coming to fulfill it. My problem was that I just did not understand the nature of that longing.

I wanted to go somewhere, and the Camino was on my list of Things I Would Like to Do. But I did not think it would be possible. How could I go away for five weeks? I did not have leave from work. How could I miss my mother's 75th birthday party? I had already planned to go to India for two months; should I cancel all those plans and go to Spain instead?

Walking to the local peak one morning, everything suddenly became clear. As I honoured the truth about what I was seeking and what no longer worked in my life, I saw my face reflected in the shining leaves on the weeping birch, bathed in sunlight. Beyond, the mountains appeared so solid and the salt water so pure and fresh. The natural elements surrounding me reflected strength and vitality and helped me listen to and act on my inner knowing.

The spark of my true life force energy had been re-ignited, from having the courage to listen to my inner truth, to making difficult decisions and acting on them. I was finally ready to embark on another cycle in life. I decided to resign from my job. And a week before the pilgrimage to Santiago was to begin, I made an impulsive decision to do it.

Ambivalence and the Beginning of a Pilgrimage

I was shivering with worry and feelings of negativity as I looked at pictures of the Camino on the Internet. I was frightened and my thoughts were spinning, 'Why am I doing this? What have I done?' I didn't mind walking for 30 odd days—a total of 790 kilometres (490 miles). However, the open landscape looked so boring and flat. After living in the gorgeous mountains of Norway, how would I feel walking through villages and cities without the companionship of 'my' mountains? I felt the challenge rise within me. I realised quickly that it was just something different from what I would normally do—and that it might be interesting, too. I hoped I would connect to something special along the route. If not, I guessed it would be just another lesson about running around doing stuff. I trusted, however, that the Camino would give me something more profound; would give me what I needed.

I could only stand in humble witness to the magnet of my divine will, how it seemed to know exactly where it wanted to go and pulled me toward specific experiences and places while my conscious mind fought my will, unable to make sense of it. Even as I acknowledged my guilt about going, about leaving my responsibilities behind, I found myself letting that guilt flow through me, and ebb away. 'Anything can happen on a pilgrimage,' I thought. By embracing the resisting part of my ego, which was trying to hold me back, I followed my heart's longing.

I didn't have a conscious plan at that point, yet in hindsight it looked as though I had in fact planned everything. I remember thinking, 'I don't know why I am doing this or why I am going here, there and everywhere, but I just have to keep on doing it.'

The words echoing in my mind were:

It is what it is and it will be what it already is.

Part 1

What is True Love?

As I was just beginning to contemplate all this, a new man suddenly appeared in my life. We quickly bonded in a physical relationship and became involved in an intense love affair—despite warning signals. But he was unaware that I felt like a fish in a fish bowl, swimming in circles, wanting to be free. Nor did he suspect that I wanted to take off for somewhere else. It might have been a mistake to get entangled with him then, but I was not fully aware of the path I needed to be on, and I didn't have the energy to sort things out clearly.

When I moved in the direction of the life I was longing for and regained my energy like an infusion of electricity, I naturally questioned my new relationship, which I thought was providing me with love. Would being in a relationship prevent me from doing what I wanted to do? Was my relationship based on an illusion of desire and attachment? Was it real or unreal? Could we walk a path to freedom together? None of the answers were clear to me.

And the core question was: *'What is true love?'* That was, of course, the very question I would soon be asking the universe—through the Camino. When I reviewed my experience later, I realised that my core motivation had always been to seek the highest truth: Love.

The First Steps on the Path

I had always been deeply connected to nature and the outdoors, but on my flight from Bergen to the French city of Toulouse I felt nauseous and out of sorts. But after grabbing a brief catnap on the plane I suddenly woke with glimpses of a new beginning and a feeling of excitement and anticipation that my life was about to change completely.

My love for nature was one thing that had never changed in my life. Despite my ambivalence I was ready to be on the move and get to Lourdes, a stunning city with a massive castle in the foothills of the Pyrenees in southern France. It is believed that the Virgin Mary has appeared here on several occasions. Despite my internal misgivings, I lined up to get close to the statue of Our Lady of Lourdes in the Grotto. Among hundreds of people, I drank and washed in the healing water. Even though the place had a Disneyland feel about it, I took a deep sense of peace from the soft yet fast-flowing river, the Gave de Pau. I felt reassured that the Camino would give me the answers to my questions. 'What is true love?' and, 'Are my boyfriend and I really a couple?' I somehow already knew the answer, but wasn't ready to face the reality; I didn't trust my inner senses yet.

As I began my journey, walking from Saint Jean Pied de Port on the French side of the Pyrenees across northern Spain to Santiago, I asked the Camino—and the land—to show me the difference between worldly love and divine love, to help me move in the right direction towards a much deeper level of love. That first day was a mixture of joyous singing and chanting, and then for the last few hours I was hobbling on my sore feet down a steep path. I arrived at a monastery late at night and it was full. But I was lucky enough to get a place to sleep in a bunk bed at a campsite. My hips were hurting and I wondered if I would be able to walk the next day. I was pleased to see the full moon appearing from behind the clouds. 'There you are,' I thought.

I stood outside and watched as the moon became clearer. The light of clarity shone through the dark clouds of uncertain times that ley before me. Then my inner knowing told me:

> *There is always light in the dark; a light that whispers in the silence. Even if you cannot see me, I am the light of inner knowing giving you the certainty to act through a tone of blissful joy. When I am far away, suddenly invisible, gone, even covered by a fog of dark clouds, remember that I'm right here with you, guiding you, even when you cannot see me.*

Grateful and surprised by this awareness that seemed to have appeared spontaneously, I felt reassured once more. And amazingly, I *was* able to walk the next day, and the secret presence of the moon did guide me. At the end of each day I soothed and healed my sore feet in the waters of fresh streams and rivers. I prayed for the water to balance my energy and each time I put my feet into it, I found myself invigorated with a new sense of life. When I was distracted by thoughts about my boyfriend, I prayed that my mind be still and purified. The beauty of the land helped me focus on the path and stay present.

After sleeping outside under the clear sky one night, I woke up with thoughts telling me that, 'Things are not always the way I think they are or should be.' I continued to walk through a landscape of castles and small villages surrounded by wide-open vistas of cornfields. And I had plenty of time to contemplate my relationship. The question that kept repeating itself was, 'Are we a couple? What do I want from a relationship? What is true love? What is my truth?'

My boyfriend's reactions of puzzlement and frustration at my desire to find my inner freedom may have been born of his idea that my actions were self-motivated—selfish at worst—but they helped increase my determination to stay focussed on my path and trust my own feelings! The yellow arrows and the light blue seashells that marked the route of the Camino reminded me to breathe and taste the nectar of moment-by-moment awareness. When I looked up into the heavenly blue sky, faith filled me with tranquillity, and in that moment, with my feet firmly on the ground, the path was my truth. At peace with myself, I was at one with my being.

My boyfriend's words echoed in my mind. He had said, 'I like you, but I am not sure if I love you at the moment.' What does that mean? I wondered. One thing was for sure, it didn't create a feeling of loving kindness. Without reacting, I reflected and again asked the Camino, 'Is this true love?' The answer was clear, but I was still not convinced, hanging on to the good times and the memories of something I thought was love.

The words ran through my head as an inner plea: 'Please take me from untruth to truth and show me what true love is.' The chain of events took me where I needed to go and opened me to the possibility of something new. Every step felt like a moment of transformation and it helped me let go of any regrets and the guilt I felt for doing what I was called to do.

The Camino marked the start of a period of intense transition for which my unconscious had spent many years preparing. Although the search for *that thing* has been and is forever a part of me, the path to Santiago de Compostela was a pilgrimage from the external world to the subtle worlds within, a pilgrimage that would take me to many sacred places, both outside and in.

A Leap of Faith

I was challenged to let go of patterns of attachment to the illusion of what I had thought my life was going to be. When I moved through my guilt, ambivalence and resistance, I thought to myself, 'The Camino and nature itself are taking care of me, guiding me. Without any worldly security, I have faith.'

By taking that leap of faith, I was learning to allow myself to trust the fruits of the unknown. I made a promise to my inner self that I would listen to any guidance the Camino wanted to show me. At that moment, I knew that for me, this was the Camino's purpose.

In one way, in my worldly ego mind, I felt disappointed that I'd had to walk the Camino in order to discover this. I didn't consciously know what this disappointment was about, but my inner being knew already. I clearly wasn't ready to listen to it just yet. There were so many things I wanted to know about my direction. My mind was craving answers, and this craving kept me distracted.

Aware of this, I grounded myself in the present and simply asked for what I needed to help me make the transition into a life that would be best for my highest good. When I surrendered to the unknown, not knowing what would happen, I fully trusted that the Camino and nature would show me what it was that I needed. I felt a strange sense of awareness that the Camino and what I came to call Mother Nature knew what I needed better than I did myself.

In the same breath I heard an inner voice, which I was learning to identify and tune in to. It told me:

> *You know, but you do not believe or trust your inner knowing. No one can ever tell you this. It must be discovered and revealed by direct and concrete experience. Only then will you know*

and anchor it through the heart of experience. At that point the worldly mind of separation, doubt and confusion will step aside.

Love yourself enough to give yourself what you truly want. Your path is one of being true to your inner self, following your heart's longing and desire. And that is where you will find me and connect with your deeper self, anytime.

It was the beginning of my practice of conversing with Mother Nature.

The Truth of Inner Knowing

Listening to Mother Nature, I smiled to myself as the silent whispers of inner knowing told me:

> *By trusting her, you go where you long to go.*
> *When you follow her, you realise she is your inner knowing.*

And this is exactly what happened. I learned that I could connect with Mother Nature in places that called to me. As I did, I knew that I would be able to relax into just being, without any false expectations. The more I trusted my inner knowing, the more effortless and peaceful the walking became. I let it all just happen, and when I actively followed my inner knowing, I witnessed how my consciousness expanded like the horizon before me. It felt endless and boundless, and I could see the infinite potential that exists in the absolute reality of truth.

Even though Mother Nature had provided me with an answer, I couldn't help myself and asked again: 'Why am I doing this?' I heard her silent reply.

> *It is nothing but the experience of being without where you are within. Part of life's journey is to just take another step. Be open and flexible; let go of the mind, the resistance and the struggle and be the love that you are. Walk lightly and it will all be revealed to you.*

With this insight I felt the need to pray some more.

'Please, Camino, tell me, show me in a natural and perfect way, What is true love? Who is my true love? Please show me what I cannot see or don't want to see. Please guide me to walk with the blessings of grace, dignity and integrity.

'Thank you for taking me where I need to go with the gentle breath of air, so we can all be illuminated by the awareness of a clear light mind. Without expectations, I accept miracles, knowing they are revealed in every step, walking in the truth moment-by-moment. In the field of naked awareness, I open up to guidance from beyond what I think it should be or is.'

Filled with deep gratitude to the Camino as it guided me onto my path of communing powerfully with Mother Nature, I whispered: 'The Camino and Mother Nature help me see through the illusion of worldly love. As I discover what true love is, I am shown what pure love is not.'

However, it was not always easy. One day, after walking 34 kilometres (21 miles), I finally reached my destination for the night. Exhausted, I dropped into a chair in a hostel by the road; my effort for the day was *completo*—'finished'—and I released a big sigh of disappointment. Something didn't feel right; my energies were misaligned and uncomfortable. There was only one thing to do—walk some more. Part of my mind wanted to complain about the inner guidance I was receiving, but after another two hours of walking, I reached a place that was just right. I got what I wanted—a bed and a shower. It made me understand that I could trust my intuition, and that I would always have what I needed. Everything else paled into insignificance.

Further along the path, I realised I was walking into the future during the present, leaving the past behind. I walked right into the inner worlds of knowing and deeper understanding just by putting one foot in front of the other. My patterns of thinking and acting became obvious. I understood the underlying motives for my fear and my love. As I walked I continued to question the meaning of life and love. These things rang in my mind like the sound of bells from a church tower I saw passing through a village. After a while I paused to glance back. Suddenly, it dawned on me that it all looked different. From this side, the village gave me new perspective on what life and love were.

I remember one day quite clearly. It was my twenty-fourth day on the Camino. I had recovered from the severe pain of a shin splint problem in my right leg. I walked through the streets of Villafranca, a pretty village in the bosom of an emerald valley. There were no fewer than four churches and two big monasteries. I wondered what it would have looked like in the past, what religious fervour must have driven the builders of so many houses of God. Now, the churches were almost empty. As I walked on up the mountain hillside that morning on my way to La Faba, I thought of my boyfriend and the ways in which we communicated.

I had been writing one day when he glanced at my notes. He had said, 'Why do you keep writing the same things over and over—repeating yourself every day—like writing a shopping list.' I had answered, 'Maybe it is a shopping list.'

The sun was almost at the top of the hill, and I had an epiphany. I knew that this way of relating did not come from true love but from the personality and its attachments. It came from fear, really. I knew that the path I was walking held the wisdom of pure love and my challenge and my lessons were to *be* love—even when someone treated me harshly or judged me. The sun was now shining on the many chestnut trees and I thought, 'I am walking in the Garden of Eden.'

In that moment the chestnut orchards represented all the little seeds of love that had been nurtured through difficult times to become trees that now stood tall; proud with chestnuts that shone like a million stars along the slope of the valley. I thought, 'What a shame that these seeds of love can so often be destroyed and sabotaged by harsh words and angry reactions.' And in that moment another realisation came to me. 'What does not feed our essence is not true love.'

Later that day I came to realise that part of my lesson was not to take personally the things I perceived as harsh. I knew then that my future could be created and my prayers answered. With that I let go and prayed for peace, love and harmony for all the pilgrims who were walking the Camino, looking for themselves.

The Camino reminded me that I was walking through pain and fear to let go of the obstacles of what my worldly mind thought was love. And as the focus of my mind relaxed and floated into the blue sky, I entered a greater field of awareness and was caressed by the nurturing sensations of Mother Nature. That's when I felt the physical experience of unconditional love and realised that my worldly relationship was not what I thought it was. The Camino helped me become aware of my dependent mind. With this observation

I prayed to be liberated from the limitations of this part of my consciousness.

Every step along represented the rhythmic heartbeat of a surreal moment where the awareness of past, present and future melted together into everything that is. Interconnected with every moment, Mother Nature revealed herself and took me from a place outside to a place within by showing me glimpses of the signs, subtle messages and teachings that are in every surrounding interaction. I accepted that I was going to be with Mother Nature all the way.

The Inner Voice

Once I became aware of the true force that Mother Nature was, I started to associate her voice with a voice inside myself—and I began to listen to what I now think of as my inner knowing. Humming like a bird in my throat, the knowing told me:

> *The longing you feel lies beyond the mundane mind and is an echo of your soul's zealous yearning for your true self. It is a calling for the 'something more' that you are. It is the deeper truth of divinity. It is true love. It is the silent voice of your heart's desire calling you home to a place where you can just be at one with who you are.*

The voice of my inner knowing went on.

> *When we are searching for something, we leave no stone unturned until we become the wholeness and perfection we feel inside. We open up to a language of higher awareness and introspection. It tells us that whatever we are striving*

for is already embedded within. It is a part of our existence, showing us that we are interconnected with a whole matrix.

I was getting restless, but it didn't stop.

True nature is the vibrational life force energy of your natural intelligence and the essence of your soul. The 'I' is who you have come to believe you are in the intellectual worldly mind. When you open to the depth of your self, true nature comes to you by following the longing of your heart. And by accepting the essence of your spiritual self, you are surrendering to who you are. While walking inwardly you allow yourself to be, expanding beyond the mundane nature of existence.

It stopped for a moment and I pondered.

I have always longed for something more. So by listening to my heart's desire, I choose to follow the path of my divine will—that is my soul's natural intelligence. It is a deeper supreme longing for something more than the illusion of worldly love wrapped in the preconceived ideas of a dependent mind.

Even though I was now listening to my inner knowing, I related to this spontaneous flow of consciousness as Mother Nature. And in her eloquent way, she said:

Yes, I am your inner knowing guiding you, until you become at one with your spirit self. At that point you will realise that this is your voice of true nature. When you discover the secret that lies in your voice—TRUST YOUR VOICE!

The message was profound and made me reflect. My greatest challenge lay in trusting my inner knowing. The habitual mental scenarios that employed phrases like 'should', 'could', 'have to' and 'if only' were never far away. Anchored, I was shown how to exist in the present moment, with no mental distractions.

Indeed, with every step I took I was practicing trust so that I could become more aware of, listen to and allow myself to be guided by my intuitive knowing. And as part of this practice, I also questioned Mother Nature. Just to make me really understand, she had brought love into my life once again. The experience of that relationship gave me the needed electrical jolt to move and make a transition. She showed me the particular path I needed to follow so that I could take the necessary steps and resign from any worldly affairs that bound me.

My mind, my thoughts and emotions, the atmosphere, the elements of nature, the light and colours and everything along the road became a reflection of how I dealt with life and my inner processes. And to my surprise, my initial idea of how boring the flat land was going to be actually turned into a series of hidden challenges and presented me with many gifts—insights, choices and opportunities to transform and let go of anything that interfered with being natural—in the moment and in the flow.

I wanted my life to be different so I consciously prayed that I could open myself to and receive divine love. This is how I came to know and realise that my inner self was on a quest for real love. As a result of trusting my truth and inner knowing, I found new meanings and approaches to life. In this way, I was able to detach myself and let go of what I had previously thought was love.

I was convinced that walking the Camino was practice for staying within my truth. The process helped me develop the strength and commitment I would need in more distant destinations and on longer journeys through harsher environments to remain on my path and not allow myself to be distracted by temptations, thoughts and emotions. I was determined to notice the answers given to me in various forms. In turn, my faith opened the gateway to the wisdom of true love, which I have come to believe is ultimately Mother Nature.

Through this knowledge, Mother Nature helped me to see the difference between worldly and divine truth. Her question still rings in my ears.

Do you want worldly love or can you allow yourself to open yourself up to walking the path of divine love?

At the end of the Camino, the answer was clear. I was ready to face the truth that my boyfriend and I were not a couple. I knew I had to move on. The Camino was symbolic of my willingness to create an authentic life.

Enraptured by the grace and venerable beauty of nature's way of life, I decided to continue walking with Mother Nature, to follow my longing to be with her further, into the mountain kingdom of the Himalayas. I sensed that with greater difficulty my vibration might lift into higher dimensions. In times of doubt, I reminded myself that the result lies in the risks I was willing to take. If I didn't do what my heart desired, I would not be satisfied.

And so it was that I followed my intuition on a deeper quest for love and truth, giving into the yearning for something more. Three weeks after completing the Camino, I was on my way to India.

By walking through foreign lands, I knew I could pursue my quest with the guidance of Mother Nature.

By practicing unselfishness,
I come to a point where I let go of guilt
I am selfish enough to follow my passion
When my heart cries
My love for nature calls me to come—I go
And I flow with the movement of transformational energy
In the moment of freedom to be all that I am, wherever I go

PART 2

Six Days in the Mountains and Valleys of Leh in Ladakh, Northern India

I could now hear nature call, 'Come to me.' My fervent longing to be free and to be who I was in the deeper, spiritual truth of nature made me listen even more. The heart of my soul was crying for its abode of being—to be with the essence of my soul's energy. I searched everywhere for that thing, but found nothing until I started to remember the wholeness of who I am. At that point I felt the spark of unconditional love awakening within me and I discovered the beauty of oneness in the heart of nature.

DAY 1
WHY? WHY? WHY?

I was on my way to India! I could hardly believe it. Was I the same person who left her life in Norway and walked across northern Spain just a few weeks ago? I had an odd recurring feeling along the lines of 'How did I get here?' But it seemed that I was also still nurturing aspects of my doubting, questioning mind. 'Why?' kept surfacing again and again. 'Why trek in India? I come from Norway, where we breathe beautiful nature.' If I had been tempted to rationalise it, this next journey might have seemed strange or crazy—or it might not have happened at all. I might have talked myself out of it, despite my heart's longing to go. Yet India's high mountains were the image that had come to mind when I asked myself, 'What next?' I realised that sometimes I'm unsure of the motivations that compel me to do things or go places.

Longing for That Thing

But this time, I was conscious that I was following a clear urge within myself—I was trusting my intuition. The well-trodden path of the Himalayan outback in northern India was a place I was naturally drawn to. This urge contained the same inner spark of free will as the one that drove me to another distant land many years ago.

At that time something beyond mere curiosity had driven me away from the comfort and safety of my homeland to work on a sheep and dairy farm in Australia. I had travelled alone across many time zones, oceans and countries to the unknown territory and vast landscape of the land 'down under'—a place I had only seen on TV. I had completed an Animal Husbandry Science degree, but little did I know that the journey would totally change my life; that I would get married, live, study and work in Australia for sixteen years.

Suddenly, in the air, back in the here and now, a flight attendant tapped me on the shoulder. I immediately refocused into the present and wondered, 'Why do I have to know, anyway, just why I am trekking in this distant place?' An answer popped into my head: 'I am simply doing what my inner knowing tells me; this is something I cannot clearly explain apart from the fact that I am looking for *that thing.*'

Landing in New Delhi

As the plane landed in India's capital, New Delhi, I once again felt nauseous with emotion. The wave of 'what have I done?' hit me in the turbulence of the landing. I had given up my well-paid contract, said no thank you to other professional career offers, closed my private practice and rented out my home. 'Am I really following my dream? Is this my real dream? Am I deluding myself, to walk away from it all, into the unknown? Have I made the right choice to follow the energy of Mother Nature, or should I have stayed with my relationship?'

Safely on the ground, I walked off the plane and listened to the conflict in my mind. I reminded myself what the Camino had told me. It was 1 a.m. in the morning and the flight to Leh was not until 7 a.m. I got my luggage and walked outside into the strong sweet air of India. All doubts and nausea dissolved.

It didn't take long before I was on the bus to the domestic terminal. There I found a chair to rest in. I knew for sure that I was in India when mice started to appear. They made me chuckle and I thought: 'My search continues. Can *that thing* I am looking for be discovered over a mountain pass or in a secret valley?' I took out my laptop and started writing, already sensing the reality of what I would be experiencing.

'I climb on from hill to hill, from peak to peak in hope and expectation, to see the view over the top and beyond. Every time I hit obstacles in the outside world, something awakens within me. The will and curiosity to find what is over the next mountaintop moves me forward, and draws me into a deeper connection with nature. While wandering, my horizons expand and I open to an unknown reality.'

All of a sudden I jumped. A mouse had run over my foot. I got up and stretched. Images of the Camino came to mind. I could clearly feel how the steps I had taken there had established the beginnings of a powerful bond of trust between my being and my body. And here in the moment, the touch of the mouse reminded me of this simple life right now. I found another place to sit, and could not deny that I was feeling sad thinking of my relationship. Even though we had only been together for five months when I left, I'd begun to feel attached. It showed me that I wanted to be loved and comforted by another—but there was a part of me that told me to hold onto my heart and not give it away too soon—that I still had most of my life journey ahead of me.

I caught myself again wondering if we had been lovers or friends. It was the same obsessive question I had asked as I walked the Camino. Maybe in the end we would be neither, but even though I knew the truth, my mind grasped for this hope, as if it were going to save me from something. Maybe the deeper part of me didn't want to be saved!

As Mother Nature had already shown me, the work of integrating and anchoring my experiences came after the blessing of insights and contemplation. I wrote: 'I still have to walk through the landscape to embody the teachings. Maybe this is a test of strength, determination and devotion.' I stopped writing and asked myself: 'Am I willing to sacrifice what my quotidian mind is grasping for and hanging onto for the sake of material security and instead put in the preparation and effort to be with her?' Without really understanding the profound meaning of my question, I recognised that ending my relationship had the symbolic meaning of letting go of the attachment to worldly love and embracing unconditional eternal love in its place.

In the same instant, I remembered what the Camino had shown me about the nature of true love. I reassured myself that beyond my mental processes, I had found the answer in the act of walking. By trusting my intuition, I was still with Mother Nature, existing in an open mental space where I felt a sense of spiritual freedom. This in itself was a choice I would not have made before, because I had been listening to my reasoning mind.

Suddenly, I jumped again. I could feel the mouse touching my foot again, or maybe it was another one. I became aware of all the people and instantly felt stressed by the thought that I had missed my flight. I quickly packed my things and rushed over to the check-in area. I made it just in time.

Leh, Ladakh—Shangri-La?

In my seat, I let out a big sigh of relief and quietly thanked the little mouse for bringing me back to the present. It was a short flight to Leh—where I was to spend six days acclimatising to the altitude before embarking on the 21-day trek across the Ladakh and Zanskar mountain ranges in the great Himalayas—a name whose direct translation is 'abode of the snow'. Leh lies in Ladakh, in India's northern state of Jammu & Kashmir, at an altitude of 3524 metres (11,562 feet).

My spiritual path over the last few years had given me a meaningful perspective on how life is different in a Buddhist culture; there is a fundamentally compassionate practice of seeing the world, the self and others. The Buddhist way of thinking is clearly illustrated through ancient living traditions, sacred symbolism and mysticism.

Buddhism is a spiritual culture that cultivates a way of being connected to a greater, more meaningful dimension of the universe in which the self is not seen as separate, but rather as a connection to an inward focus on wholeness and solidarity. In essence this means a belief and value system with a deep-seated sense of compassion and cooperation rooted in the identity of the culture. The non-dogmatic teachings are often expressed and practiced through a mix of complex symbolic art, architecture, ritual, prayer, dance, masks, festivals, music and meditation.

I was starting to piece together connections between potent sacred art, signs, images, and symbols relating to inner worlds of various traditions and cultures that I had come into contact with. I had found many little glimpses—insights that came like lightning strikes, reminders of direct experience—that revealed subtle messages through experiential awareness or inner knowing. I was looking forward to feeling this more directly and physically.

As I approached Leh from the air, I saw that the land of white covered mountains was engraved with peculiar patterns that seemed woven into the earth. It made me believe I was watching the heavens from above. Irregular thin strips of lush vegetation were flowing like green gushing rivers across the bare and brown landscape from the top of the mountains, creating fields of land. I thought to myself, 'Maybe there is some truth to the saying that Ladakh is Shangri-La or the closest thing to it.'

It was a smooth landing. I stepped out onto the tarmac, and the pristine pure air caressed my face. With a deep breath, I looked up into the clear blue sky, and exhaled a sigh of freedom full of profound joy; relief rushed through my body like a contented stream from the glaciers I had just seen.

I was immediately reminded of my experiences in Bhutan that had introduced me to the bounty of Buddhism in 2004. The small Himalayan kingdom, nestled between China, Nepal and India, had given me lasting impressions. I had never known that a land could have a soul until I had been there. I still think today that it must be because Bhutan is the only country in the world that embraces Tibetan Buddhism as its state philosophy. Amazingly enough, Bhutan was totally isolated from tourism until the 1960s when the King changed the rules, although tourism is still restricted to a certain number to protect it from outer influences. Not only that, it continues to intrigue me that the government's focus is on Gross National Happiness as opposed to Gross National Product.

Even though this is not usually the case in northern India, I could smell the atmosphere of Tibetan Buddhism in the fresh air as I walked into the terminal building in Leh. It was not at all like a Western airport terminal. At the entrance I was greeted as a queen with smiles that exuded peace and compassion.

A man and a woman dressed in a traditional Ladaki costume welcomed me by placing a *khata*, a white silk scarf used for offering, gently around my neck while handing me a silver cup of water and biscuits. 'You are blessed,' they said and smiled. I immediately felt embraced by their caring nature and sensed they were people who wanted to make me feel at home in this remote location. This was really a place from another time and dimension where I could leave behind the modern fast pace of routines, demands and expectations.

As I was waiting for my luggage I admired the woman's traditional *perak* headdress. They wear it for special occasions and for rituals, weddings and festivals. It is made of turquoise and silver accessories stitched onto a coral-coloured cloth or a leather band that curves from the top of the woman's forehead, over her head and down her back. It symbolises a blue cobra ready to strike. And I learned later that the amount of turquoise represents a woman's status.

In Bhutan, they say they spend a lifetime searching for *that thing*, for that which we have possessed from time immemorial and that has been and is with us all the time. This dimension of hidden truth is a mystery. It is part of life's philosophy, mythology and traditions, not only in Bhutan—the land of the Thunder Dragon—but wherever we wander in mind, body or spirit. The Thunder Dragon is Bhutan's national symbol, based on the tradition of the Drukpa lineage of Tibetan Buddhism. The national flag features the Druk— The Thunder Dragon of Bhutanese mythology.

I found myself again in a region that breathes many levels of ancient Tibetan Buddhism and which has only been accessible for tourists since 1974. As I opened to the powerful energy vibration I could feel concealed in the divinity of this land, I caught myself thinking, 'Is this it?' At the same time I was aware of repeating, 'I think this is the way.' My mind was telling me I was looking for a way, thinking there was only one way. Then Mother Nature added, as if flowing from the gentle stream of higher consciousness.

> *There is no way called 'this is it'; only the way of heart consciousness which the mind does not know or understand, but loves to THINK it knows. The mind takes refuge in attaching a (false) significance to it.*
>
> *Don't be fooled into thinking you know what I want. Flow with me, for I am your core vibration. Then, you shall find the keys and open the seals to your secret energy. Only then will you rest in the essence of true nature hidden in the current of divine intelligence coiled within.*

A Whirlwind of Energy

I picked up my luggage and found the guide who was taking me to the hotel. After a warm welcome and a delicious lunch, I went for a stroll to familiarise myself with the small town. I was with Mother Nature, alone but not alone. As I walked around, I entered a whirlwind of electrical currents, a different world; I was travelling in another dimension, as if I were in a wonderful dream.

My habitual mixed feelings appeared and then transformed themselves into intense energy. Though strange, I also sensed a familiarity and remembered something ancient moving through me with that energy; something like the naked awareness of an empty mind. I felt the pulsating vibration surging like high-voltage electricity. It made my body shiver and tingle with waves of vulnerability.

Cold with shivers and an immense pressure in my head, I thought my reaction might be a result of altitude. I knew there was much more to it because I had never felt this strangeness before. I thought of faith, and I remembered to trust the higher forces of nature. Instantly, I felt safe.

Later, after night had fallen, I returned to my room so I could ground myself in this energy vibration. I lit a candle and burned some incense I had obtained from my first trip to Peru to clear the air, so to speak. It felt natural to do a little ceremony or prayer to the moon, which was shining on the altar I had made on the windowsill.

Praying to the Moon

Each of the small objects I had placed on my altar carried a symbolic meaning, that of shedding the old skin like snakes do, so I could make the transition into newer realms. I looked at the broken glass snake that had come into my hands in Bangkok on my way home from Bhutan in 2004, and prayed for wholeness. The silver bangle engraved with sacred wisdom contained my life while I lived in Australia. I prayed to let go of the past and open myself to the empty sky beyond my intellectual mind.

When I walked the Camino, I had been using a *mala* from Bhutan to recite a daily planetary mantra. A *mala* is a string of 108 prayer beads commonly used by Hindus and Buddhists to concentrate and focus attention on the meaning and sound of a particular mantra while chanting the associated syllable of a deity or a prayer. As I began my little ritual, I held the string of prayer beads in my right hand and with the *mala* draped over the middle finger, I used my thumb to turn the beads clockwise, while I silently repeated the mantra. In Sanskrit this practice is known as *japa*.

I prayed to the moon that I be rooted and grounded in balance, safety and inner security. And I whispered: 'Please connect me to the power of nature and the unseen mysteries of the life forces in the alchemical process of earth, water, fire, air and ether.' I played the hummingbird flute from Cusco in Peru and called on the potent unconscious power of a greater intelligence beyond my worldly mind. And lastly, I held the little glass dog that my eight-year-old niece Amanda gave me as a gift before I departed. It reminded me to pray for unconditional love for all the beautiful children held in the womb of Mother Earth.

Wrapped up in my woollen underwear, I lay down on the bed under two sets of covers. Without doing anything I started to breathe consciously as I felt the presence of a very heavy energy. Suddenly, I got an image of what I understood was an umbilical cord between my ex-boyfriend and me that needed to be cut. It was hard and painful and I resisted doing it until Mother Nature said: *It is easy, just do it, don't think about it, release it and it is gone.* And as soon as I did, I was filled with lightness and all the pain disappeared into nothingness. Other painful memories of people that I care about came and went, as I passed them on into the moonlight.

Silently, Mother Nature told me: *Truth is in your breath, because that's where I am.* As I looked at the moon, its pure beauty and fullness sparkled like static electricity through my body. And even though I felt secure, there was something going on. With a deep sense of gratitude I felt the moon shedding its light on me. I was clearing the old and connecting with the new.

My First Spiritual Face

Enmeshed in the moonlight, I began to 'see' a faint face in the moon—an intuitive vision—of someone who reminded me of both a man and a woman. Simultaneously, the moon held me while the intuitive wisdom of the unconscious gave me strength to go beyond my conscious mind. It was a strange feeling, this physical realisation that the feminine and masculine together were the oneness of God. I was also aware that this was something I was afraid to reveal to myself. Totally surrendering to the presence of Mother Nature in a palsied state and with a splitting headache, I still felt grounded—but in a new kind of consciousness.

I thought, 'This is just the beginning—she is literally jolting me into a state of higher vibration.' I felt like crying but didn't know why. I seldom cry. I started to breathe deeply and soon I was at one with the flooding tears. Then, Mother Nature said: *What is it my sweetness?*

'I don't know,' I replied. I could feel her powerful vibration, yet my eyes burned and I just wanted to be. I continued to breathe and the lump in my throat grew, but eventually the tears released the contraction. Strangely enough it felt good. In the weird land of the moonlike vibration, something was happening. All I could do was flow gently with humility to something greater. I just cried, as I understood that there was something deeper to connect with. Cradled in the arms of Mother Nature, I entered into the new.

Again I prayed to the moon, asking for a gentle transition, illuminated by the moonlight. I felt a subtle shift in consciousness and connected to the vibrational frequency of the soul. I was overflowing with the happiness of pure ecstatic love and joy. In this space, I found the energy of Mother Nature in consciousness and light. My soul resonating in harmony with all that is, the truth was revealed by the immortality of stars dancing in the sky. I was aware then of the confluence of energies of the moon and the sun, like the female and male energies, and I surrendered again to the movement of the fluid white light energy—and fell into a deep sleep.

DAY 2
LEH — FINDING SHANTI (PEACE)
3524 METRES/11,562 FEET

I awoke at 7 a.m. feeling embraced by the warmth of the sunlight shining in through the thin curtains. I couldn't help but contemplate the sun and the moon; they seemed to symbolise the conscious and the unconscious play of consciousness. Maybe it was the masculine and feminine energies of the universe that came together to create balance and harmony in the perfection of nature's wholeness; as the mind and heart integrated into a single consciousness.

I felt calm and wondered what kind of whirlwind energy vibration had moved through me the night before. The pure love I had received felt like that which I would feel for a child. It had a different vibration from what I usually think of as worldly love.

Without really wanting to move, I stood and opened the curtains and lay back down on the bed bathing in the higher vibration of warmth radiated by the sun's rays. With open arms, I received strength for the day about to begin.

Soon I got up and went to sit on the veranda. I ordered my breakfast, and truly felt on top of the world. It was certainly a place where I could practice patience and acceptance to go with the flow, rather than fighting what was happening. As I enjoyed the tasty onion and tomato omelette and cups of mint tea, I relaxed into the heart of this new and unfamiliar feeling and the vibration of nature's grace, with all its knowledge and wisdom. Slowly, it dawned on me that Mother Nature had taken me to another dimension, affecting me profoundly on a cellular level.

Silently questioning Mother Nature in the back of my mind, I spent the day exploring Leh and learned that it was also referred to as 'Little Tibet'. I found the single main street, and could understand why. The Leh Palace, and other brick and mud houses that looked more like ruins, dominated the old town centre. Signs and symbols of a Tibetan Buddhist culture and identity were embedded in everything from the manners and habits of the people to the colourful clothing, fresh vegetable produce sold on the road, and corner shops selling Tibetan ornaments and art.

I walked to the colourfully decorated gate in the town square where I found several large prayer wheels. Some hunched elderly people walked around the huge cylinders that contain myriad copies of mantras and sacred texts printed on rolls of thin paper. I could hear their mumbling prayers as they turned the heavy wheel with one hand and simultaneously moved the prayer beads on the *mala* held in the other hand. Some of them also used a small hand-held prayer wheel. Spinning the written form of the mantra around and around in the wheel is an important part of their daily spiritual practice.

Despite the poverty and the extraordinary mixture of beauty and harshness, tenderness and wildness I could see in people's faces there seemed to be a different level of consciousness here. There was something about this culture that portrayed a genuine generosity, a capacity to be present in the moment and to value the simplicity of a complex life that was subtly reflected in the rituals and symbolism. Their calm, peaceful, yet powerful natures reflected a sense of deep connection to the soul and to the sacred reality of their faith.

Apart from admiring a young Indian boy sitting on a corner making a few rupees from polishing shoes, there was little to remind me that I was in India. I would later find out that Tibetan Buddhism had only survived in the most isolated and remote places in the Himalayas where modern India had not yet taken over. Surrounded by wild and beautiful mountains on all sides, I gradually worked my way to the huge white monument—the *stupa*—that I could see at the top of a hill in the distance. I took my time and bought a sheepskin vest on the way. It was an impulsive purchase, and something I regretted later.

There are many different *stupas* (also called *chorten* in the Tibetan language). The intention for these spiritual structures, their symbolic significance, is to help support devotees in their spiritual practice and in the making of offerings to liberate themselves from suffering. They signify the powers of the universe, the elemental forces of nature as well as Buddha's teachings and protection. Some are more elaborate than others—an enlightenment *stupa* for example symbolises Buddha's attainment of nirvana or the awakened state.

This particular monument was known as the peace *stupa* (*shanti* translates as peace). When I got closer, I began to feel awe at its reverent presence of liberation. It was not like any other *stupa* I had seen so far. It presented the perfect setting to contemplate the mixed feelings that had arisen in this desert-like lunar existence, way up high in the Himalayan outback.

At the top of the stairs, I started walking the *kora*—moving clockwise around any sacred monument, deity image or temple at least three times to accrue spiritual merit (*karma*) for others and ourselves. *Karma* evokes the concept that every act of body, mind and speech has a cause and effect. Therefore any spiritual practice such as walking the *kora* and repeating prayers is viewed as good *karma* and fortune. I had naturally become accustomed to this integral part of Buddhist devotional practice and daily ritual, which is believed to increase ones spiritual merit. It is also believed to help one to be reborn into higher realms and enjoy a better existence in the next incarnation.

Lost in contemplation, I walked around the *stupa*. It had elaborate symbolic art that represented the Buddhist ethos of detachment from any form of suffering caused by desire, ignorance and anger and to live compassionately so one can ultimately reach enlightenment. The circular motion apparently reflects the form of the cosmos.

Before going back, I sat cross-legged at the base of the *stupa* and admired the amazing view. Apart from a monk, I was the only one there. The monks here are devoted to the Buddhist teachings prescribed by their lineage or order. On the surface it struck me that the rather monotone and dry landscape high above the treeline and the white brick and mud-plastered houses scattered in clusters was a stark contrast to the rich architecture and to the culture I could feel on a deeper level. And as I sat there I prayed for peace and looked up into the sky painted in royal blue ink. My eyes took in the dramatic snow-capped mountains in the distance. The austere beauty of the naked and ragged desert landscape and the daunting contrasts of the strange land made me shiver. It was a surreal feeling that drew me into another realm, which felt surprisingly familiar, filled with a rare sense of sacredness and protection.

With a feeling of being able to reach right up to heaven with my arms, I got up. It was time to move on and get back to the hotel before dark.

I returned to my hotel at dusk. After a lovely dinner and a pot of tea, I made some notes on my laptop. But after writing a few pages the electricity cut out, then came back again. I tried to restart my laptop a few times but the power kept failing and I repeatedly lost my work—because I didn't realise that my computer didn't save it automatically. And I had not saved it soon enough. Also my battery had a very short lifespan and wasn't worth charging. The power cuts were apparently normal here, in a place where electricity was not to be taken for granted. Little did I realise that I was going to be without electricity for most of the next three weeks.

I glanced at the altar on the windowsill and thought of my experience the night before. 'Surrender to the vulnerability,' I reminded myself. By connecting to the predominant power of nature's elements, I could stay grounded in what felt like another dimension. I had no choice but to trust that Mother Nature knew the way. With a deep sigh, I slowly relaxed into the pulsating new vibration from the 'broken moon' land—a place that is cut off from the rest of the region for several months of the year due to the heavy snowfall.

I finished my tea and got ready for bed while praying to Mother Nature that I would meet the mystical and almighty vibration of this land with humility, gratitude, truth and love. The stillness of night permeated my being and I lay down. I relaxed and started to breathe slowly into the prayer of peace—*Om Shanti Shanti*. Silently repeating this mantra, I was lulled into sleep, and my body gradually became cocooned in a warm liquid sensation as the light of peace caressed me.

DAY 3
Monasteries East of Leh

I woke up on my third morning in Leh feeling fresh and ready to spend the whole day visiting four different monasteries east of town. In the Tibetan language they are known as *gompas,* or solitary retreats for peace and constructive reflection.

After another filling breakfast, with Stansen—my guide for the day—by my side, we drove about 50 kilometres (31 miles) through incredibly scenic and intense terrain along the Indus River to the first monastery carved into the mountainside in a place called Hemis. Just before arriving we passed cultivated fields where local women were harvesting barley at the end of the short summer growing season. We stopped so I could take pictures, and I admired how they stacked the harvest into neat cone-shaped bundles in patches that reminded me of sacred geometry.

The luxury of travelling by car during this first part of my journey allowed me to contemplate many things more profoundly, without the distraction of physical exertion and frustrations that typically come with walking at high altitude. When we finally arrived at Hemis and I entered the secluded sanctuary, imposing Buddha statues welcomed me with radiant, benevolent eyes. Humble monks appeared from nowhere and hurried me past bolted doors and into the heart of the temple towards the shrine—typically a small place of worship. The monks' respect for the great teachers made me feel humble as well. Their apparent absence was perhaps a gesture to show silent devotion before the masters and the teachings.

A shrine is a sacred or holy place, dedicated to or dominated by one or more deities and various other icons. There are many different shrines within one monastery. The walls are covered with ancient murals and *thangkas* (Tibetan paintings on cotton or silk, usually depicting a Buddhist deity, famous scene or mandala) as well as statues and carvings. The art conveyed Buddha's teachings and the path of enlightenment through complex sacred symbols. The *thangkas* were created as tools for meditation and contemplation, and had great spiritual significance. I knew they represented the invisible spirits of great teachers, gods and goddesses. Many of the deities depicted here had frighteningly fierce faces.

Even though I found little resonance or connection in what felt like physically lifeless and spiritually austere rooms full of statues or objects, I could see beyond the fierce faces and gestures of the deities. I felt their invisible formless energy balanced in the mystical atmosphere. The cold and arid darkness reflected the warmth from inner beams of light shining through the slightly open door. The pulsating butter lamps and the musky aroma added to the mysterious mood of feeling something more than I could see.

As I moved from one room to another, the desolate stillness that usually permeated the monastery was suddenly broken by the lively activity of a *puja* (worship and offerings conducted by a *lama*—a respected high monk or spiritual teacher), filling the silent air with a rising sound of echoing prayer gongs, drums and distant chanting. It was a ritual calling forth the energy of compassion and wisdom.

I followed the sound of the distant hymns and found the small *puja* room on top of a roof where a *lama* worshiped Buddha nature (past, present and future), gods, goddesses, protector deities and masters with rituals and offerings of sacred texts in the form of music, prayers, hymns and mantras.

The door to the *puja* room was half open. I stepped inside the entrance and paused. The serious old *lama* was about three metres away, chanting hymns while playing the drum and a gong. I saw a pretentious-looking mask, large and fierce and garlanded with countless silk offering scarves *(khata)* around its neck. The male animal head was black, with a red nose and lips. It had a wide gaping mouth and white teeth, and a red, white, black and gold third eye on the forehead between the golden eyebrows. While the third eye relaxed me, the big white round eyes looked like they were going to jump out at me. I knew they wouldn't and instead the mask started talking to me—or maybe it was Mother Nature.

> *I am the power of destruction and protection of the divine. Nature is fierce and destroys all evil where deemed necessary to uphold the ultimate reality of the divine, ruling over the mundane.*
> *I am creative and destructive, sweet and calm, fierce and horrifying. When you embrace the good and bad, it frees you from illusions, arrogance and fear.*

Totally absorbed, I found myself witness to what exists beyond the veils as the hymns became fainter and gradually dissolved into nothingness. For a moment I was left with an empty mind. Abruptly, I returned to the present when my guide, Stansen, called me.

I gathered myself and walked across the rooftop. Puzzled, I didn't see the ladder at first. I found it and climbed up to another area of the monastery. Stansen sat amongst a group of women. Everyone was laughing as they welcomed me. They were enjoying a tea break as they worked to restore parts of the temple. I was invited to sit down and was immediately offered different types of tea—salt, butter or milk. They had three huge thermoses and some battered pots. I was worried that I'd have to drink one of the special teas. The traditional butter tea called *chang* (made by churning butter in a long, wooden churn with milk, tea and salt) was too strong for my stomach.

Eventually, I was given the sweet chi tea with its many different flavours. I enjoyed the moment immensely. The women kept looking at me and couldn't stop smiling and laughing. They were in no hurry. My cup was filled again and I was offered biscuits. I could see how much the happy and peaceful, yet tired-looking and hard-working women enjoyed sitting together chatting, drinking and eating. They reminded me of something very important in life. After a little while we moved on.

A Perfect Teacher

We entered another shrine and wandered among the many deities and the mystical atmosphere. Stansen suddenly said, 'Buddha is an enlightened being who is a perfect teacher. You know we don't believe in God, but we believe in teachers who are perfect. For example, to fulfil a class we need a teacher, a text and students, and then we have a class.' He then asked me, 'When do you say you have a good teacher and when do you say you have a bad teacher?' Surprised that he had asked me, I replied, 'When the teachings come from the heart and when you feel understood, then you know you have a good teacher.'

He replied, 'Why does it only come from the heart of some teachers and not others?' Stansen answered the question himself.

'Is it because good teachers understand the psychology of the student? A good teacher knows what kind of teachings his students need. He teaches with keen interest, studying the students themselves; he uses appropriate methods to understand the student. A good teacher uses different methods to impart the message or knowledge. You will always find different natures of students. Some have a compassionate face, like Buddha, and others a naughty face that doesn't want to understand. A good teacher finds different methods to teach differently natured students who have different experiences. Like Guru Rinpoche used different methods to overcome the evil spirit of bone religion that existed before Buddhism in Tibet. Otherwise many teachers come to the classroom and give lectures and deliver speeches without getting through to the students' minds and hearts.'

Quietly I thought, 'I have never found a perfect teacher or what is considered a guru.' And with the benefit of hindsight, I could see 'I' (the ego-driven part of me) had looked in all the wrong places, searching for something or someone outside myself to give me the answers. I could see how I related to negative external influences, internal confusion and the fogginess of life—how I wasted time by overlooking the teachings that were right under my nose in daily life.

At this point I knew that I had finally turned inward. Teachers and teachings are everywhere and in everything I encounter. This vast land is giving me glimpses of the new, showing me the way beyond a clouded mind, where I am encouraged by nature's benevolently powerful vibration to trust the flow of things.

I wondered if our scientific ideologies and our ingrained religious beliefs were disempowering us, preventing us from seeing the deeper meaning of the spiritual land. This tainting may inhibit our human understanding of one another and ourselves, and suppress the connection with the inner nature of being human. Maybe too much intellectual knowledge freezes our growth and the evolution of natural intelligence. My senses were opening to something unknown and invisible. Layers of my deeper nature were being revealed in the bare and naked desert of my awareness.

We left Hemis Monastery and moved to another. The deep red colour of the monks' robes followed us. Eventually, after a long day we returned to the hotel. Even though I felt exhausted, my mind was calm and clear, free from distracting thoughts and emotions. I was experiencing freedom in my mind. The sound of the prayer gongs and the chanting of ancient Sanskrit texts and mantras had started to echo through my consciousness. By recalling the sound, I could feel the pulsating heartbeat of drumming and the light rhythm of the bell that brings harmony.

That night, sitting on the balcony, I gazed at the blue-black night sky. My breathing was steady as I took in the translucent air of active wisdom and compassion. With an open mind, I connected to the new and I could see Venus—a sparkling diamond, bright and clear. Before getting too cold, I went to my room and got into bed. I felt perfectly tranquil in the broken moon land and floated into a reality beyond the physical, asking: 'Who are you? Who am I? Where do we come from?'

DAY 4
Nubra Valley — North of Leh

I was fast asleep when a knock on my door roused me. A soft male voice called, 'Ma'am, breakfast is ready and your driver is here. Can I take your luggage?'

It was my fourth day in Leh and I was going north to the Nubra Valley where I would spend the night. This area only opened to tourists in 1993. I was told last night that we had to drive an alternate route as the main road was closed due to road problems. It would take about five hours. However, I didn't mind, as we would cross another pass.

My driver was a friendly, young Ladaki family man with a wife and one child. He spoke little English, so I was only able to understand a fraction of what he said. I had chosen not to have a guide as the day before had given me more than enough.

The morning was glorious, and I was ready for a two-day adventure before the 21-day trek in the Himalayan outback began. The sky was perfectly clear and the temperature was cold in this dry, high altitude climate.

We drove through town, already fully alive at 8 a.m. with people performing their sacred rituals and others who had opened their stores. We followed the same route as yesterday, hugging the river until we took off in the direction of the valley. With loud music playing, the atmosphere seemed positive and upbeat as I admired the passing brown meadows with animals grazing on patches of green grass.

We meandered through quaint villages. The flat roofed mud and white brick plastered houses were tiny and rather basic, with Tibetan Buddhist symbols scattered around. At one point we stopped so I could take pictures of different *stupas* and prayer wheels.

Shortly afterwards we started the zigzag ascent to the pass. Lulled into a sense of this being a long journey, I was not prepared for the sharp surprise that was soon to come. I kept turning my head backward to watch the magnificent mountains; I just could not take my eyes off them. As we drove, the dramatic view of the majestic Stok mountain range, draped in white silk, faded. When we were about to cross the mountain pass, I turned back once more and suddenly a large male face—as if engraved in the snow-capped mountainside—spontaneously appeared. 'Oh my God, this is incredible!' I gasped.

I asked if we could stop the car so I could take pictures of what had just leaped out of 'heaven'. It was too cold to go outside, so I took photos from the car window. I didn't want to leave, but felt better, knowing I had a picture of what looked like a king engraved in the snowy peak. We crossed the pass, as if nothing had happened. Along the way we saw workers pushing boulders and debris from the rocky road so we could drive through what seemed like a rushing river.

At the top of the pass, rainbow-coloured prayer flags inscribed with mantras and symbols were wrapped around poles. The two supporting poles sagged from all the offerings, yet despite the strong wind, only the messages flew away with the sound of the fluttering; the wind blowing the flags helped spread Buddha's messages of wisdom, compassion and peace.

I was still thinking about the face in the mountain. Although unusual, I realised I didn't have any particular thoughts about what I had just seen. I didn't wonder who it was or why it had appeared. For now, I just enjoyed the ride and the ever-changing and expansive view. I could not stop staring at the weirdly shaped mountain rock and pinnacle formations. The constantly changing colour and form made me wonder about the millions of years of erosion—that left the landscape looking like a smudged oil painting. When we descended from the pass it struck me just how extreme the landscape and life was.

We reached a place where we needed to cross the river. Although the bridge had collapsed, the driver found a way around. Just before we entered the valley—the home of two rivers and their vast sandy confluence, we passed what looked like a hidden jewel. It was a tiny village at the end of the descent, nestled between the mountains. The emerald, terraced fields created by the melting glacier sparkled with wonder. The idyllic, picturesque scenery consisted of a white cluster of buildings with a temple and other tiny houses placed up against the mountain cliffs. I pondered what it would be like to live there. It was hard to imagine how people could survive in such an isolated place.

The intriguing surroundings continued, opening up even more as we followed the narrow, curving road carved into the mountain cliffs. A landslide could happen at any time.

Among the living sacred symbols of prayer flags and *stupas*, road signs appeared. I smiled to myself as I read them. Despite the fast moving car, I managed to note them in my journal.

'Life without vision, courage and depth is simply a blind experience. Hurry and worry go together. Drive like hell and you will be there. Diverse in nature, united in hearts.' The idea of the zen road signs made me think of the ridiculous signs along the roads at home. Wouldn't it be lovely to see a sign that said, 'Grow in accordance with your inner directives' or something like it? The signs here definitely confirmed the different philosophy and way of thinking that I experienced.

Being Present, Like a Child in Wonder

The sense of foreboding in the road sign messages stayed with me as we finally reached the fog-bound Deskit Village. When we passed the village and its military presence, the atmosphere felt heavy, like my mood. The level of tension building inside me was tangible, with a knot in my stomach and an unexplainable sense of menace. My body was tight, tense with chaotic emotions, and my head felt like a steaming pressure cooker ready to go off any second. However, as soon as I knew that we were going to what looked like a green oasis with trees in the middle of a desert, not too far ahead, I relaxed.

After a short drive, we reached Hundar Village and as far as I could go as a tourist. I was relieved and pleasantly surprised when we got to the organic camp among the green trees, where we were staying overnight. From the outside, I felt disappointed but as soon as I walked into what was a serene and beautiful garden, I felt a sense of familiarity. I was hungry and after a delicious five-course lunch my emotions settled.

On my way to the tent for a nap, I stepped lightly on the stones in the lush garden, and brushed against the colourful and lovely blooming flowers. In the tent, I removed my outer layers of clothing and quickly got under the blankets. I sank into the surprisingly soft and comfortable bed. As I lay there it occurred to me that the tent looked more like a room with a wooden floor. The fine white curtains that covered the tent opening moved gently in the light breeze, and with the sun shining onto the orange tent, I was infused with what reminded me of the golden temple light.

The remoteness made me feel I was closer to the absolute. The perfumed scent from the pretty roses heightened my senses and I lapsed into another time and space. Here the fragrance transformed into pure love and I was transported into the feeling of nurture I had felt as a child in winter, when my father warmed my ice-cold hands under his armpits.

As I recalled the prickling sensations of warmth coming back into my fingers, I was suddenly disturbed by an uninvited vulnerability. Safety and vulnerability at the same time! Not knowing what had come over me—curled up under the thick quilt on my bed in the green oasis, I chose to concentrate my attention on the peaceful sweetness of the trees and flowers. I allowed the quivering within my body to be soothed away by the sounds of the running water, birdsong and the sighing of the wind as it made its own music. By letting go and accepting the way it was, I again drifted off, asking Mother Nature to hold me.

Soothed like a child, I surrendered my thoughts and emotions to Mother Nature. In the next moment I was captivated by what she then said.

> *I am nature's help; my colours and sounds will gently and slowly dissolve your tension—lifting your energy vibration from darkness to light—so I again can see your smile radiating*

rays of light over the mountain landscape, making true nature laugh with blissful joy, showing you that the more you wonder, the more you will discover the outside, within yourself.

I show you where you are and as soon as you become aware of me, you know where you are and which world you are in— the worldly or the divine. By being aware, you can observe your thoughts and emotions and choose where you want to be, regardless of where you are in the outer mind of distraction (restlessness, heaviness and confusion) or the inner higher mind of consciousness (fresh, light, spacious and alert). Awareness is to be fully present and beyond thoughts and emotions, where you find truth in depth of your being.

As I lay there it was as if my sadness turned into pure love rolling through me on waves of silk. I listened intently as Mother Nature continued.

You shall see me in the invisible. Move with the longing tears of something more, deeper and unexplainable, beyond what you think you cannot see, and you shall find me in your higher consciousness. When you connect with the rhythm of your breath, you shall feel me in the balance and harmony of your vibrational energy.

Surrender to me and I will show you the way. Come with me. By fighting what is, you only resist the natural flow of your true nature. Come. Flow with me and listen to the sound of my whispers in your body, mind and heart. Embrace yourself in the arms of this new and unfamiliar feeling, in the vibration of nature's soul's resonance—the knowledge within and therefore without. And you shall remember your core energy vibration, that of nature's eternal bliss.

Like a beautiful lily unfurling to the brightness of the sun, I was now beginning to feel safer and much calmer. I was released from my earlier anxiety and found a space of beauty within me, as clouds lifted from my mind to give me clarity. This is exactly what my much-loved father had once done to melt and relieve the immense pain of my frozen hands.

Slowly I started to move, but Mother Nature kept my attention.

Longing is the soul's love for the supreme ultimate reality, calling you to come home to the world of your true being. It is a language of love that the mind does not understand with its logic and reasoning.

I am whispering in your ear, divine love is waiting for you. Like a true lover, fervent longing helps you to realise that there is something more to be revealed. It is a search for unity with conscious oneness. Nurture your longing and you shall hear your heart's desire. Nourish it with patience and you will be with me in the essence of your true nature.

Devotion is your longing and your soul's love for me.
I am the selfless devotion you find in unconditional love.
I am what you are when you focus your intention on attaining a natural state of mind.
I am the impossible that becomes possible.
I am the divine will of nature's perfection.
I reside in true intelligence.

Nurtured by Mother Nature, I was rocked with tender motions of self-compassion. Like a baby tucked up safely inside a warm blanket in a wooden cradle, I thought of my grandmother. She now seemed like a beautiful rose who had seen and heard me clearly. It was only later in life that I became aware that she had, through her loving actions, cultivated my worthiness and connection to natural intelligence, innate within each and every one of us.

Struck by such an epiphany, it dawned on me that I was now being touched in the same way by nature's intelligence. It was the experience of energy transformation in action. I felt like a butterfly. With an affectionate gentle stream of unconditional love flowing through me, I was filled with goose bumps of anticipation. Although physically weary, I suddenly became aware of the time. I was supposed to go on a camel ride! I forced myself to move, and started off half asleep. On my way to the sand dunes, I noticed the distractions of my mind had passed. By seeing or witnessing the thoughts and emotions, I understood how they only block the freedom of mind to flow with our natural wisdom and intelligence. Once again, I was free and I was flying with the imaginary butterflies. 'Maybe my grandmother or father is one of those,' I wondered.

There were hundreds of stones or slabs along the way that were carved with Sanskrit texts of mantras or other holy images that made up the *mani* walls. *Mani* walls were found everywhere in significant places around the barren, sandy landscapes and villages. Some were short, and others stretched out in longer rows. As I passed them, the *Om Mani Padme Hum* mantra or prayer repeated itself automatically like an echo in my mind. The sacred land of a spiritual tradition was encoded with the language of symbolism. After a short stroll, I stopped by the large and colourfully decorated prayer wheel and slowly moved around it clockwise in circles, three times, while turning the heavy wheel (made out of a metal drum). It is believed that turning the drum or rows of smaller drums, is equal to reciting prayers of one *mala* (string or necklace made of 108 beads).

I continued to murmur the *Om Mani Padme Hum* mantra, and at the same time, as I walked, I thought of its meaning and visualised holding a lotus and a jewel in my hand. I had learned that this was the literal meaning of this mantra. (*Om* symbolises the purity of body, speech and mind; *Mani* is the Sanskrit word for jewel and sets the intention to become compassionate, loving and enlightened; *Padme* means lotus and symbolises wisdom; and *Hum* signifies the unity of method and wisdom). This is the mantra of the *Avalokiteshwara* deity that signifies the mind of enlightenment, great compassion and loving kindness.

As my feet touched the earth, one step after the other, my energy became lighter. In contact with the vibration of the earth, I was aware of my internal world changing as I interacted with the enchanting energies that moved through me. With the mantra dancing on my lips, I wondered if its sound vibration really did have the power to purify the mind and the heart. It was a mantra more usually used for the practice of spiritual development and for opening the heart—a fact I didn't know when I was first drawn to recite it.

I reached the camel station and felt the strangeness of the desert sand that grounded me. It also seemed to soften my mind. And being around animals made me feel totally at home. I was helped onto the back of one of the camels. We set off, and even though the slow movement of the camel was a bit comical, the gentle rhythm allowed me to breathe freely and take in the scents of the animals and the environment. As a result, I sank further and further into the experience of the sand dunes.

Simultaneously, I felt lifted into a light atmosphere, totally present. I could simply be, by breathing in the stark contrasts of changing light shining on the naked majestic mountains all around. I opened my arms and felt the warmth of compassion in my heart, shining with golden light rays. My view expanded and I could see into the many levels of blue-sky consciousness. The vastness of the valley gently filled me with space as I melted into oneness with all that is. For a brief moment, I experienced being totally at peace.

Happy with the camel ride and blessed with lightness in my heart, I walked past more *stupas* and *mani* walls. Just before the bridge that marked the sensitive border post to China, I turned. No foreigners were allowed past this point. I rode up the mountainside to a deserted small shrine above Hundar Village. The shrine felt eerie and different; it seemed more like a cave for meditation. Apart from the impressive golden statue, it was empty. Relieved to be alone, I knelt down in front of the Buddha and experienced the presence of a higher guidance, which I had not felt in any other monastery so far.

I wondered if it was Mother Nature. Then, I heard the firm and clear words:

Breathe with the Divine Breath of Truth.

These refined and exact words echoed repeatedly like a mantra in my mind. I didn't even have to write it down in the journal I always carried with me.

Yes, I knew it was Mother Nature. I was in harmony. I also knew my earthly thoughts were not far away, replying: 'For now, anyway!' I made my bead offerings and realised the point of being there, beyond the consciousness of my rational mind. Grateful for all the beautiful signs of aliveness, I knew I was not alone. I was so present it was easy to notice distractions. And by breathing the divine fresh air, I could let the buzzing inharmonious energy vibrations, as well as the harmonious ones, flow through me.

On my way back to the green oasis I pondered, 'Maybe the truth of who I am is shown in whatever nature mirrors back to me? By being present, like a child in wonder, I move freely with Mother Nature. Free from distraction and conditioning, I am focused about where I want to be.' Back in my tent, I curled up in my sweet idyllic haven among the sparkling flowers and babbling stream. Instantly, I was soothed and the sensations took me back to a childhood memory where I was sitting on my grandmother's lap, eating porridge with raisins. Enthralled, I snuggled up right there in my tent, as if I were cuddling close into the bosom of my grandmother. It was the exact feeling of being nourished by Mother Nature's comfort and love.

As I relaxed even more, I drifted back to the memory of playing with my grandmother's long thin greyish plait that was resting on her flowery worn-out apron. In that moment, every cell in my body remembered the deep unconditional love I felt in her hand softly stroking my hair. As I re-entered the memory of this loving communion, I felt the same thing at a divine, impersonal level, which helped me realise that the vulnerability of nakedness, the freedom of emptiness, had led me to my true wisdom and knowledge. I was receiving what I had been searching for—true love. Fully embraced by total peace, I fell asleep.

DAY 5
KHARDUNGLA PASS
5602 METRES/18,379 FEET

I woke up early after a good night's sleep, with a clear mind. My first thoughts of the day were to remain in a state of gratitude. We started on the return trip to Leh right after breakfast. After a short drive we stopped at Deskit Monastery, tucked into and clinging to the hillside above the village. It is the oldest and largest monastery in the valley, with over 100 monks in residence.

The location and the way the buildings seemed almost stacked on top of one another was fascinating. Even the architecture was a feast for my philosophical mind; it contained intricate, complex layers just like the process of consciousness clearing I was experiencing. I climbed the stairs and simultaneously turned the small prayer wheels aligned in rows along the monastery wall. The monks in their red robes were a stark contrast to the sandy beige of the desert landscape. I reached the top of one of the flat roof buildings, and stopped to admire the splendid view. 'What a magical place,' I mused. In that moment I could imagine what the green and fertile landscape would look like totally frozen in winter.

'Maybe the land has different personalities, just like the mind,' I wondered as I continued to walk up the stairs to the main temple entrance.

I was taken to the Gonkhang Temple, dedicated to the protector deities, those with particularly wrathful countenances. The entrance was carved and elaborately decorated to emphasise the shrine's sacramental significance. As the big padlock was opened, I removed my shoes and quietly said a prayer of thanks before I entered. Here in the monastery's inner sanctuary I recognised a familiar sense of something I couldn't put a name to. It was a large room filled with mostly veiled deities and masks pledged to protect the teachings and the teachers. Ancient faded murals embellished the walls and unusual ornaments were scattered everywhere.

I spotted a place on the floor that seemed to be waiting for me to meditate among all the images of the wrathful deities. With a beam of golden sun shining on me, I floated into the powerful esoteric presence of ancient wisdom. My mind was comfortably empty, clear and calm. I had no need to understand the meaning of these colourful, complex, yet simple images hiding behind the veil; I was content to have just a vague impression of them. By focusing on my breath, I remained deeply relaxed. My intuition told me that the masks emulated the profound and luminous teachings of the Mother that were camouflaged by the intellect.

Even though I had to keep going, the calmness and depth of the stillness in that room came with me as I moved through the rest of the monastery. Little did I know that Mother Nature was going to lift the veil and reveal the faces of a higher consciousness.

Nakedness

We continued our drive and started the steep ascent toward KhardungLa Pass—acclaimed by some to be the highest motorable road in the world. It didn't take long before I noticed another road sign: 'God made Ladakh—we connect it to the rest of the world.'

I caught myself reflecting. 'We are all a seed created by God or some other universal force, and it is up to us to connect ourselves with the best of who we are. To feed our essence with what it loves is the only way for the flower to shine and blossom.' It is not always easy to know how to do this since our cultural heritage has a tendency to suppress the female part, covering us with layers and facades.

As we drove up the steep narrow road, a feeling rose; I knew I was actually conquering the biggest mountain—the one within—and so learning to master the mind.

The incredibly dreamlike landscape we were travelling through felt hypnotic and led me into an inner experience of feeling totally bare and naked in the nothingness or emptiness. I had never been able to fully comprehend either concept—emptiness or nothingness—with my reasoning mind. As I merged with the landscape, there was nothing to bind me, to grasp or hang onto. I felt totally free. I could see how I had been vacillating between these revelations of true freedom and support and the doubts lodged in my old mental paradigm.

I saw that whatever I put into a space of openness, it is transformed into an experience, and then mirrored back to me by nature, beyond either the barriers of the mind or the walls of the shrines. Firmly anchored in the presence of earth and willing to go beyond, I was ushered into the land of being, where I was free from the contractions and reactions of the mind. I understood that I was still looking for the very essence of myself, for the experience of my absolute oneness with true nature.

By weaving together my outer and inner experiences, the real and unreal merged into emptiness, which then opened into everything; there was no longer a separation between the two worlds. I had a feeling of being without form flowing with the fluid energy of higher consciousness that took me beyond and into the universal ecstasy dance of realisation. Coming into form and dissolving out of it were both amazing experiences.

I knew that only in the stillness between my thoughts did Mother Nature's voice, my higher consciousness truly speak to me. Even with a trembling bladder, on the bumpy road, I dwelled in the ground's power of existence. I felt the pulse of Mother Nature and the heartbeat of love. Between thoughts, she spoke again.

> *Your true nature is the heart of the self, pulsating with currents of vibration. When you find the rhythmic heartbeat of your inner self, the unreal becomes real. Then you will know that I pulsate in your heart with nature's force of natural intelligence, beyond thinking. Your intellect is a mere instrument for true nature, just like external nature is a vehicle for internal primordial energy.*

Khardung Village

We approached Khardung Village and it felt as though I was entering the womb of nature's creation. With the experience of being held by Mother Nature, I connected to the awesome vibrations of sheer energy that surged through me with an unconditional motherly love.

The village was seated on a plateau surrounded by steep mountains. A gorge was carved out far down in the steep valley. Below, I could see the stream of water flowing through the earth like divine consciousness flows through humanity. It occurred to me that this was a dynamic and universal energy dance without fear of the unconscious; where the heart was in synchrony with the mind.

Then, without warning, I was thrown around in the car. The bumpy road was getting worse. And what was I supposed to do with my bursting bladder? There was nowhere to stop. Again, the open landscape spoke to me with her words.

Born pure in heart, it sometimes takes many lifetimes of work to purify the mind, body, spirit and speech. When you open up and give birth to the universe of wholeness, you become at one with your inner self. This means a commitment to be true to self.

I immediately related to what Mother Nature was saying, and she continued as if she was singing a sonorous lullaby.

To have the will to stay on one's path of truth and walk with integrity, one must allow the old to die and give birth to the new. That is simply nature's cycle of life.

And her gentle voice of higher awareness didn't stop.

The layer of self-love is an absolute along the way, as you connect with and experience your true nature. Love for oneself means to nurture self like a child, so you can value yourself as 'worthy'. Self-love and care is connected to your higher consciousness, and without it you will not pass or overcome the obstacles of the mind (preconceived thoughts and emotions).

I could accept this idea as it made complete sense of my need for integrity at this time of my life. Nature's cycles and paths were being shown to me all around, through the astonishing mountains, the meandering streams and the small moving dots of white clouds in the alluring blue sky that seemed within reach.

Tightly squeezing my legs, I thought my bladder was going to burst any second. What could I do? The answer I received was this:

Look at me and you shall look into the essence of your heart. Tell me the truth and I shall reveal it to you. It is hidden deep within the story of creation, written in the scriptures within you. The heart of nature is a mirror of you and the shape of your essence. Layers of consciousness unfold and nature's intelligence reveals wisdom in the petals of knowledge through experience.

I forgot about my trembling bladder and contemplated what Mother Nature had just said. The image of compassionate self-love that she painted in my mind had become more than just an idea. To love the self was not something I had consciously started relating to until my heart was shattered into a million pieces. Since then, I have learned through patient self-awareness that self-love is an absolute for growth and nurturing the child part of my inner self. And now, through Mother Nature's teachings, I was beginning to experience even more strongly that loving self is a gateway necessary for a connection to divine consciousness. Without self-love, I am disconnected from my inner essential self.

However, I was not sure at this point if I could absorb and understand all of the additional information I was given. How could I overcome the obstacles of the mind?

My trembling bladder spoke loudly again, 'If there is a God in this place, please give me a toilet.' I sat on the edge of my seat and squeezed my legs together even tighter. And finally, not long after we reached Khardung Village, my prayer was answered. Needless to say, I was relieved. After a short break to eat a chocolate, stretch our legs, breathe the fresh crystalline air and briefly interact with some local characters, we continued the zigzag ascent to the pass.

What is Nirvana Anyway?

As we moved through the landscape like a hissing cobra, I felt physically more comfortable and entered a contemplative state of mind. It was impossible to write while driving on this road, so I used my digital recorder. As I spoke into the recorder, the voice started talking through me, as me, as easily as I might inhale the fragrance of a rose.

> *Just like nature of creation, you cannot think you are going to have an insight. This is the obstacle to attaining the goal of ultimate reality. By limiting the freedom of mind, the energy of nature is suppressed, creating a barrier for the natural intelligence of pure consciousness to flow.*

'Yes,' I mumbled, 'but going beyond, cutting the chain of conditioning and walking past the obstacles of fixed thoughts and negative emotions takes patience and a strong sense of discipline.' In Tibetan Buddhism this is referred to as 'nirvana' or 'enlightenment'. And here, in this land of pure, untouched and pristine energy vibration, the consciousness of enlightenment lives on the food of nature's intelligence; mantras, prayers and daily rituals of worship and devotion to something greater than the worldly mind.

Quite frankly, who knows what enlightenment is and where we end up? My thoughts told me that my worldly ego—I—did not believe in such a thing. But in spite of my ignorant mind, I was after all walking the sacred land of Tibetan Buddhism imbued with the belief that every soul is reborn to overcome suffering and to learn lessons until it reaches enlightenment; possibly within this lifetime.

As we continued driving, I clung tightly to my backpack, camera, video camera, small laptop and recorder on the bumpy road. Physically, it felt as though I was falling apart. I must have needed the roughness of the road to shake up the ego part of my mind that was hanging on to the automatic way of thinking. Again, my consciousness drifted to the naked land, and I witnessed the flowing stream that crossed my inner landscape. I thought: 'Laziness, boredom, fear, doubt and frustration are only excuses for the disillusioned mind to cling to what it believes is the truth, so that it does not have to do anything about changing actual facts based on illusions of an entrapped mind.'

I could see how life could often be like this jarring, bumpy, curving, crazy road. While being bounced around, we were still ascending! In the midst of it all I reflected: 'When I allow myself to be seduced by the intellect, I get nowhere. It is like a co-dependent relationship where two people are mutually dependent psychologically upon each other in an unhealthy way—I become attached to ideas that do not serve my highest good and at worst suppresses my true self.'

With crystal clarity, Mother Nature's teaching started to flow like a stream.

> *True nature cannot be forced. Its natural intelligence is to flow into existence, letting it come, like a flash of lightening; an insight is instantly borne in an open, free and flexible mind. Just like the creation of the universe—enlightening experiences*

and electrical currents of divine love come into existence in an instant from the manifestation of cosmic play. If it is controlled by reasoning or figured out by thinking about it, creation will never take place. Only beyond the intellect of the mind can the power of nature create, through the secret energy of nature, inherently within everyone. This is only activated when you long for the ultimate potential, hidden in supreme freedom to just be.

When we climbed higher up the mountainous road it was as if I could see how the obstacles of the mind dissolved. I could feel how when I surrender, I instantly connect to the higher wisdom that is simply there, especially in nature.

Just before the pass, I turned back and looked into the blue horizon. The clear view of the solid and forbidding mountains told me that everything I wanted had a form of attachment. The valley below seemed deeply forgiving and loving and encouraged me to let go of my old thoughts and simply trust. It was similar to the way I had been relieved from my pressing painful bladder. I saw that with compassion and acceptance, I could embrace and release whatever came my way.

'How amazingly magnificent it is to be a witness to the creeping disillusionment that wants to seduce me,' I concluded with great pleasure and enthusiasm.

Spectacular KhardungLa Pass (5602 metres/18,379 feet)

Finally we reached the top of KhardungLa pass. My perception expanded in all directions through the sound of what seemed like thousands of prayer flags, fluttering on strings in the cold, fierce wind. As they spread prayers to the world to purify mind, body and speech, my energy went with them.

As soon as I entered the temple area at the summit, two women came forward and greeted me with warm hugs. 'We are so happy to see you,' they said. Even though I had never seen them before, I just smiled and felt a homecoming to that nurturing heart-space. It wasn't long until, between the flapping strips of green, red, yellow, white and blue cloth, some torn and faded, I found myself rolling around in the snow like a gleeful child—with these two women. It felt like a magical celebration of joy and unity. Bonded, without separation, I looked into the eyes of another living culture of Indian women and goddesses. My eyes opened onto a mystery within.

And with this visual picture, I stepped inside the small temple filled with a peaceful, airy atmosphere. I was not the only one. Many people had gathered here to connect with the spiritual forces the mountain pass symbolised. Before departing, I left some of the 108 prayer beads that made up my *mala*. The necklace had one day unexpectedly shattered while I walked the Camino de Santiago in Spain. I had collected the beads, sensing they would be important later. And now the time had come to leave these wooden beads (usually made from seeds of the rudraksha tree, the wood of the tulsi plant or the lotus plant, yak bone, or different crystals and gems), that carried my prayers for detachment and freedom, and to come into union with aspects of my higher being.

It was tremendously cold, but I wasn't ready to leave. I wanted to get to the real peak of the pass, so I climbed higher and higher in my gold running shoes. With both of my arms, I reached into the royal blue sky. 'There is no limit!' I exclaimed. 'Just remove the obstacles and here I am, on top of the world!' My toes were freezing, so I hurried back down, and I was very happy to jump back into the warm car.

The Goddess of Stok Kangri (6120 metres/20,078 feet)

As we descended to Leh, I became fascinated by the magnificent panoramic view of the Stok mountain range that soared up towards the sky around us. It seemed we were in a fantasyland. Without warning, the invisible became visible. Excitedly, I blurted out, 'Wow! I can't believe it—I can see another face on the highest peak, Stok Kangri.'

The face was so vivid; I handed the camera to the driver and asked if he could see it through the lens. Silly me. He handed the camera back and just looked at me. What I saw was a small delicate face of an old looking man staring at me from what looked like the throat of the mountain.

As we continued down the winding road, I kept searching the craggy mountains and I could not believe it when I saw yet another face staring at me; it was the third one! The goddess' head covered the mountaintop as if resting. Her face toward the sky, a silky veil covered her eyes and draped down the mountainsides. Out of nowhere, like a flash of lightening, I could see both the physical and spiritual. It seemed like a natural phenomenon—something I had always seen and known.

My mind felt empty, like a void. I could say nothing! I could think nothing! Instead, I was quietly drawn into the silent landscape of the inner and outer worlds. I watched with deep concentration and a state of total calm. Then it happened again. Another amazing vision appeared. It looked like a serene man wearing a headpiece.

Carved like a sculpture on the surface of the mountain, the image turned into a meditating Buddha in a lotus position (cross-legged, with feet resting on thighs).

I gasped. 'Is this what can happen when the mind is at peace and free from external stimulation and any interference from preconceived ideas, conditions and expectations? Perhaps the mind really can open to perceive the reality of higher consciousness.'

As we descended, we entered a lush verdant paradise and drove between avenues of trees. The familiar hustle and bustle of Leh greeted us. I was still seeing the vivid faces and the goddess shining in what had now changed to the red-gold light of dusk on the mountain peaks. I experienced an aspect of freedom I hadn't known; I was seeing beyond the world of distortions, through layers of the world's artificial images and illusions to nature's mystical images that were no longer hidden to me.

So what had I just seen? Was it a glimpse of a new dimension and a new, mysterious part of myself? I felt I was seeing with 'new eyes', with 'spiritual eyes', or even with the 'eternal eye'. Had I witnessed a dimension only seen by the holiest among us? I could only wonder. I decided that it was rather pointless to analyse the matter any further. I would put these events aside until something started to make more sense naturally.

Hotel Holiday Ladakh

Back at the hotel in Leh, I was jolted into what felt like the mundane ego mind—that way of thinking and being that most people take as normal, in which we feel separate, vulnerable, fearful and self-protective.

Part 2

I was not happy when the male representative from the mountaineering company turned up at dinner and told me that there was another person joining me on the trek. A French woman was going to come with us the next morning. Even though I had pre-booked a guide and specifically made arrangements to do the trek on my own before I left Norway, I had already arrived at Schiphol airport in Amsterdam when I read an email from the company in which they had asked if a man from Austria could join me. Despite strong physical contractions through my whole body, I had agreed. Now with the French woman included, we were three people doing the trek, in addition to the trekking team, which would consist of the guide, horseman, cook and an assistant, plus six ponies.

Although deeply disappointed, I couldn't get myself to complain. Instead, I justified why I should let it go. It was a lot of resources for 21 days when others also wanted to do it. But I really wanted to do this alone and my heart was screaming with frustration. The good thing was that they were only going with us for the first ten days to the halfway mark, Padum, the capital of Zanskar.

It was still dusk and I stayed on the balcony for a while. I reminded myself to breathe and just let things happen. As I listened to my breathing, I watched the mountains and felt the energy of Mother Nature. I could still see the mountain goddess bathing in the gold-red light on top of Stok Kangri.

'Must I hang onto my thoughts and emotions so tightly?' I asked myself. Then, I remembered the liberating feeling associated with the release of my pressing bladder. In that moment I could let go by releasing the worries that were just as painful to hang onto. In that moment it was as though I was driving past a road sign that said, 'Let it go!'

Automatically, the *Om Mani Padme Hum* mantra started to repeat in my mind, and the thoughts and emotions dissolved. The mantra is meant to protect or guide the mind, and this is exactly what I experienced. By continuing to breathe and chant under my breath, I became more relaxed and continued to gaze at the mountain goddess. With her illuminating presence, I knew instantly that Mother Nature would come with us. My awareness told me that everything was perfect the way it was. I felt the energy of excitement rise and instantly I knew that 'Mother Nature is the mountain goddess I can see on Stok Kangri; she is the mystery of inner knowing guiding me.'

I hardly noticed the cold, although it was getting late. I went inside and finished packing, and thought about the visions that had appeared out of the rocky and snowy mountains. Very clearly she told me:

Faith and devotion are actions that bring you closer and closer to your ultimate goal, as you approach freedom. Just walk and everything will unfold.

I smiled to myself and replied:

'Walk I will—guided by Mother Nature who shows me the way. Strange isn't it? Searching for who I am, I see her. And not only that, she helps me to see how easily I can fall back into the insignificant worldly mind of the ego. But when I watch her glowing there on the mountaintop, I can observe and become aware of another reality of truth. It shows me that I can also be a witness to my heartache, and at the same time embrace it with an unconditional loving acceptance, as my cognitive perception changes, without attaching any significance to it.'

I had witnessed something extraordinary, and with this direct experience, I was moving in and out of different dimensions—*within* the real and surreal landscape. I was not dreaming. Something that was not there one moment was very much there the next. I wondered if I was the only person seeing it—and if so, why.

I was tired from the intensity of the days so far. The electricity was out and I didn't feel like speaking into my recorder. I finally got into bed. I glanced at the precious gems that were still on the altar I had made on the windowsill. The clear light of the moon made the silver bangle inscribed with a prayer of good luck shine with layers of consciousness; a perfect round universe granted me visions of freedom.

DAY 6
Lamayuru — West of Leh
3420 metres/11,220 feet

I was full of energy when I woke at 6 a.m. and the first thing I did was open the thin curtains. The clear blue sky filled me with excitement and joy. Was the goddess still there on the mountaintop? I quickly dressed and went out onto the balcony. And yes, she was there! It was a good time to do a prayer and set my intention for the day. I was grateful for what I had seen and I thanked Mother Nature, the moon and the sun.

My fervent longing, now so powerfully awakened, brought me to ask the same question again, 'Who is it that I am seeing? Am I seeing the seer, who lifts the veil and reveals the reality of truth?'

It didn't take long before *Mother Nature* surreptitiously answered my questions.

> *The veil is being lifted and your visions connect you with the divine source. Watch and you shall find me. You are what you cannot see through a polluted mind. You are the invisible core, the vibration of earth, water, fire, air and sky—you are the*

reflection of a pure mind, crystallised in the molecules of water, and yet so much more than that.

I wasn't quite sure what she meant, and I uttered in my mind, 'But how can this be?' She immediately replied.

I am the experienced reality of the divine self—the secret energy of nature, hidden in truth beyond the unreal. I am changing your perspectives and transcending old patterns. The world of your new reality may be thought of as strange but the strangeness is an act of the divine, of unseen magic. Only through experience of another reality do you understand nature's wisdom with your inner knowing—a source of super consciousness beyond mundane thinking.

I found myself apologising to Mother Nature for rushing to get ready on time for breakfast. While carefully packing my gemstones, I prayed for an open heart and clear light awareness to accept others and myself unconditionally in every step taken.

The driver came at 8 a.m. and the French woman was waiting in the car. I had accepted the situation and decided that this was how it was supposed to be. On entering the car, I was barely greeted with a hello. Our relationship was tense from the beginning. However, I remembered the message from Mother Nature and surrendered to the way it was. Then, I felt fine.

The drive to Lamayuru, west of Leh, would take about six hours. It was the only road that would take us to Srinagar in Kashmir if we continued past Lamayuru. We stopped at a couple of striking monasteries along the way that housed great Buddha statues and artefacts such as butter lamps, complex masks and *thangka* scroll paintings.

They reminded me of the calm mind I aspired to. Nevertheless, I felt restless and in a hurry to reach Lamayuru.

Since the French woman gave no impression of wanting to make conversation, the fascinating landscape once again triggered my intuition.

The Grasping Mind

I thought of what had happened so far and could not help but notice that in the midst of these precious experiences, my mind constantly backtracked to old, fixated thinking patterns. Surrounded by the stunning landscape, I caught myself thinking I had paid too much for the sheepskin vest. I was annoyed with myself for buying it. Not only was it more to carry, but on top of that, I didn't need it.

In a split second a feeling of self-compassion blossomed within me and I let go of the frustration for purchasing the vest. The man needed the money and I could forgive myself for not being more aware at the time. It simply showed me how easily I could be seduced by the worldly mind if I was not grounded. I was amused that I could obsess about this trivia and feel frustrated in this land of enlightenment! It occurred to me how quickly I could shift from higher consciousness and bliss to lower states of worry and sadness and vice versa.

The first step was to pay attention to whether my internal physical, mental and emotional energy levels went up or down. I had noticed that this could manifest in various ways. For example, my shoulders would be stiff, and my thinking would go into overdrive and I would start to obsess and worry over little things. Or I would feel nauseous, restless and overwhelmed with confusion and doubt, so I could not concentrate on anything else.

When the mind grabs hold of something it thinks is important, it fixates on worry, doubt, guilt, frustration and so on, and that creates low physical, mental and emotional energy levels. That tendency to fixate feeds the ego's obsessive and obstructive nature, cluttering the clearer parts of the mind. When this happens, I find it is impossible to hear my inner knowing.

It is easy then to fall into a kind of addiction, or become stuck in a loop of negative thinking habits. By being vaguely aware that this was not right—and maybe more importantly that it wasn't *me*; I could see the attachments and let go of what felt like a lifetime of old patterns that related to wanting to be loved.

The kind of journey I was on now, in the challenging Himalayas, was my antidote. It had a miraculous power to cut through addictive thinking patterns. When I walked in unfamiliar territory, my mind had to expand and this helped me break old habits. New ways of thinking emerged, as well as new ideas and visions.

Taking Care of Myself

In hindsight, I realised that my internal physical, mental and emotional energy level had decreased when I first said it was okay for another person to join me on the trek, and then again when I repeated the situation. I had listened, but ignored the disappointment and heartache that had created a major contraction in my body, emotions and mind. The dishonouring of my voice and heart's desire seemed so habitual. How long had I been doing that? Or was I being too hard on myself? I was here, right? I had acted on my deep knowing and strong signals to go to India.

By putting others' needs before my own—in an attempt to be

unselfish—yet failing to trust myself enough, I had disrespected my inner self, which was something I had worked hard to connect with. This was a habit I needed to pay attention to. When I allowed myself to go on the Himalayan journey I took care of myself in a loving way. Yet I was still discovering how to love myself enough to avoid falling into habitual mind traps. In trusting the physical, mental and emotional signs of contraction and expansion, I became more aware of how to discriminate between when it was okay to say *no*, and for that matter, *yes*.

For the time being, I could allow myself enough compassion to see that everything about the current situation was the way it was supposed to be. It simply was the way it was—uncomfortable, disappointing and even lonely at times—so I could practice purifying my mind and opening my heart.

I started to experience the way awareness became an evolutionary process that took place as I walked forwards, backwards, sideways and upwards. Walking the Camino was a great example of this. It had made the illusions about what I thought was love very clear. I had noticed though how easy it was to forget this when I returned home to my habitual patterns and environment. Maybe that's why I wanted to make this even bigger journey to India—to fully integrate what I had learned.

I also realised that the Austrian man and the French woman were teaching me how to take care of myself. I did not forget the mental and emotional contraction of agony in my body when I had said yes. In a similar situation later, I remembered this and said *no*. In the end I was grateful for becoming more aware of my intuition and how to trust my inner knowing.

The Moon Land

As we approached the little village of Lamayuru, my jaw dropped. I was awestruck by the claylike, light brown rock formations. They were shaped in round, sculpted curves that were alive—to me—with faint, white faces hidden in the darker brown mountainside. The mountains seemed to move with animated faces that came in and out of focus, as I flowed between conscious and unconscious states of mind. It felt like I might be on the moon.

There were silhouetted forms present in something that reminded me of soft human shapes without distinct lines. These figures overlooked the moon faces and I thought they might be protective deities. I felt hypnotised by the strange presence of these deities with their silhouetted human forms and vague faces. What I was seeing made me think of the protective wrathful deities I had observed in the monasteries. Usually they were kept veiled, obscuring the fine details of their features, which would only be fully revealed at a festival once a year. Some were never revealed.

The vision I had seen on top of Mount Stok Kangri appeared in my mind, where I had seen the veiled goddess, or the Mother. I wondered then: 'Did the mountain goddess on Stok Kangri ever appear without her veil? Perhaps the veil has another meaning.' The natural landscape and the visions I had been witnessing always seemed to reflect the moon and the mystery of existence. It made me wonder if there was a connection between the feminine, nurturing moon energy and the veils I had seen on the protective deities. Could it be that to penetrate the mystery we had to use our feminine awareness?

The sun had also given me experiences and visions on earlier travels to Brazil. I lay on the beach one day and the sun literally came into my belly, filling me with the powerful energy of fire, transforming some emotional pain. The sun and the moon definitely symbolised something within me. But then another question popped into my mind: 'Why was all this coming to me, now?' Mother Nature firmly interrupted these thoughts with a request.

> *Please don't ask how this suddenly reveals itself. You can trust that the answers will be revealed to you. You are connecting to something familiar, a core vibration you are remembering. Trust the moon energy. Trust the energy of fire from the sun.*

The not knowing was certainly a challenge to my reasoning mind. I wanted to know—now! But perhaps my inner essence recognises or remembers what I want to know on a cellular level. Maybe the sun and moon were awakening some sort of deep physical memory. Could I learn to hear my intuitive voice more clearly? Did the monks have experiences like this as their consciousness expanded in meditation? If they did, maybe they just witnessed their visions without doing anything. I saw that my mind had a strong desire to capture and keep my experiences, when perhaps they were only ever meant to be transitory. It occurred to me that if this is true, then in the end it does not matter.

A flash of doubt, frustration or worry passes the same way a glowing light of peace, love or joy eventually fades. Just like a flame. The mind, however, does have the capacity to be still. In a harmonious state, the mind does not interfere, but rather witnesses the flame objectively.

Lamayuru—the Monastery

The spectacular view of the Lamayuru Monastery opened up and I felt like an excited child on the edge of her seat. The building was perched on a spur on top of an eroded clay landscape of sculpted cliffs. There were other adjacent white brick houses varying in size, cascading down from the monastery. It also looked like there were caves carved into the mountain. I could see, in a lightning flash, the intricate layers of the mind within this design.

Once there I got out of the car, stretched and reached my arms far up into the blue sky. As I breathed in the fresh air, I saw new possibilities in the vast uncluttered mountain plateau above the treeline. The sound of the laughing, playing children made me smile and I was drawn closer into this compelling place.

The Lama

It was early afternoon and we were free to do what we wanted. After saying hello to the quiet and friendly Austrian man who was joining us here, I started to explore the monastery. When I entered the assembly hall, the place looked deserted. The huge red temple door was not bolted and a pair of shoes was on the stairs. It struck me as a little bit eerie. I removed my shoes and went into the big room filled with precious statues, colourful *thangkas* hanging from the roof and big glass cabinets with ancient texts.

I followed the distant sound of a drumbeat and wasn't sure if I would be allowed to enter the back room. Carefully, with butterflies in my stomach, I entered and found a lama at the end of the room carrying out *puja* worship rituals. I gestured to ask if it was okay for me to enter; he nodded. Before him was a low table with various instruments and tangible artefacts, including offering bowls, a skull bowl and the sacred texts. The *ghanta* (handbell) and *vajra* (known as thunderbolt, symbolising the absolute) are essential objects of wisdom and compassion used together in prayers and rituals to uphold harmony.

I leaned on the wooden pillar in front of him and listened to the chanting and drumming. My eyes gently closed for a brief moment. The sound of the bell took me into a land of purity and peace, where I could feel my heart dancing with the music of life.

Afterwards, he proudly showed me the butter sculptures he had made for offerings. Then, without knowing where I was going, I was guided down a steep path to the *Sengge-Gang* (lion mound) temple. We meandered past the ruined buildings and found the oldest shrine, tucked away. I watched as the lama opened the huge lock with a big key. The dark ruby entry door was so tiny that I had to bend down to go inside. I was later told that doors and windows are kept small to keep out ghosts and demons.

I was astounded when he left me there all by myself. The small rooms felt like deep caves and the faded and damaged murals on the walls reflected a primordial wisdom in the nine-hundred-year-old shrine. Even though it was cold, I sat down in front of the white skeleton painted on the brown wall. I contemplated the image, and dropped into stillness. There was a magical presence. It was as if my wants had been heard; to be guided by a lama and left in peace with no one around.

After a while the lama came back and took me to the main area with many different sized white *stupas*. He didn't say much. When we turned the small prayer wheels, placed in rows around the outer walls of the monastery, the lama's shyness and the sound of the squeaky wheels filled me with giggles of joy and innocence. Two older monks dressed in their red robes joined us and as we moved around with broad smiles on our faces, the door to the heart of my compassion was opened even wider. With deep humility and gratitude, I felt blessed. The monks nurtured me in their innocent way with the same feeling of unconditional love that Mother Nature was awakening within me.

I loved being around them, but I needed to meet the others. As soon as I reached the dining room where we were having dinner, I noticed that the atmosphere had dropped to a sombre mood. I acknowledged this and like a flash, the image I had seen of the mountain goddess, on top of Mount Stok Kangri in Leh, came into my mind. And in that moment, I could see the gold-red light from the goddess shine on everyone in the room. It seemed as though the light were emanating directly from the image of the mountain goddess. I watched the energy change from dark gloom to golden light. For a few seconds, I was transmuted into a space of something that felt like eternity.

The guide's faint voice brought me back as he prepared us for the next day. Half listening, I thought, 'Wow! This is really seeing a different perspective.' Could I really be seeing this, or is it just an illusion? After all, there were no windows in the room and it was dark outside.

I returned to worldly affairs, and heard the guide tell us that all the supplies including the tents and food we needed for the entire journey were in place for us to start the trek in the morning. And the whole team had arrived. One more night, and we were going on foot even further into the isolated, treacherous Himalayan kingdom.

It was early September, so I wondered if we would make it across the mountain passes before the winter snows set in. Anything could happen.

Protective Deities

On the way to my room, I noticed the moon shining on the naked landscape, as if Mother Nature was radiating her inner light on everyone. It was a good moment to pause, and as I took a deep breath I could see that the three linear stars nearest to the moon were sparkling bright. It occurred to me that they represented the intuitive wisdom of the unconscious, pulsating quietly but brilliantly. My surroundings glittered and I felt like I was inside the heart of the soul. The intimacy I felt from this granted me real freedom and oneness.

Walking to my room, the squeaky floorboards welcomed me. As I opened the door, I felt strongly drawn into the room; the big space inside had a royal presence. I walked over to the windows facing the courtyard of the monastery, and closed the torn and semi-transparent curtains that didn't quite cover the windows. The large bed was inviting and even though it was my last opportunity to use the computer, I allowed myself to just lie down.

Immediately the light images from the mountain goddess of Stok Kangri and the moon lit my mind like a light bulb turning on. I smelled the rose fragrance of unconditional love from the lama's burning incense and sank deeper and deeper into total relaxation. I drifted into the light with vague images of deities floating above me. As darkness took over, a deep silence penetrated my cells. The velvet texture of peace flowed through me like something liquid and pure— perhaps golden honey. I felt transparent and formless. I rejoiced in the guidance of higher consciousness that I was merging into.

PART 3

The 21-Day Sacred Walk: The Himalayan Kingdom of Ladakh and Zanskar

May we trust the intuitive guidance of the white moon faces so we can walk onward, lift the veil of illusions and receive the life force energy from the faces imprinted in our unconscious mind and hidden in the rocky snowy mountains—guarded by Mother Nature's divine consciousness.

DAY 1
OPENING TO THE SACRED WALK
GROUND ZERO: 3524 METRES/11,562 FEET

I awoke early to distant sound of gentle chanting. The softness resonated seamlessly with the loving and peaceful energy I felt within from the night before. The echo of the rhythmic chant sounded like an eternal, reliable expression of loving devotion. It gave me a sense of tranquillity and comfort, almost like a lullaby—partly perhaps because I had now heard similar chanting recited so many times in sacred places.

I rose with the dawn and stretched. My body was still not quite awake. I went over to sit on the windowsill and looked out. Incense was burning on the flat rooftops around the monastery. I breathed in the aroma and felt an urge to connect with nature and receive whatever guidance it might offer me. How might my unconscious be trying to prepare me for expanding my horizons?

Slowly I gathered all my things: laptop, camera, video, recorder and writing journals. As I put them into my backpack, I mumbled: 'God knows why I am carrying all this on a trek that is considered to be one of the toughest in the world!' I was aware of thinking that they were material attachments I needed to let go of. Yet a part of me absolutely knew that this was what I had to do, that I would need these things.

I was listening more deeply to my inner knowing even though it came and went like the glittering stars in the night sky. Despite what the worldly mind said, I could now register my critical thoughts, let them float and dissolve like white fluffy clouds. I could continue to cultivate a practice of patient awareness and trust in the present. By relaxing, I could allow the wisdom of the intuitive voice to enter me more fully, and decisions and action came more easily.

Ready, with my trekking boots on my feet and dressed in many layers of clothing, I went outside. While I knew I would soon have to face the intense cold at higher altitude, I was more worried about how I would protect my face from the fierce sun. At the same time, the depth of silence I had experienced during the night and the memory of the meditative moon landscape comforted me. I felt a sense of belonging and freedom—freedom just to *be*.

A Prayer for Permission

I walked over to the main monastery to do the morning ritual of turning the 108 prayer wheels. As I repeated the *Om Mani Padme Hum* mantra, compassion awakened deep in my heart. Simultaneously watching the smoke from the rooftops, I breathed into the gratitude I felt rising all around me. I offered my prayer for permission to enter the mountain kingdom and be protected from evil spirits and bad luck, and it dissolved into the clear sky.

Maybe I had already been blessed by the greater presence I had felt floating over me during the night. Although it was a bit weird to think there were fierce-faced protective deities dancing around and above me, I was at peace. I realised that this was my intuitive mind, accepting what I see, sense, think and hear when it aligns with my reality.

I could see that the surrounding moon landscape reflected the unknown potential that lies hidden in our unconscious. I could hear the echo of people's questions, too. 'How do we know and see what is true? How do we know what is real and what is not?'

Most of us have been programmed to think that what we see is real. This is a phenomenon of the intellectual mind. The truth can only be understood by experiencing our own reality in connection with our true inner nature. This is a process of experiential learning and understanding the mind by cultivating self-awareness, acceptance and intuition.

Imagine watching the moon as it moves from new to full. Although we can't quite see it growing, we know it does. Unconsciously we trust the process, and just know, without rationally thinking about it. Our consciousness expands naturally like the moon becoming full; we develop wisdom and become more conscious as knowledge floats in from the unconscious. As we experience this connection, we may feel a joyful richness and fullness that infuses us with calm, clarity, freedom—and that gives us a sense of happiness, goodness, peace, love, vitality and strength. This bridging and expansion is what I believe to be the silent voice of our inner knowing, intuition, true nature, soul or higher consciousness, that opens us to our truth; it is as unique to each of us as our DNA. To access this higher dimension of our mind we must connect to the essence of our true nature.

With this in mind, I was starting to believe that the sacred Sanskrit syllables in the *Om Mani Padme Hum* mantra could manifest certain powerful cosmic forces. It is believed that by reciting the six mystic words or by engraving them on rocks, one can be liberated from harm and disease in this life and ultimately be led to a state of Buddhahood in later lives.

I let that thought sit there and decided to connect with my own prayers. Silently praying for good weather, excellent health and divine strength, I was ready to start the 21-day adventure walking across the remote and almost inaccessible Ladakh and Zanskar mountain ranges. I was not the first to walk through the hidden valleys of sparsely populated barren land and experience the rare enclave of rich Tibetan culture and Buddhism. Many great Tibetan Buddhist teachers, saints and masters had traversed it long before me.

PrikitingLa Pass (3700 metres/12,140 feet)

As I walked that morning, on the first day of the trek, the pristine beauty and the heavenly azure sky struck me. There was no one around. The path was empty and silent like the open, austere landscape. However, I soon spotted some women harvesting the barley crop. The fields were decorated with lovely square patterns made from the bundles.

Despite the heavy backpack containing all my technical gadgets, I was excited and had a sense of courage and relief at finally starting this journey. Secretly, I was hoping to find *that thing* I felt stirring deep inside and to be set free from the life of suffering that didn't give me what I wanted. Usually a happy-go-lucky person, I at times entered a state of despair and grief over why I couldn't have a happy loving relationship and a job that satisfied me.

The strong drive for *that thing* had intensified over the last few years. I could feel the greatness of something coming in my life;

destiny was around the corner but I didn't know what it was. I was following my inner knowing more and more, but was also feeling waves of fear and resistance about being who *I am*. Something bigger than the little me definitely wanted to be expressed.

The transformation I was experiencing on these treks felt like both a gift and a burden. It was a process of resistance and surrender. Every time I turned a corner or crossed a mountain pass, *that thing* felt bigger and bigger. I was impatient. I desperately wanted to understand and know, but I discovered that the answers were not logical and took their own time in coming.

The nine passes we were crossing reminded me of the summit of higher consciousness, towards which I was climbing inside myself. In tune with contraction and expansion, ascent and descent, peaks and valleys, I was still walking blind through the process of letting go of worldly attachments such as my love relationship, daily demands and work responsibilities. I was, however, increasingly aware that these commitments and the illusions that kept me holding on to them had separated me from who I truly was. The real challenge was to stay true to myself and in the process wake up to the simplicity of everyday experiences, which paradoxically offered me new visions.

I had learned courage and perseverance, so I had no fear of physically walking. I was more than willing to walk. Rather, I was dealing with the fear of allowing myself to embody the greatness of divinity I felt within me (which I now know is within everybody).

With my long flowery cashmere shawl wrapped around my neck and head, I was hiding from the sun. Only my mouth, nose, sunglasses, and parts of my off-white headband were visible. I thought of the shaved monks and nuns who strip away all their outer symbols of attachment and the distractions of individuality. Would I be able to be as devoted and dedicated to the sacred path, and move beyond the wanting, grasping mind?

In between my panting, I wondered: 'Is this what will happen on my journey?' Just thinking about shaving my head aroused fear in me. I thought some reassuring thoughts—that if I shaved my head then that would be absolutely perfect at the time. And symbolically it could mean that another mask was removed on the healing journey of revelation and freedom. After all, I was longing for the simplicity of life that this spiritual land reflected.

Winded from the altitude, I stopped to catch my breath and drink some water. A light breeze suddenly came to cool me down. For a brief moment the passing wind reminded me of how awareness comes and goes and helps me release negative thoughts. The bare desert landscape showed me how whatever floats to the surface of the mind can simply be released over and over until it is gone. I had not forgotten how fantastic it felt when I had released my pressing bladder!

As I looked up into that heavenly sky again, I realised there is no need to hang on to anything. I promised myself that I would never again allow the ego mind to deny the wants of my heart. I turned around and saw the others not too far in front of me, so I continued to walk and heard myself mumbling: 'Whatever comes, it will be just another thing to let go of.'

As we reached the first of nine passes, I felt surprisingly light. The top of the pass reminded me of a narrow gateway. Steep mountains rose on each side, with just enough space to walk past. A small cairn with one big rock shaped like a diamond and many other loose rocks stacked around it was placed right in the middle of the path. It looked like a *stupa*. I had learned that this kind of spiritual monument or landmark, on a windy desert mountain pass, was believed to offer protection from evil spirits and ensure travellers safe passage.

The view to either side was breathtakingly beautiful. I looked back over the landscape I had walked and, in amazement, I could see how perfect everything was—and always had been. On my in-breath I asked: 'How did it happen?' And on my out-breath, the answer was clear: 'When I let go and surrender to the powerful forces of nature, it is what it is—if I let it be so.' I loved this technique of finding the question and answer connected so closely!

I faced forward again and gazed into the horizon of the unknown that my intuitive mind was leading me towards. The towering jagged peaks, forming into waves of mountain ranges, reminded me of ice pinnacles sticking up in the air. As I started to move, I thought: 'Maybe the truth I am seeking lies in the depth of my own being.'

In that moment, I stopped and spontaneously reached into my pocket to get some of the prayer beads I had kept from the *mala*, which had broken when I walked the Camino de Santiago. I threw them into the luminous air and murmured into my shawl: 'Please let me walk in harmony, so I can discover *it* and rise to a new level of consciousness.' I realised I was asking Mother Nature to help me see clearly and break free from habitual behavioural, emotional and mental patterns that no longer worked in my life. It was partly frightening, but I knew it was my truth.

As I opened to the intuitive part of me, Mother Nature was becoming a natural part of my consciousness, allowing me to be more accepting and compassionate towards the critical and judgmental mind, and toward the other people I was walking with. By walking, high and low, I understood that she was my intuitive guide toward greater awareness, unconditional love and full presence. I was with her now, moment-to-moment.

Mother Nature was moving through me with her natural strength. In unity with her, it felt as though I were gliding effortlessly through the naked landscape like a serpent shedding its skin. Only later would I realise, to my amazement, that she was in fact awakening the innate life force energy believed to be dormant and coiled at the base of the spine, like a serpent. It is called *kundalini* in the Sanskrit language.

Wanla Village

With tremendous lightness, I zigzagged down from the first pass. I literally felt as though I had left all my attachments up at the summit by the rock cairn. Suddenly, I saw a *yin-yang* symbol engraved into the dry claylike mountainside. It reminded me that opposite forces are complementary. Light and dark, fire and water, and male and female forces are examples of this.

I danced along with great joy and the bareness of the naked landscape filled me with a sense of raw beauty. I breathed the amazing wonder I could feel oozing from the land. With every step, my prayer to let go turned into repeating: 'Just walk…let go…just walk…surrender…just walk…the movement will set you free.'

I passed more white *stupas* with square bases and domes at the top. Next to them was a big flagpole with a single red prayer flag swirling around the long thin pole. It was a shockingly gorgeous contrast to the royal blue sky and the brown desert land.

After a three-hour hike, we reached Wanla. The entry to the village was marked by an open brick square with three small *stupas* inside (copper, white and silver). And here was another flagpole with two long prayer flags, one blue and one yellow. We found a place to sit and ate our simple pre-packed lunch. I tried not to complain about the white bread and enjoyed the potatoes, hard-boiled eggs and snacks.

We had a short rest and then slowly made our way up the steep path to the spectacular views of the valley from the shrine—the local solitary retreat temple. I had to stop several times to catch my breath. As I reached the top, rays of energy radiated from *Avalokiteshwara*, the shining Buddha of compassion. The strong sun effortlessly dried the apricots placed on the flat rooftops.

I recited the *Om Mani Padme Hum* mantra, which is also supposed to charm *Avalokiteshwara* and build a stronger connection to this living image of compassion. I climbed the ladder to the rooftop of another small building. The sun was strong so I made sure the shawl covered my face. I sat and chanted the mantra while I contemplated the rushing river that ran through the small village. My eyes shifted to the red and yellow berries on the distant rooftops that seemed to make the mantra seed syllables echo even more strongly. The berries also reminded me of the prayer beads I was carrying. In hindsight, I was making a trail of blessed seeds for a protected journey and a safe passage across the mountain passes.

From where I was sitting, I could also see that the rooftops were a place to dry fruit and store grass, firewood and the dried cow, yak and goat manure that is used for heating and cooking during the long winter months due to the scarcity of trees and the absence of firewood.

Before leaving, I went back into the small temple and left some of the prayer beads by the feet of *Avalokiteshwara*. My mind was surprisingly empty. I eventually went back down to find the campsite. After unpacking my sleeping bag, I found a place to sit on the rocks by the river where the locals were washing their clothes. I admired them; they made me think of the good old days when I grew up on a farm. The soothing sensation of the cold water on my feet balanced and energised me. I connected to the flowing stream of consciousness. The feelings of longing for simplicity in life and my love of nature started moving inside me like the water I was watching. I drifted and a film from the past started to play itself out on the screen of my mind.

My life growing up on the farm had been rich with the fullness of beauty and peace that nature gave me. Any contact with nature and animals had a special way of stimulating me into unconditional love. In that moment, I could feel the prickling, warm sensation when a calf had licked my hand with its warm, smooth tongue. I could even smell the newly cut grass that filled me with the energy of living, and taste the warm, thick and creamy milk that my kind mother squirted into my mouth when she was milking the cows.

Here, on this trek through a landscape so different from that of my roots, it was so oddly similar—whichever way I turned, nature provided the same inner peace, harmony and compassion.

Watching the River

Life today is so different than it was in my early days. Our modern busy life makes it easy to dwell on the past and worry about the future. The present moment—like this moment of being by the river, with my feet in the water—is so easily forgotten in the hurry and rush. When I sat there, in that place on the rock, I heard myself saying: 'My goodness, how much I have missed this.'

I could hear a soft buzzing in my ears and felt I was flowing with the constant moment-to-moment change of energy. Light shimmered on the river like little stars and I was filled with peace. The river music from the stars told me that the past, present and future constantly change and are transient. Nature has its own way of harmonising as long as it is not disturbed. Like the river, the less I interfere with negative thoughts and emotions, the easier I flow; the river constantly moves, naturally and effortlessly. All I need to do to be in this flow is just *be,* and not *do* anything.

Sitting there on the rock, it was easy to see that if I tried to change the direction of nature's flow, it would only create obstacles. Until I learned to go with the natural flow of life, I would experience snags or whirlpools. I could see that my still mind did not try to change the natural flow, but simply trusted its transient nature. Rather than being hard on myself—an approach that only feeds me illusions of the past, which are conditioned by a lack of self-worth—I could let myself be nurtured by Mother Nature's soft presence and her unconditional love.

I gazed back up at the temple I had visited earlier and noticed that it looked like it was hanging in the sky. I thought: 'Trusting life's highs and lows, I am only as solid as the monastery's precipitous crag, with its existence going back to the 11th century.'

When I understood that there is nothing to hang on to, I could instead flow with the cyclical change of impermanence, which could take me further, beyond any illusions of past, present and future, into a truer existence which is already perfect.

Being present by the river, I could embrace my heartache and illusions with compassion. In a meditative and relaxed state everything becomes transient. There is nothing to hang on to or worry about. How I carry the past and the future therefore depends on how present I am. When I surrender to the teachings of Mother Nature, I no longer fight who I am. And as I sat by the river musing over these things with my feet immersed in the ice-cold water, I knew that this is what it was like to be a child of wonderment, freely breathing the flow of harmony into my life.

DAY 2
HANUPATTA VILLAGE
3970 METRES/13,024 FEET

After a hearty breakfast of porridge, omelette and tea, we started the second day on a dusty road running alongside the river. As I walked through the village of Wanla in silence with the guide and my two fellow trekkers, I looked at the monastery perched on the cliff. I tried to make conversation with the French woman but she was still not interested and seemed happy only when she could speak French with the Austrian man. It didn't take long before I dropped behind and was separated from them.

When I passed the *mani* walls and *stupas* found in most villages, I made sure that I followed the ritual of walking on the left side of the *mani* wall (the long rows of stacked stone slabs inscribed with the *Om Mani Padme Hum* mantra, prayer and sacred texts) and the two *stupas* with their flagpoles, wrapped in colourful prayer flags.

I started to hum the mantra. A little girl ran past with five ponies. I could see carpenters sitting inside dark rooms eating their breakfast. Other locals were already harvesting and carrying big bundles of barley on their back. Further along, young girls ran around with bowls full of apricots.

The guide had suggested that I put my laptop in the bag carried by the ponies, but I didn't want to risk it. Even though we were not going to have any electricity until we reached Padum, I wanted to carry it so it didn't get damaged.

As I entered the next valley, I passed another prayer wheel and walked around it clockwise, three times. I felt light and my mind was clear. With the loud sound of the rushing, bruising river next to me, I realised I still had to walk and move through challenge after challenge to find the answers. When I take action, I face my reality and purify. When I fight and disturb the natural flow, it only creates obstacles in my mind. By going with the flow, I set myself free from disturbance. I again thought of the act of dishonouring my heart's desire and asked myself a question: 'What is it about you that allowed you to do that to yourself?'

No answer came, but it didn't matter. I strolled happily through the beautiful valley, feeling a greater internal space to receive nature's goodness. I had walked for four hours when I reached a place that looked like the beginning of a gorge. There was something that looked like a small, antique, holy altar engraved into the mountainside along the road. I immediately knew that this was the place to leave my broken glass snake. First, I looked at it and then held the brittle snake in the palm of my hand against my chest, and set my intention silently. If it had been a real snake, it would never have snapped. I prayed for the amazing movement and resilience of the snake to move me forward.

For a moment, I felt the snake's flexibility to move and naturally find its way. With my eyes closed, I asked Mother Nature to gently transform and heal me so I could become whole and my inner rhythm could become intertwined with the rhythm and harmony of the outer world. Guided by symbolism, I continued on my way, snaking along the narrow, eroded and dangerous trail.

I started to reflect. 'Faith determines my conscious choices as I make and accept every step of the journey. Intention is really a deep wish or a prayer to supreme consciousness to grant me what my heart longs for. Since mundane existence is not pure in its form or intention, but rather is often disillusioned by lack of awareness, fogginess, fear, greed, doubt, anger and confusion—purification must take place. A wish may be granted in many ways by nature, teaching me lessons I do not want to face. But when I nurture my essence with self-love, being and acting in resonance with who I am, I receive what my heart desires.'

Then Mother Nature injected a simpler, slower wave of thought into my stream of consciousness.

If your desire comes from your mundane mind, separate from your divine will, I cannot give you what you want.

If your desire comes from your pure heart, in devotion and love for me, I will give you in abundance that which will nurture your pure heart.

I passed another *mani* wall, and started humming the *Om Mani Padme Hum* mantra of compassion and purification.

The Crown—A Golden Gateway

I continued to walk the ascent to our destination just past the tiny village of Hanupatta. I thanked the fluffy clouds for being here. It was perfect with the sun shining through only now and then. And for sure, it was much easier to walk than in yesterday's scorching heat.

Without warning, the atmosphere changed. I was walking into something that I could only feel the presence of. As I gazed at the jagged mountains covered in a mystical mist, it didn't take long before my mind expanded into another realm.

My eyes caught sight of a pinnacle that reminded me of an amethyst crystal. Around it towered mountains of different shades of pink, green and brown. It was like watching layer upon layer of mountains within one mountain. And even though I was stretching my imagination, maybe I was watching the secret treasures of consciousness within the mind, revealed in another reality.

Below, into the valley, the water had carved a deep gorge through the eroded clay. I could hear and see the beautiful clear, blue-green water rushing down the Zanskar River. 'It's got to flow,' I mumbled. I felt more and more that everything I became involved with should flow effortlessly. If it is right it will flow easily, without the need for struggle. Earlier, the Camino had shown me that my relationship required too much effort and had not been flowing well.

I smiled and entertained myself by watching the dramatic scenery as I walked. My vision expanded and I saw a ridge that led up to a place that reminded me of a forbidden fortress. The narrow path twisted around giant rustic, iron-coloured pinnacles. I felt the sensation of connecting, and needed to make sure I had my feet on the ground. It made me feel as though I were entering a sublime crystal energy. In that instant, a 'spiritual home' opened and greeted me with a visual image of a bridge that took me to a castle. It was bathed in green and golden-white shimmering light on top of the high-reaching peaks in the distance.

I was short of breath and had to stop for a moment. My bag felt heavy and my neck was sore from gazing up. I hadn't realised I was dehydrated. As soon as I took a few deep breaths and drank some water, I felt renewed.

I turned and looked in the direction we were heading—up into the narrow valley. I spotted the guide ahead of me. He and the other two trekkers were on their way down to the river. He waved for me to come. I caught up with them and we all had lunch by the river. I found a rock to sit on. The French woman and the Austrian man kept speaking French. Their presence didn't feel comfortable and I chose not to analyse their behaviour. Instead, I reminded myself that everything is perfect the way it is. As usual, I ate quickly. I was not happy with the typical soggy white bread with cheese, but I enjoyed the potatoes, biscuits and chocolate. The flowing water gave me a feeling of balance and my roots were again anchored in earth.

After a short break, I walked ahead of the others, but soon they passed me. As I reached Hanupatta with its small cluster of houses, I could see a white-golden mountain formation upon which a crowned head appeared. I was simply awestruck by the beauty, and realised later that I'd hardly noticed the village itself. What was this showing me? What was it mirroring? Perhaps it was a gateway, opening into the depths of consciousness. I wondered if the thin golden white lines I could see resembled energy grids or planetary ley lines.

I walked the remaining short distance to the campsite and intently stared at the crown. Then, something less tangible appeared above it. The impressive peaks of copper, iron and silver seemed to represent a protective wall around a castle of gods and goddesses. The whole place was throbbing with the earth's *kundalini* energy.

What was I seeing? Could this be the ultimate reality of another dimension? It occurred to me that I was being shown the crown of supreme consciousness. At the same time, I was feeling restless. My energy told me something was afoot.

I realised that although I had experienced a dogmatic Christian upbringing, I had never had a deep certainty that God exists. In this moment, I could see that my belief in God had been based on an intellectual understanding and not on true, pragmatic experience. I was now learning that a spirit realm of gods and goddesses really does exist. Maybe the reality I could see here was showing me that God is in nature—everywhere. I felt a perceptual shift in my consciousness. At the same time, I felt a slight stab of fear about this change.

My mind calmed as I reached camp and went to help the others set up the tents. The ponies were happy grazing after a long day. I wandered around and saw a woman and a couple of children in the field below. I decided to join them. The woman gave me a big friendly smile and continued to harvest the wheat. I sat down on the ground and enjoyed watching the children perform a little dance for me.

In contrast, I was aware of the feeling of discipline and devotion that the surrounding mountains created. The hard-working woman with two long black plaits falling down her back wore a ragged, traditional, long brown wrap-around dress (*chupa*), a sweater and a down vest. In addition, she had a well-worn, white woollen yak skin that covered the back of the *chupa* from her waist down to the back of her knees. It was shaped like a square with a band around her waist to hold it in place.

The deep wrinkles on her face told the mystical story of an ancient soul using her lines as a natural decorative art form. Her pretty earrings, made of many small bone-coloured pearls on a red string, complemented her disordered teeth that were visible when she smiled. Her turquoise beanie reminded me of the snakelike headpiece (*perak*) that I had seen worn by the lady who welcomed me upon my arrival to Leh.

The little children couldn't eat the food I gave them fast enough, while the woman kept pulling the wheat with her strong, bare hands. At the same time she looked at me with her gap-toothed, glowing smile. I thought to myself that her energy was congruent with the earth's power. I was intrigued by these people's ability and capacity to be self-sufficient in such a harsh and extreme climate.

The guide called me, so I waved good-bye. It was late afternoon and we were going to have some noodles. Afterwards, I found a place to sit on a rock to relax and drink my tea. I didn't feel like doing anything other than just looking at the ponies and the scenery behind them. Wherever I looked there was something to see. But it didn't take long before the crown formation in the mountain landscape captured my attention again.

It was beautiful, glittering with golden colours in the sunlight. Even though it was not moving like the ponies, it drew me into a meditative trancelike state in which I could see the many layers and energy lines of the formation. They were similar to the lines on the woman's face, only much thinner, with multiple layers upon layers.

Still sitting on the rock, I saw a vision of a door opening at the base of the mountain and what looked like a cave mouth or entry. Without physically moving, I was there, sitting by the opening. I felt myself becoming one with the golden gateway that led to the innermost cave of the soul. Total stillness embraced me with powerful arms of protection that offered permission to enter the higher realms of supreme consciousness.

For a fleeting moment I was where I knew I belonged—in union with my divine self. With no conception of time, I don't know how long I sat there before I started to feel the cold rush through me. The sun had gone down and it was getting dark. I hurried to my tent before I got any colder. I needed to sleep and I didn't even go outside for my usual washing ritual. With all the different layers of clothing, I slipped into the sleeping bag and nodded off quickly.

Later in the night, I woke, restless. I tossed and turned and felt choked by my clothes. It was difficult to breathe. My lips were dry, and I questioned why I was doing this. What was the point of it all? I knew now that the visionary glimpses I saw were a reality of another dimension. But what were they showing me?

I finally found my headlamp and reached for a tissue to rub my sore eyes. Half asleep and still lying on my side, I held the recorder in my hand. When I pressed the recording button and started speaking in a whisper, I noticed that it was difficult to swallow. However, my energy changed as I tuned in to Mother Nature's vibration of unconditional love.

DAY 3
Photoksar via Sir SirLa Pass
4850 metres/15,912 feet

I was already awake when I heard the guide's voice calling out, 'Good morning, here is your tea.' The thought of a hot cup of tea got me moving. I opened the tent zip and stretched my hand out into the open. Still in my sleeping bag, and now with my purple down jacket on, I sipped the hot tea, peeking out through the tent opening. It dawned on me that I had been in my worldly, critical mind again, trying to make sense of what I was experiencing. I also realised that the doubts had faded as I connected with the earth's aura or subtle luminous energetic field.

It was easier to get dressed when I felt warmer on the inside. On my hands and knees, I crawled outside the tent. For a moment I stopped moving as my eyes fixated on the golden crown in the mountainside, which was still there. I admired this incredible creation that touched me so deeply. It struck me that it could also be a mountain head or 'godhead'.

I felt linked in to the intricate and complex energy patterns that I could sense and feel, which existed beyond what I could see with my two eyes. As I got moving, the land buzzed with an energy that evoked a sympathetic resonance in every cell of my being. I thought of the sound of a hissing snake, moving smoothly and confidently through the landscape. I could feel a pulsating movement like fire inside.

After a delicious omelette and *chapattis* (a flat round bread originating in northern India, made of wheat flour, water and salt), I was ready to start walking. It was a glorious day with a clear blue sky. My vibrating cells let me dance along lightly, as I recited the mantra *Om Mani Padme Hum*. Grateful for being in the presence of Mother Nature, the following words came to me: 'In silence I cry for you. In action I walk with you. In moments of despair you embrace me with your healing art.'

With the freshness of the wind gently swirling around me, I knew for sure that I was not alone. I had the 'perfect company' that could not be seen. I purposely lagged far behind the man from Austria and the woman from France. I was in no hurry.

As I kept walking up from the wide valley floor, I could see the pass in the far distance. With my backpack and the camera bag dangling around my neck, the walking became harder. I had to stop frequently to catch my breath. It didn't look like a steep ascent but it was a very long one, and the summit often seemed out of reach. My worldly mind had reared its ugly head again. By walking slowly, I worked hard both physically and mentally to keep my mind from going in different directions. Despite the heavenly blue sky, I felt frustrated. By slowly letting go with each step, the struggle became an opportunity to concentrate more deeply on my breath. I repeated the mantra of compassion that helped me maintain focus and move more easily. *Om Mani Padme Hum; Om Mani Padme Hum; Om Mani Padme Hum...*

I prayed: 'Please give me lightness, so the wind can blow me up the mountain.'

As I found a steady rhythm of breathing and walking, I realised that just being and living, without the masks of ignorance and illusion, was the key to freedom. And once again I found myself entering the flow. I noticed that every time I focused and connected with my breath, the stillness cleared my worries and the coolness I felt from the others. With my mind calm, the energy of the serpent I felt inside navigated my every move up the mountain.

Finally, as I reached the Sir SirLa Pass, the heat of excitement surged with a strong current through my body. Every movement had a divine spark that awakened the energy of fire within me. But as soon as I walked onto the huge plateau the gusty wind hit me like a tornado and the cold icy welcome from the others almost knocked me over. I had to concentrate just to keep my feet on the ground.

The big cairn caught my attention. It had a swaying flagpole garlanded with strings of colourful prayer flags and many *khata* (silk offering scarves). I quickly went over and started jumping up and down. The cold wind was shaking me up with the sound of the fluttering flags that matched the excitement of the fire I felt inside. Letting myself show my internal state, no matter that it might look crazy to the others, affirmed my desire to be true to myself.

With the help of the tattered flags, prayers and an extensive *mani* wall (with hundreds of stone slabs engraved with sacred texts and mantras), Sir SirLa Pass gave me a whole new openness to a higher state of consciousness. The alluring snow-clad mountain peaks were now closer than ever. With that in mind, I found a place to leave some prayer beads at the highest point in between all the rocks.

I decided to leave the *khata* I had been given when I arrived at the airport in Leh. As I tied it to the prayer pole, I prayed that all beings be free of suffering and the causes of suffering. At the same time, I visualised the golden crown head image that had been imprinted in my mind. I asked for a clear vision. Without any particular expectation, I murmured: 'Please help me to recognise and know my divine self.'

The strong wind made me bend at an angle, like the flagpole. A parallel gust of trust surged through me as I gasped at how nature could radiate through the incredible landscape and me. I noticed that the others were looking at me. And in that moment compassion toward them circulated inside the whole of my body. The fierce wind had changed my state of mind into a loving stream. I accepted that my behaviour was vastly different to theirs. They didn't carry a *mala* or turn the prayer wheels, nor did they make offerings to the land. I never talked about my experiences so I don't know what happened for them apart from the fact that we were all awestruck by the surrounding beauty. Yet I sensed that anyone who walked this powerful land would somehow be touched in a profound way.

I was getting more and more convinced that both the Austrian man and the French woman were helping me to be loving toward those who I didn't feel comfortable with. They showed me that it was my right to walk my own path without judgment towards self or others. I didn't have to please them in any way. We were together but we walked separate paths.

We didn't stay long at the pass. The others had already eaten and were starting the descent. I quickly ate my lunch as I wondered about the mystery of the mountains. The vastness made me think of nature's deep layers of consciousness and how they affected my state of mind and being. I happily descended from the pass, and walked on through the heavily eroded landscape. It reminded me of how an alchemical transformation can spontaneously happen. 'That is what happens when a shift in consciousness takes place,' I told myself.

I had walked for hours when I noticed that I was getting impatient and tired. My mood fluctuated and my body had started to change from feeling light to heavy. In the rise and fall of my breath, I noticed that my energy was low and I felt contracted. It didn't help to realise that we were not staying at the campsite in sight. Our destination lay on the outskirts of Photoksar Village, at a place that I could not see. I watched as the guide kept walking on and I couldn't see the others either.

Nature's Jewel

The riverbed that flowed down the valley had made so many trails that it was difficult to find the right one. I started to think that I didn't really need the guide—who wasn't there to help me anyway. However, I noticed that he had not turned right where the trail disappeared into the steep-sided gorge down toward the village. After some searching, I found my way across the river and spotted an ascending trail. I moved slowly, and panned across the incredible scenery. Drawn into the neat patches of green fields that bordered a huge crevasse in the landscape, I couldn't believe what I saw on the banks of the gorge on the other side. I stopped and got my camera out of the bag. As I squinted through the lens, I could see even more clearly. I spotted what seemed like a tiny white shrine tucked away into the mountainside in the far distance, beyond a small village. I assumed this was the gorgeous village of Photoksar, secreted among the sheer cliffs of the towering mountains. Had I taken the wrong trail, I would have ended up far away from where I was supposed to be!

The soaring mountains commanded my full attention, and I followed the zigzag trail up from the village, through the lens. I went beyond the shrine and my visual field opened even further to the absolute vastness in front of me. The mountain shapes and formations made the cluster of white houses in the village look very tiny. The stark desert landscape came alive and exploded into a display of rainbow colours and patterns of light and shadow from the afternoon sun.

'Wow!' I gasped. I could feel how the multi-coloured thin deep lines created structural patterns against the mountainside like veins. The mountain looked like a huge white jewel sculpted into the land. It had similar colours and structures to the golden crown, but seemed like another layer somehow—leading to a deeper area inside the cave. The mountain was predominantly brown, with a combination of swirling waves of white, gold, silver, copper and purple. I thought it represented the almighty presence of a higher consciousness that had, once again, so powerfully lifted me beyond the lower territory of the illusionary mind.

I wondered if I had walked into a living art gallery. The magnificent mountains reminded me of paintings—ones that expressed a secret energy. They had the power to stun and awaken me. Maybe it was the same powerful serpent energy that transported me like a vehicle, moving my feet and pushing me up the slopes. Keeping my eyes on the spectacular scenery was the connection to nature's vitality that helped me walk across this desolate land.

With more energy now, I continued to walk slowly as I breathed the thin, fresh air. At times I paused to sip some water and admire the mountains as they gradually disappeared behind me. With the sun at my back, I started singing. As I got closer to the camp, the orange tents came into view. I eventually reached the campsite one and a half hours later. The others had already set up the tents and the cook was busy in the dining tent, preparing dinner. After a cup of tea and some snacks, I found a rock to sit on to write in my journal. It was cold and already the light was fading on the distant mountaintops. I contemplated the waves of energy lines and patterns. I didn't have much to write. And that was fine.

Even though I had not been pleased to pass by what I thought would be our camp earlier, this was a great place between mountain passes. It felt like I was sitting on top of a giant peak where I could watch the mystery. Wherever I looked, I could see amazing deep purple, jade green, white and golden waves in the rocks. The colours and shadows made the earth feel so alive. Thinking about the visions I had experienced, I could still feel the joy that had ignited the flow of fire inside me.

I reached into my pocket for the recorder and uttered a prayer to just be. And without warning, I heard myself say, 'I can see something!' I saw a new vision of lines that reminded me of roads going up to a monastery on top of the mountain. Someone with a large human head and an animal body was leaning toward it, praying while resting their forehead on the top. The reflections turned into written words on the page. 'Maybe the divine is real with a living earthly presence.'

I stopped writing and went back to the tent. A washing bowl filled with water had been placed outside. Still in a state of deep wonder, I found my towel and soap and splashed my face and body. The cold sent shivers through me and at the same time thoughts flashed through my mind. 'Perhaps the unknown reality is more secure than the illusions of security itself.'

I quickly finished and went into my tent to scribble down my trail of thoughts. The last line I wrote was: 'So why do I fear reality itself?' With this, I sat in silence for a while. No particular answer came and dinner was ready. Later, from my tent, I watched the bright sky with its millions of stars. I hadn't noticed how tired I was and with a mind that didn't need to figure anything out—at last!—I felt peaceful. It was pitch black and even with my torch it was not easy to wiggle into my sleeping bag with all my clothes on. I eventually settled and prayed for healing light from the stars.

DAY 4
SINGAYLA PASS
5090 METRES/16,700 FEET

I woke up feeling relaxed and energised after a restful night's sleep. We started to walk around eight o'clock. The air was as crisp as the sound of the thin ice breaking as we crossed the frozen streams. I stopped to look at the tiny blue flowers growing in the dry brown earth next to the path. The shades of light kept changing the landscape like thoughts ebb and flow. White mountain flowers reminded me to breathe in the beauty and the immense open space. Why would I ever worry? There is no need, I told myself. And as I turned around, another mountainside appeared with dramatic views.

I passed by another wide, longish *mani* wall, and remembered to chant the *Om Mani Padme Hum* mantra. The symbolism reminded me to connect with the presence of the divine rooted in this revered land. Here, people believe in something greater than themselves, beyond the reasoning mind, and yet they also are true to themselves. I felt they understood what it means to be a human being. This was something to pay attention to!

The ascent to the pass ahead seemed endless and it literally took my breath away. I stopped for a moment and with a deep tired sigh, I mumbled: '*Om Shanti…Shanti* (peace)…the steepness is hard…*Om Mani Padme Hum*.'

I breathed in and out, and focused on a prayer to be set free from the complaining mind. This got me into the same rhythm as the day before. The landscape flattened out and I moved above the snowline with a sense of detachment. I could hear the twittering of birds and my perception flowed spontaneously. I spoke into my recorder as I walked.

'We move uphill again, one step at a time; slowly I breathe the thin air. I know we will reach the top. Another pass this time, another view, another feeling, and another atmosphere opens the horizon and consciousness.'

I tucked the recorder in my pocket and looked at the reddish earth against the blue sky and the snow-capped mountains. The serpent fire energy moved me forward and I asked myself: 'Can I experience the fullness of being present in times of challenge?' Every breath and every step was a matter of discovering my core self.

Nevertheless, I was struggling and breathing heavily. I paused to catch my breath again. It was quiet. I merged with nature's stillness and prayed for lightness to blow me up the mountainside like a breeze. And I whispered, *Om Mani Padme Hum*. As ponies passed me, I felt the warmth of the sun on my back. Almost there! I heard the sound of flapping prayer flags from the top; some breathing hymns started to sing in my mind.

Breathe and focus your mind.
Let each breath of fresh air carry you.
Breathe the air of who you are.
Let the earth breathe you, so you can breathe the earth herself.

Guided by my connection with Mother Nature's breath, I eventually reached the top of the pass feeling exhilarated and joyful. I walked over to the others who were standing by the large *stupa* and the cairn next to it. The monuments were covered with strings of torn prayer flags (white, red, green, blue and yellow) and *khata* (white silk offering scarves). The gusty wind and the sound of the flags instantly released my struggle, and once again I left some of my prayer beads among the hundreds of rock slabs that were inscribed with prayers and mantras.

We took some pictures, sat in silence together and ate our lunch. However, with the stunning artistic panorama around me, I was not very hungry. The place had a stimulating effect and had I not been walking, it would have been hard to keep myself grounded. It didn't take long before I started to feel some intuition wanting to surface. I got up and found a spot away from the others where I could speak into my recorder.

'I move up and down mountain passes and it becomes another reflection of my life that goes up and down like the landscape. And when I reach the highest peak, I clearly see the beauty, everywhere. In the end, on the plateau of ease and grace, I don't even notice going up and down. Because after all, when the mind is calm, there is nothing to hang on to, and nothing matters—not even who I am.'

Before leaving, I went to the *stupa* and the cairn, and left the small stone from home, inscribed with, 'Who am I? What is my vision?' But first, I breathed into it and prayed: 'Please take me from untruth to truth. Please take me from the unreal to the real.' I looked into the blue sky. I felt trust. It was time to move on again.

As I walked, the steep zigzag descent made me feel uneasy. I leaned heavily on my walking poles and felt somewhat comforted. Captured by the mighty mountain scenery, I gasped, 'Wow! This is incredible.' It was hard to keep my eyes on the ground but a lurking fear reminded me to watch where I put my feet. 'I must stay present on the path,' I reminded myself.

As I walked slowly, I was again drawn into the spectacular colours—a river of purple flowed down the valley. The light draped down like waves of silk curtains from the rugged mountainsides. Abrupt clay spurs and dramatic cliffs were painted in silver, gold and copper. What I thought were flower fields of pink, green, purple and red, were actually rocks! This reminded me that things are not always as they seem. I whispered: 'I breathe in all the amazing colours and breathe out compassion, peace, balance and harmony.'

By now, I was in a natural state of flow; I almost didn't notice that I was walking on a flat narrow trail. Without realising, I had entered another realm, where I thought of my surroundings as an enlightened state of consciousness and experienced the joy of connecting to the universe of wholeness.

The Lion Woman

Totally lost in my own world, I walked along. I had fallen behind the others as usual. Deeply engrossed in the magical land, I was suddenly jolted back to the present. I saw an incredible image of a woman in the single copper rock formation in the middle of the field. She was vivid and had a golden glow about her. This beautiful goddess enthralled me. Her hair was blowing back as if she were riding on a lion. She was like a younger version of the mountain goddess on top of Stok Kangri.

I took a picture to capture the image. I wanted to stay there, but instead felt the need to rush on so I could reach camp before dark. Constantly turning my head to look back at her, I quietly thought: 'Another dimension of perception that just comes spontaneously. When I am looking for something, wanting to see something—it does not happen. When I try too hard, or think too much, the flow of natural intelligence becomes suppressed.'

The Orange Star Camp

I reached camp and the orange tents were far away from any villages, at a plateau in the wilderness at an altitude of 4200 metres (13,779 feet). Somewhat bewildered, I was still lost in the rock formations that now reminded me of apostles. Now, in the distance, small orange, star like shrubs were dotted everywhere in the sandy desert around me. I contemplated how old this land was; how nature's forces must have been at play over millions of aeons. 'Who painted this landscape inside and outside me, and united them into one?'

I could feel the life of the earth moving through me. 'Maybe everything is energy moving through us,' I scrawled in my notebook. I drank my tea and ate some biscuits quickly so I could organise my tent, wash and change my clothes. That way, I could just get into my sleeping bag after dinner. By this stage, I was always starving. And I was not disappointed. The cook presented a three-course meal with a curry dish made of vegetables and delicious Indian spices.

On my way back to the tent after dinner, I noticed that the shrubs that had looked like orange stars by day had faded into blinking, radiant stars by night. They gave me hope. It felt like my first day on earth. I stood outside my tent for a few minutes.

The stillness penetrated me and even though it was cold, I felt the warmth exuding from the earth. I breathed deeply into my belly, and felt my body waking into a new state.

I quickly opened the tent zip and went inside. With my headlamp on, I made some notes about the orange stars and the goddess I had seen. I wrote: 'Her rising hair reminds of the fire I feel inside. When I see her through the eyes of my soul, she awakens me with her flame of energy.' My glasses started to fog and the pen stopped working. I hoped that it meant I could now go to sleep. As soon as I thought this, the flow of intuition stopped, and I became very sleepy. My inner and outer worlds were in harmony.

It took a few minutes to make sure I had whatever I needed during the night, before I wiggled down into my sleeping bag. I was dressed in my woollen underwear with the additional clothes I kept in the sleeping bag to put on—warm—in the morning. Not only that, I also had my camelback (a flexible bag made of plastic, with a capped mouth for filling water, a hose and a bite valve at the end to drink from) filled with hot water. To keep the batteries for my electronic equipment charged, I had them tucked into my body, touching my skin. I had figured out that the batteries wouldn't last very long if they were left in the cold.

After adjusting to the crowded condition inside my sleeping bag, peace flowed through my body like a wind of love, and Mother Nature whispered:

> *Truth is in your breath, because that's where I am.*
> *In every breath you take,*
> *I am deep within the mist of your unconscious.*

A Sword of Light

A few hours later, I woke feeling hot and my eyes were burning. It was still pitch black and I suddenly felt trapped and uneasy. I realised that I was 'on fire'—inside a ball of fiery energy. At first it overwhelmed me. However, I soon came to understand that this was Mother Nature's way of showing me how spontaneous transformation takes place. I instantly surrendered to the energy.

And then, out of nowhere, there she was with her gentle guidance.

> *I am the breathing energy consciousness you gasp for—*
> *Breathe and I will give you strength and vitality.*
> *The fire you feel is your natural healing power—*
> *I am a force greater than you—*
> *Innate within the earth—*
> *Innate within you and everyone else.*

In a trancelike state, I let nature's energy work through me with what felt like a crystalline vibration cascading from the mountains. Rays of multiple rainbow colours radiated their beauty and magic above my body. Despite feeling numb, every part of my being was permeated with an ecstatic vitality. In the remote isolation, which felt close to nonexistence, in the middle of nowhere, I had little choice but to surrender to Mother Nature's force.

I sensed the presence of the mountain goddess from Stok Kangri over me—with a large sparkling, white star just above her head. In her left hand she carried a shimmering sword of white, translucent light. I drifted off, and saw a flash of movement as she moved the sword above my whole body. From top to toe she made motions of an infinity symbol.

This didn't stop until I felt an immense, abrupt pain in my diaphragm. Flashes of loss, fear, pain and despair appeared simultaneously. The idea of stepping into the power of who I am felt like a deep wound. I felt nauseous, and knew the only way through the pain was to embrace the feeling and surrender in love and devotion.

In that moment I thought of the two little boys who had come to my tent in the late afternoon, herding sheep from a nearby village. I wish I had saved my lunch for them. All I could give them were biscuits and an apple. By thinking of them, I found myself breathing in compassion and breathing out fire. This was something I had learned intuitively: to transform my internal energy when I was trekking.

Still in the dark of night, a sudden purple beam of light entered the top of my head with a sharp, electrical current and ran down through me. My whole self vibrated with the changing hues that rolled down into the valley—purple, copper, iron, silver and gold swirled together with rainbow colours. They filled my diaphragm with serenity. I watched as the all-powerful energy also flowed into people who came into my consciousness at the time.

In a flash, I saw the vision of the Stok Kangri goddess' translucent sword cutting through the illusions of my mind. A mountainside cracked open and released the contraction of fear from deep inside me. It was like an erupting volcano. I was witness to an unfolding new reality, as a face appeared from what looked like a gigantic, circular-shaped black rock.

As this happened, I became a bright, shining white, luminescent snake, that after a few seconds, turned into a blinking star on top of the mountain peak. Within this star, I looked into the diamond-shaped luminous essence of my soul. And out of this, Mother Nature's presence appeared spontaneously. She talked to me as if it were my own voice. Without hesitation, I sat up and fumbled around for my recorder. Sitting cross-legged, knees splayed to the side, I didn't even feel the cold. And in the dark mist of the mysterious night, I started to speak with her voice.

> *You are awakening to the inner strength and healing memory stored in your body, mind and spirit. I am a reflection of what is within you. You will find everything in nature and you know how fire works. You can no longer hold your breath and suppress the power of nature's intelligence. It is time to release and let go of the deep fear, just as you can let go of your pressing bladder.*

Then I replied: 'Why am I so afraid of awakening to my own true nature? Why do I fear a new reality?' She answered:

> *You know this very well. Attached to who you have become, you are afraid of being rejected by the world around you. You are already rejected, so why be afraid. An obstacle of conditioning, related to lack of self-worth, has been deeply engrained in you from the beginning of time. And without awareness it will drag you back into a conditioned state of separation, fear and loneliness, if you allow it.*
>
> *Expansion has always been the issue.*
>
> *Until you really trust deeply in your heart and understand that the life force energy you breathe is who you are, you are disillusioned by the intellect.*

Before I finally lay back down, I had flashes of how separated

I had felt from the others on this trek, how rejected, and how true Mother Nature's words were. My life had been lived so far largely to try to avoid rejection.

DAY 5
Lingshed Monastery via KiupaLa Pass & MargumLa Pass
4400 metres/14,436 feet

In the morning my body was stiff and numb. So much had happened during the night that I felt an odd mix of being slightly exhausted and having been healed at the same time. I started to move about slowly, and got dressed in the cold crisp air. The feeling of being 'on fire' inside a ball was totally gone but I still felt I was in the 'dream' I had experienced so powerfully just hours before. The transformational energy I had felt was something totally unrelated to altitude sickness. I heard the sound of the gas fire from the camp and emerged from my tent.

My mind drifted. 'In one sense, it is easy to go with the flow without being attached to illusions that hinder me. By letting life happen, the amazing grace comes. When I am connected to nature's intelligence, the visions, insights and experiences from higher consciousness come spontaneously. Sometimes they come when I am least resistant and most open, like last night.'

I came back to reality and rushed to pack and get ready for the day. Breakfast was waiting and I was starving; my wish for porridge was granted. I definitely needed that comfort food after my intense night. Most often the three of us ate in silence with the occasional comment, and this morning that was a relief since I was still partly in the 'other world'. We heard that a French group had become lost but were now safe in a nearby village. The trekking team usually had their breakfast after we had finished, but with their proficiency they would clean, pack up the camp and catch up with us surprisingly quickly.

The last thing I needed to do, before leaving, was to fill my camelback with boiled water. I added purifying tablets to ensure that the water would be fine to drink in about an hour. With everything I needed for the day in my backpack, and my camera bag around my neck, I was ready to go. When I started to walk, I again admired the orange shrub dots. They reminded me of prayer beads, and I could feel that my trail would unfold like the 108 prayer beads I had planted like seeds along the way.

I quickly got into a steady rhythm of walking. With the *Om Mani Padme Hum* mantra echoing in my mind, the magnificent scenery drew me inward. I could feel the earth and sky meeting and right at that place there was an ecstatic, electric tingling sensation; it moved through my body as if I were making love to the earth. There she was again in my shifting, morning consciousness.

> *I am your life force energy, the vibration and the fire that drives you.*
>
> *I am the passion that makes you cry with ecstasy, vibrating in every cell of your being.*

I felt immense love from Mother Nature rush through my body with currents of heat. Automatically I asked: 'Please forgive me for any wrong-doing or harm I have unknowingly caused, and release me from the limitations and attachments of the mind. Awaken me to the divine dance, which I know is only obscured by doubt, impatience and a restless mind that drives me in all the wrong directions.'

With every step, I listened to my breathing and focused on the experience of peace, with an acute awareness of belonging to this fascinating land. I was on a plane of heightened reality beyond illusions, where I could observe the beauty and at the same time, detangle passing, inner reactions without struggle. I had nothing to wait, wish or hope for.

The experience during the night made me even more aware of nature's mystical allure. I could feel nature's joy, simplicity and peace. I continued to breathe the captivating mystery displayed in a painting of dancing colours and patterns of energy waves swirling around me.

We followed the trail high above the Zanskar River and passed rows of white *stupas*. Now the shape of the mountains had changed. The new rounder and gentler form exuded softness and peace; I imagined it might feel like velvet if I touched it. Three hours later we crossed another awe-inspiring pass. Looking down into the steep valley from the top of KiupaLa Pass, I saw a tiny village with only a few white houses and patches of green fields. The surrounding landscape was something from another world. It reminded me of a lotus throne, holding the seat of supreme consciousness. The copper, iron, silver, and gold painted an enthralling picture of energy flowing down from the stunning peaks. I wondered what it must be like to live in that power spot and constantly receive that level of earth energy. What would it do to the consciousness of the people?

It was so magnetic! 'If only I could experience the fullness of that!' I mumbled.

Before leaving, I did my usual ritual of setting my intention and I left prayer beads by the *stupa* and the cairn, with colourful prayer flags flapping around the swaying flagpole.

Lingshed Monastery and Nunnery

We zigzagged down the steep descent into the valley. I moved slowly as I leaned on my walking poles. It took some of the pressure off my knees. The narrow path was perilous in places and made me even more careful as to where I put my shaking feet. Down in the deep valley, I stretched and drank some water. After a short rest and another ascent, we reached the top of MargumLa Pass. From there we could view Lingshed Monastery, placed right up against the mountainside, gripping a sheer cliff. Its many pristine white buildings seemed stacked on top of one another, as if tumbling down into the fields. Lingshed is one of the most remote monasteries in the region of Ladakh, with about sixty monks in residence.

We made a short descent from the pass to the monastery entrance, where the monks in their ruby red robes, welcomed us brightly and warmly. The monastery was surrounded by large white *stupas*, *mani* walls and prayer wheels built into the walls of the monastery. It was a village tucked in between the rugged mountains and bare landscape. How precious this place was! The only way to get here was by walking and the place was totally isolated during the winter.

We camped right next to the monastery. Another group of trekkers were also camping there. We explored the village, which was spread out, and visited a small nunnery half an hour's walk away, tucked down into the neat green barley fields. The nunnery had a step like form. I admired the nuns as they tossed the crops high up in the air to sort the grain from the chaff.

I heard the sound of a trumpet, and told the others I was going back up to the monastery so I could join the *puja*. They followed. The Austrian man, the French woman and I found the *puja* room, removed our shoes and entered the crowded room. All the monks sat on the floor. We found a place to sit at the back. I was filled with joy as I heard the monks singing and chanting.

As part of the *puja*, two sweet, friendly boy monks moved quietly and quickly around the room with large battered kettles and served tea. They soon came to me. Finally, I could enjoy a hot cup of Indian chai made of milk and many different spices served in a big mug. I closed my eyes and savoured the cinnamon scent and rich taste. I was in heaven!

I sipped my tea as many of the monks turned their heads to look at me. I exchanged smiles with them as I watched the sandalwood incense smoke spiral in the sun, shimmering with different shades on their faces. The monks simply glowed in the sunlight that came through the large glass windows; the sound of the chanting penetrated deep into my consciousness and soothed me. My eyes became heavy and closed gently.

My entire body was floating in relaxation. It was as if I was held by an ocean of water, without the need to do anything. As I floated to the surface and opened my eyes, I knew that I could no longer get away with ignorance or fear. That day, on the trek, I had sensed that the mountains and the sacred art and design of every monastery demanded that I face myself. I understood that it is necessary to honour myself and my surroundings with devotion.

I breathed in the many blessings that were present. My teacup was refilled many times. The children's big, radiant smiles, kind eyes and compassionate, genuine gestures soothed my being. I felt like I had just received several big, warm hugs.

I finally noticed that the others had left and the sunlight had faded into the dark night. I walked back to the dining tent and thought about how the monks sensed that every day was a fresh new beginning, just like a lotus flower opening to receive the light of the day and closing at night. Their daily devotion allowed them to experience the presence of holiness in everything. When I merged into their calm nature, I could immediately feel grateful for my recent mystical connections and visions.

It occurred to me that the monks as a collective force were as powerful as the spirit of the mountains. Later, after dinner, inside my tent again, I sat upright. My mind wandered back to the night before. I reached for my recorder and continued to speak where Mother Nature had finished earlier that morning.

'Expansion was always the issue. Silently looking from an expanded sphere of consciousness the window opens. I may look out and yet it is contained within me. My history. Reflecting on the process and watching it from a detached perspective increases my awareness. By entering the field of awareness, from the position of an observer you, I and everyone else has a personality blended in unique ways of many particles and stories interwoven into each other. It is like a kaleidoscope of many colours and forms. Through this conceptualisation, I can watch from a detached perspective beyond the theatre of the mind, and the clear view illuminates the wounds taken in the battlefield of each wound that needs healing. Not only the wounds taken in the moment of now but also those that were inherited from other situations, places and circumstances that were not sufficiently harmonised and zeroed out in those lifetimes.'

With a sigh of relief, I put down the recorder, and tucked myself into the sleeping bag. As I closed my eyes, I knew I was in for a peaceful night.

DAY 6
HanumaLa Pass
4950 metres/16,240 feet

The night's sleep had been tremendously deep, and I felt rested when I woke. The morning rituals were effortless and I had time to wander around the monastery after breakfast. That morning I heard that the other trekkers who were camped near us were suffering from bad altitude sickness. I was grateful for my good health; apart from a stuffy nose and slightly sore lips, I was feeling great. Nevertheless, I offered prayers for the others by turning the prayer wheels with even more force, while humming the *Om Mani Padme Hum* mantra. A boy monk was playing by the lovely shallow stream with lush green trees all around. It struck me that I didn't know what day it was, and it didn't matter.

My bag was packed so I was ready to go when the guide called. We walked through the small village and the striking emerald fields. People were up, working their land and turning hay.

When I had walked for an hour, I stopped to savour the sight of Lingshed Monastery one more time, before it faded into the distance behind me. It looked like a dazzling diamond, full of energy, against the mountainside. The verdant terraced fields sparkled against the bare, desert-brown, reddish landscape. I could still hear the blessings and chanting from the monks ringing in my ears.

As I walked on my own, up and down and across the windswept plateau that looked like sand dunes, I thought about the decisions I had made that led me to this adventure. I had broken through my early conditioning to work hard and feel secure, and had set myself free from limiting thoughts and emotions. By noticing the frustration of doing what no longer worked and by listening to my heart's desire, I was transformed. I could now walk on this trek, so symbolic of the way I wanted to live, more in synchrony and alignment with my truth.

I slowly moved up the next mountain with my shawl wrapped around my neck and most of my face. I was calm; I was right where I needed to be, and I was still moving forward. I could watch my thoughts rise and fall like my breath, and I could accept and release expectations and judgments. Life was unfolding just the way it wanted to.

I reached the end of the plateau and could see the snakelike trail zigzagging up the steep mountain in the distance. This was the path that led to HanumaLa Pass. I thought of the brittle, glass snake and prayed for the strength and power of a real serpent to move me sinuously up to the top. However, in order to get to the base of that trail to start the crooked ascent, I had to first get through a section of the path that looked like ice. It tilted straight down into a steep crevasse, and it looked like I might need crampons.

My guide had disappeared, as was usual for him, somewhere up ahead. I felt a deep fear that almost overwhelmed me. Alone on a slab of tilted ice, I could see myself lose my grip and slide into the infinite abyss. I told myself: 'Stay with it. Are you breathing? Keep your head cool. I know I'm learning to let go, but not that much!'

Dizzy and bound by tightness, I kept my balance and focused on my breathing. Adrenaline was rushing through me. I placed my full attention on what I was doing. I put one foot slowly in front of the other and hugged the earth with my boots. There was nothing to hang onto. Yet, with every step, I connected with the earth—and I stayed present. Words came to mind, repeated over and over, and led me forward with trust.

Be here now. Watch your steps. Keep your balance. Focus. Breathe.

I imagined that I had glue under my boots and started to regain my internal balance. By connecting with the earth and the sky, I was brought back into sync with nature.

In midst of it, I felt anger toward the guide and his lack of safety consciousness. It was not a bad thing; it shifted my focus away from the fear. Step by step, I walked through my fear and anger. When I reached the bottom of the descent my agitated mind had settled down. Now at the base of the HanumaLa, I looked back at my experience, and could see how my consciousness contracted when I was caught in fear.

After a short rest and a snack, I felt recharged and began the ascent. Slowly moving up the steep airy mountainside, my adrenaline started to pump again. I got dizzy and had to stop before I fainted. I thought of other times I had fainted in 'safe places', and I knew no one could save me if it happened here. The path was narrow, and it felt like I was trying to balance on a tightrope. If I fell, it would be a long way down into a deep chasm.

While stationary, I avoided looking down. I repeated some phrases to help calm me. 'Connect. Breathe. Relax. Focus. Flow with what is. Stay connected to the earth and the sky. Be present. I trust the earth under my feet. I trust her. She carries me.'

I moved forward cautiously. I was breathing deeply and my chest hurt. I stopped again and sipped more water from the camelback hose hanging over my shoulder, even though the bite valve was covered with dust.

My palpitating heart and my pulse rate slowly settled. I gradually reconnected and became more present in my body. My concentration returned as I centred myself in the moment and regained balance. Almost motionless, I kept moving, extremely slowly, higher and higher, toward the pass. I let my thoughts and feelings rise and pass while repeating *Om Mani Padme Hum.*

The path finally became easier, although higher in altitude. At times my legs wobbled and I really wanted to give up. But where would I go? I started to think of the serpent path I had seen zigzagging up the mountainside; in between my breaths, I could feel a mysterious will and perseverance at work—something that came from a deep part of me; something I was just learning to recognise. With every step, inner strength pulled me upward. And oddly, at the same time I accepted that sooner or later, I was going to die.

I realised I was walking a tightrope. A little instability could cause imbalance in my mind and body—and then it would be over, and I would be tumbling down the steep mountain. By hugging the earth, by merging into the earth, I could create a feeling of safety and lightness that lifted me into a lighter vibration and onward up the mountain. I continued to pant my way to the top, and reassured myself: 'Remembering where I am—I am focused. Trusting the natural flow—I am not distracted. Present in the moment, I am calm and connected.'

The horseman and ponies passed me at one of the narrowest places. I was amazed how they climbed like goats. I could see the others ahead. Like a breath of sheer silk moving through the air, Mother Nature came to support me. She took my mind away from how I was feeling. The wind was not too bad, so I stopped and found my recorder and started speaking.

When you are trapped by the mind, it can pull you off the path of truth and take you away from reality and your ultimate potential. The surreal feeling of trekking in the ancient land of mysticism requires and demands total presence and commitment to keep firmly to the path. Here, you simply cannot afford to let the mind wander or be distracted by thoughts and emotions of fear, frustration, doubt or beauty. Walking the path helps you develop the skills to master these distractions; to focus and concentrate the mind to stay on the path is of utmost importance.

This is also reflected in daily life. It is easy to get off the path and get side-tracked by distractions and people. As you let attachment to thoughts, beliefs and emotions interfere with your reality of truth, it is also easy to get lost in those desires and illusions. If you do not become mindful and aware, you end up feeling stuck and getting nowhere—feeling prey to life. And you may or may not get a second chance this lifetime, depending on the situation.

'Yes, this is right,' I thought. I had been forced to pay attention and stay present on the narrow path of truth, where my higher nature ruled over something I thought I had no control over.

As I reached the top of the pass, breathing became easier. My heartbeat was calmer, more even. I was literally on top of the world, watching the astonishing view, just being in pure awareness. It was amazing how the panoramic view could influence me in such a way that I instantly forgot the hard work. I was jumping with joy. Again, I was reminded of what it was like to be under nature's power to influence and change my perception of the world. Then, Mother Nature captured my attention.

> *It is a lesson for everyone in everything; no matter where you traverse—high and low—life is about encountering learning experiences. Listen and you will connect with me, wherever you are. When you listen to your breath, you grow and unfold into the fullness of being your ultimate potential. The walking and breathing are part of your natural internal tools to overcome the mind's obstacles. To benefit fully, however, requires you to practice awareness and walk with the intention to benefit all sentient beings. Remember that with practice, your consciousness subtly shifts and you become it—the flow, the peace, the joy and the love. Yet, it requires your presence and attention to be in harmony and balance. In a natural state of mind, the stillness of your inner knowing guides you into the realm of higher consciousness, beyond the worldly mind.*

I was beginning to understand what she meant. After a good rest, eating my pre-packed lunch while admiring the infinite beauty around me, I began the gentler walk down. Relaxed and in silence— I was beyond the limitations of preconceived ideas of how I think life ought to be. Walking over the passes so far had taken me past some major internal psychological barriers and I felt much lighter.

After a few hours of descending through some wide-open vistas, the path closed in and became rocky. A spectacular river gorge appeared and I reminded myself to stay present. It was getting more difficult to walk, although it was also a nice change. I meandered along the narrow trail by the river. I felt like I was walking in fairyland on a mystical path with natural caves and bridges made of rocks.

I wondered where the camp was and finally, after descending through the gorge for a while, I could see Snyertse camp. It was in the middle of nowhere, tucked on a small ridge, far from any villages. The orange tents were already up and the boys were preparing food. It was always nice to reach camp after many hours of walking. Thankfully, today, I had no physical aches and pains.

It was already late, and I was getting cold. I unpacked and got a washing bowl of warm water that had been prepared. The campground was very small, so I rested in my tent until dinner. I nodded off and when a strong wind took hold of the tent, it brought me back to the present. I was called for dinner and it was a bit of an effort to go out into the cold night again. However, wrapped in all my clothes, with my headlamp in place, I made my way to the dining tent.

The others were already there, also wrapped up. It didn't take long before we could loosen our clothes and take off the outer layer. The gas from the cooking made it much warmer. As I walked back through the chill to my tent, Mother Nature's words came like an ethereal mist touching my face.

Trust me!

When you go to the land in the realm of the divine, it means that you dwell inside the essence of yourself, wherever I am. Trust me, I hear your prayers and the glimpses of inspiration confirm my existence, something more real that your essence feels. This is your true nature, giving you faith to carry on. And with every breath you take, consciousness expands and a new reality is revealed as you unfold. When you trust the signs you are given, your reality of truth shifts. The surreal and spontaneous true intelligence flows in tact with life's evolution, which you are a witness to.

'Yes, I understand,' I thought. First I learned to walk and then I ran, only to learn how to slow down again. But how do I overcome the obstacles of preconceived ideas and the strangling limitations of the mind to find the rhythm and harmony of true nature?

Spontaneously, she answered.

The answer has been revealed by becoming more of who you truly are, so you can flow with the stream of consciousness and reconnect with your true nature in the present moment. And when you do, you connect to your unique energy and strength. You have many tools for overcoming the obstacles of the mind. The colours you see and the sword of white light are also tools for you to heal and cut through illusions of the mind. You will know how to use the white light and the colours you are infused with. I will show you.

What Mother Nature said surprised me. I could sense that my consciousness was starting to expand. By thinking differently and acknowledging my feelings, I realised that there was more to life than I could understand with my limited worldview. And that's when I began to trust even more what I didn't actually know.

A few minutes had passed and I had stalled in my tracks from one tent to the other. I had been watching the night sky full of stars, and I forgot how cold it was. It didn't take long before I was in my tent. With my headlamp in place, I scribbled down what Mother Nature had said and my own reflections. I felt relaxed, but at the same time I felt the anticipation of what was to come.

I wrote: 'The unknown is becoming a new reality. In only three more days we are going to be in Padum, at the halfway mark. I will then be on my own, without the others. The thought of this makes me feel lighter and excited.' I put my journal away, but within close reach. I fell asleep, with mantras dancing on my lips and the wind howling like a pack of wolves.

DAY 7
PurfiLa Pass
3950 METRES/12,960 FEET

The sound of the restless wind woke me and not long after that I heard the guide saying, 'Good morning, your tea is here.' For a moment I didn't know where I was, but it didn't take long before I was half out of my sleeping bag, still keeping my legs warm. I leaned over to open the tent zip, and looked out. The sunrise was shining on the highest pointed mountain peaks. I took a deep breath and savoured the moment. It was such a magic, wild morning that I felt like jumping up and down outside and hugging and kissing the earth. Instead, I reached for my cup of tea. With both hands wrapped around the cup, I sat and gave thanks for the warmth and the energy it gave me to get going.

When I got dressed, I stopped to write in my journal. 'The rays of the sun grant me awareness in the present so I can appreciate the beauty nature fills me with. The wild mountain peaks remind me of the wrathful and veiled deities' presence that I have seen in the monasteries.'

Then the guide called to see if I was ready. 'Coming,' I said and quickly packed my sleeping bag and paraphernalia. I hadn't realised

I was late. The others were already eating breakfast and within thirty minutes we were on our way. The guide told us that today's climb up PurfiLa Pass would not be a great challenge. I soon found out that a different kind of concentration was required.

Ponies passed us on parts of the trail where it wound around extremely narrow ridges. We had to move right up against the cliff so they could go by. They disappeared into the distance in a cloud of dust and the sound of fading bells.

The *Om Mani Padme Hum* mantra had become a tool to help me move beyond distracting thoughts and maintain balance. The steady walking kept me grounded and present. After crossing PurfiLa Pass, the valley of Zanskar revealed itself. We walked on a trail down the valley to the banks of the river. Not only did I notice that the landscape had changed, but today I could observe my mental waves of thought without getting involved. It was like watching nature's energy.

The gravel ground was almost white now. And this was incredible to see—a wide, pristine turquoise river flowing effortlessly, dominating the eroded and wide-open plains with unbelievable spur and cliff formations. Nature looked and felt alive. With my eyes fixed on the surrounding beauty, I prayed for the flowing river to focus my mind and balance my body.

On top of one of the ridges, I stopped to look down into the Zanskar River. There I saw a small boy bathing on the banks. The clear water was so inviting. Nevertheless, I continued, and the others were, as usual, ahead of me.

We had walked for six hours and the camp was, as far as I understood, not far, when I spotted a little white sandy beach next to the river. Tempted, I walked off the path and made my way over.

It was a relief to remove my boots and sweaty, dusty socks. 'This is just what I needed,' I said to myself.

The soft sand felt like heaven and sent nurturing and tingling feelings through my body. The clear, cold, turquoise water soothed my feet and totally relaxed me, physically and mentally. I lay down and sank deeper into the sand. Every cell in my body knew what I was thinking and feeling. Composed, placid and clear, I let myself drift. The sand felt like a soft warm bed and my senses became alive in the moment of nothingness.

I didn't want to move but I felt compelled to report to the camp. I grudgingly put my boots back on and walked for another twenty minutes. The campsite, called Hanumil, was on a broad shelf on the bank of the river but I could not see a village anywhere. We were still in the wilderness and no one was there apart from the cook. The tents were up and the others had gone bathing in the river! I dropped my bag and noticed that the campground was big, and for the first time flat, with some grass and trees.

The cook had made a table from one of the containers they use to carry cooking pots and food. He had even placed a tablecloth on it. The green sleeping mats had been placed neatly on each side of the table to sit on. He quickly served me noodle soup. Hungry, I ate fast. After a short while I found my journal, moved one of the mats and got comfortable lying in the sun outside my tent. It didn't take long before I felt tired and moved inside.

Even though we had not had dinner yet, I crawled into my sleeping bag. I noticed that my mood was dropping like the temperature and my mind was starting to question things again. What was the point of all this? Was it the 'I'—the old—that I was tired of? Despite my distracted mind, I was aware of Mother Nature's comforting wisdom that came over me like dusk.

There is nothing you can do other than just keep on walking, so that you can travel the inner life of your experiences. With expanded awareness you will find the answers within the core of your being.

'Where will it take me? Will I ever find what I want to do in alignment with my true self?' With this question, I sat up and started writing. 'I don't know. It is just something I have to do. Maybe my true nature is a place where I can just be to feel the sensation of Mother Nature in the sand, and smell newly cut grass or the fragrance of a rose.'

Mother Nature's invisible presence returned and she told me:

When you unfold, you open like a lotus flower, blossoming with self-knowledge and wisdom of joy.

I thought about it for a minute and wrote: 'I am not convinced, but it occurs to me that by questioning and doubting—there must be more to let go of. I am shedding layers, and wandering up and down through those layers of consciousness, so I may as well enjoy nature that reflects who I am on the way. Will it ever end? I don't think so.'

My thoughts then changed direction and I questioned, 'Why do I bother listening to my own nagging when it only creates low vibration and dishonouring of myself? Why do I go into struggle when I don't have to?'

Aware of my lower vibrational misery, I noticed that I had become a witness to the fighting thoughts and emotions that were still not at peace within me. Without resisting or fighting the thoughts, I didn't tend to identify with what was happening. Then I could surrender patiently and accept wherever I was.

'Tomorrow is going to be different,' I reassured myself, even though my critical mind was thinking that nothing was coming from all this. I thought, 'Maybe I am just fooling myself looking for *that thing* that does not exist. Am I deluding myself? My thoughts and emotions—my obsessive worldly mind thinks so, but my divine will knows another reality and keeps pulling me toward *it*. Maybe I have even become too obsessed and worried about who I am.'

I paused and scrawled, 'What can I do at a time like this?' By writing it down, I realised I was really asking Mother Nature to show me how to move from a lower energetic vibration to a higher one. Also, the writing helped me to practice patience. I could then more easily register my thoughts and acknowledge my emotions— and watch them pass and dissolve.

I was tired of sitting, so I put my journal down and curled up in my sleeping bag. Self-love started to flow like a warm sensation through my body, and I heard Mother Nature's words.

> *Stay with it. Feel it. Be with it. Move with it. Touch it. Listen and let it flow through you. Allow yourself to sway with the wind, without fighting nature's forces, until the softness of love fills your heart and transforms your pain.*

I knew this instruction by now and was aware that my old painful feelings deserved to be honoured and experienced like any others. Therefore, I willingly embraced the feeling of despair. This part of me felt lonely, sad, hopeless and separated from my true nature, and I wanted only to disappear from all worldly concerns into a safe and protected hollow shell. I felt raw and exposed.

Unlike my daily treks, there were no mountains in here, no scenery in which I could take refuge. Suddenly, I thought of the gateway into the cave of the golden crown. In that moment, Mother Nature spoke again.

Feel the pain and let go, whatever it is that you are holding on to, release it. Breathe in—let—and breathe out—go. You have the permission to surrender. You are safe.

It was like a song that reminded me of being held in my grandmother's loving arms. I surrendered and felt myself lifted into a transparent chiffon cocoon of calm, unconditional love. I embraced the whole of myself with that same motherly love. Within seconds, I heard the soft sound of a babbling stream. Immediately, I found myself in the river I had sat by earlier that day. With my eyes closed, I could see a vision of the clean, fresh turquoise water flowing up and down my spine. It felt like life force energy, cleansing me. My tension dissolved and I was released from the contraction of emotional pain.

I could just be where I was, without being anywhere. For a moment I experienced myself curled up like a tiny baby seed inside a conch, a spiral white shell on the bottom of the sea. Secure and protected within this shell, I simultaneously observed my body that was still curled up inside my sleeping bag. A warm tenderness entered my physical body.

Out of the blue, my consciousness shifted and I was holding the conch in my hands. It had a fragrance of something totally new. I placed it into my chest and the hard shell gently melted. I felt the softness of a baby's skin. From the heart of my being, I felt the rising compassion of divine love. The sweet fragrance of a new-born baby brought a state of blissful ecstasy within me and made me feel transformed into a translucent being, full of pure energy.

I paused and sensed that Mother Nature now was softly singing a melody.

When you remember your core vibrational frequency and feel the earth you step on, you know it is a part of you. Purified and cleansed by the water, you know that, too, is a part of you. By feeling the warmth of the sun, you know it is the flame of a fire that burns inside. By breathing the air, you know it is your life force energy. By looking up into the blue sky, you know you can surrender in faith to something more, something beyond what is readily perceived by your two worldly eyes. In worship and sacrifice, the third eye is the window of higher consciousness. As you travel inwardly you open up to the cosmic eye and become at one with wholeness.

My breathing slowed until I felt entirely tranquil and safe. Suddenly, the guide's loud voice jolted me out of my dreamy state, as he called me for dinner. I started to move and went outside. It was time to face the cold reality, although it felt good to stretch and breathe the fresh air. I hadn't noticed I was so hungry. After eating another hearty meal of rice and a variety of different cooked vegetables, I knew I would sleep well that night.

I smiled to myself and thought, 'Maybe I can get back into the feeling of being in the conch shell on the bottom of the sea.' Just thinking about it, I could feel the sea washing over me. The salt water purified every part of me.

DAY 8
PISHU VILLAGE
3470 METRES/11,384 FEET

In spite of waking up to another glorious day, feeling refreshed, I began to anticipate what was going to happen when I reached Dharamsala. I observed myself thinking about what might or might not happen in the future. I let the thoughts pass. I knew it would not happen the way I *thought* it would. The only requirement was to be in the moment where insights come unexpectedly and spontaneously like flashes of lightning.

I was a bit annoyed that my mind wanted to know what was going to happen. But my consciousness shifted when I heard Mother Nature's words.

> *It will all unfold as you just keep on walking. When you want to know it leads to annoyance. That is good. Becoming aware of being annoyed is even better.*

The penny suddenly dropped. It is not so much about the thoughts I have, but the awareness about what I am thinking that is important. I saw that by attaching significance or meaning to thoughts and emotions I became those thinking patterns rather than just flowing with my inner knowing. In this open, mountainous space of possibilities, I could let everything happen more easily—to remain in the flow.

I reminded myself that thoughts have the habit of repeating themselves over and over. I knew that the mind was playing a game to sabotage the truth. And therefore I avoided my true being by thinking that nothing was happening. This is, I thought, an illusion because true nature is constantly turning the wheel.

So then, by taking one step at a time there was nothing to be afraid of. What held me back was thinking too much, and I was more aware of the thoughts that took me into a lower state of vibration. With this reflection, I was opening my mind to the mystery beyond my immediate thoughts. This made me tingle with exuberant joy. The elements of earth, water, fire, air and ether showed me how to recognise the divine self, where to go, how to spontaneously heal wounds and master the mind. This natural intelligence is innate within all of us.

I had by now finished my morning ritual, and I was packed and ready for breakfast. I had been so engrossed in contemplation that I had not realised that my tea had not arrived this morning. And no one had called me. I wondered why and went over to the dining tent. They told me they were running late and I needed to dismantle my tent. Soon after that we had breakfast and started walking. The walking was easier as we got closer to the halfway mark—Padum.

As I walked with a gentle stride along the Zanskar River that morning, I could see that here, like everywhere, life changed constantly. Colours and light, wind and weather were like consciousness, interweaving and creating intricate patterns. I felt part of everything around me and I thought I could hear the sound of chirping birds. Even though I could not see any, I surprised myself when the humming of the *Om Mani Padme Hum* mantra translated into a prayer to Mother Nature.

'Please, let me be here now, where I can just be. Please feed me the essence of true nature—and let the earth, water, fire, air and ether fill me with the universe of cosmos.

'Please let me be the earth I step on. Please let me be the water I drink. Please let me be the sun I am. Please let me be the fire I am. Please let me be the air I breathe. Please let me be at one with you—the pure colour I see in the sky. No longer separate, I am whole together with you. Please let me be a raindrop that dissolves in a lake of pure consciousness. Please let me surrender in love and devotion to you. Please let me be here now, with my true nature.'

It turned into a melody that silently buzzed with tones of delight as I walked. I eventually stopped to get my recorder. The flat and featureless ground made it easier for me to walk and talk into the recorder at the same time. I talked to Mother Nature as if she were right there with me.

We approached Pidmo, one of the more remote villages, and I tucked the recorder into my pocket. There were only a few houses scattered around. By now I had caught up with the others. We paused for a drink and watched the local harvesting. A young man was threshing what looked like hay with the help of four yaks (*dzo*) with thick, long horns that walked around in circles, and two horses. When I saw the women sifting and throwing the crop up in the air, I realised it must be wheat or barley.

We soon resumed our walking and stopped to have lunch on the sandy banks across the shallow riverbed. I truly admired the local people's skill and knowledge of working with the desert land in such a way that they could make a living. When we started to walk again, I purposely lagged behind the others, as was my habit. It was only a five-hour walk today, and I was almost there.

A mountaintop appeared in the distance shaped like a pyramid. It was in the mountain range behind a village called Zangla—once a tiny kingdom. The pyramid's apex was a pattern I had started to recognise. By trusting my higher consciousness, I allowed it to awaken memories I didn't know existed. I knew it was a portal to the sacred energy vibration. The golden crown had showed me this and made me believe that it was true.

I stopped to take some pictures of the pyramid-shaped mountaintop and a castle that looked like a ruin atop a clay crag on the outskirts of the village. And this time it was a real castle—not a vision! I admired the river and the torrents of sand that formed into pyramids. I continued to walk until I reached the campsite opposite Zangla, across the river. It was a large open, flat grassy area with plenty of space for all the tents. White *stupas* dotted the landscape.

I dropped my bag and walked around. The guide had told me that Padum (the halfway mark) was to the south, in the direction of the shiny towering snow-capped peaks. To the west, an extraordinary formation brought to mind a passage to a womb in the heart of nature. My visionary field expanded and a layer of my perception awakened. I didn't even need to look through my camera lens to see the deep ruby-coloured jagged peaks that formed the opening of a triangle pointing downward. I did not know the significance until later that night.

It was still early afternoon and I went to explore the nearby Pishu Village and take some pictures. There were a few local characters around, dressed in scruffy clothing. I found a school with children and after saying hello, I walked across the fields to the nunnery, which consisted of a few white buildings. Happy to see me, the nuns offered tea. We sat in silence and peace. Although we could not understand each other, one of the nuns made it clear that she would like to have my socks. Unfortunately, I didn't have another pair so I made some other offerings before I made my way back to camp. The light was already fading.

Spiralling

As I went to sleep that night I found the loud, shrill voices and laughter at the campsite particularly disturbing. It was unusual, and for the first time I got my headphones and listened to my own music. Out of nowhere, I fell back into my grief, and the images of my relationship. Tears welled up and choked me as I felt the lost love. The wave took me down in a spiral into the mysterious womb of earth.

The message came: 'There is something wrong with me,' and 'something is preventing me from fitting into normal life.' I knew it had nothing to do with the people here, my family, or friends. I had learned that every time I experienced something difficult I went deeper, lifting another veil of illusion. Releasing the pain I found within strengthened my self-awareness practice and the connection to my core being. I understood that this was Mother Nature's way of teaching me how to embrace my soul's essence.

By resting in what felt like the arms of Mother Nature's unconditional love, I surrendered and trusted that she knew what was best for me. As I lay there in my sleeping bag, my body felt grounded and rooted in the earth.

Suddenly I saw the conch shell from previous evening, at the bottom of the sea. Then the whistling sound from the conch changed my perception and, I saw myself sitting in a cross-legged lotus position inside the womb of the soul. Not on the bottom of the sea but in the middle of the ruby mountain passage I had seen that day. I absorbed the essence of that particular vibrational energy and a gateway opened to her divine transformational power. In a state of silence I was connected to the sacred space of divinity hidden in the layers of the mountains, and deep inside the layers of my true being.

In a trancelike meditative state I held the white conch with both hands resting in my lap. My attention focused toward the sky as I gently lifted the conch that looked more and more like a translucent chalice or cup. Energy flowed like waves of golden light from it.

And then a vision appeared in which I stood under a waterfall shaped like a conch. Mystical healing water poured vitality and strength over my head, running softly over my face and onto my lips. I opened my mouth and tasted drops of divine nectar. Everything was in perfect flow with harmonic resonance. Embraced by the magic healing energy and protection, I must have fallen asleep.

DAY 9
KARSHA VILLAGE
3650 METRES/11,975 FEET

A soft sound of what reminded me of the whistling conch shell I had heard the night before, gently woke me up. I immediately noticed that I felt different. It was as if an exquisite stream of divine intelligence had been poured into my body, and I felt surprisingly strong and harmonious. Slowly my body awakened and I opened my eyes. It was going to be a short day—only four hours of walking, which now seemed like nothing! I got dressed and packed. As I moved outside the tent the guide came with a hot cup of tea. Sipping slowly, I ambled around the campsite looking in all directions. I bowed in gratitude and knelt down on my knees and touched the earth. Then the guide called. It was breakfast time.

Afterwards, we all started walking together through Pishu Village. People were busy with their chores. The rows of huge *mani* walls and *stupas* decorated the landscape before us as we strolled along the flat and windswept plain. Today the path was as natural and simple as my quiet mind.

It didn't take long before I lagged behind the others again. The amazingly blue sky made me smile. Even though the wind nagged at me I was at ease, breathing gently. I followed the dusty road and again the thought of the whistling conch shell put me in a heightened state of consciousness.

As I got closer to Karsha Village, I could see the spectacular monastery clinging to the mountainside. It was an incredible image of white buildings carved into the sheer cliffs. I turned off the dirt road and followed a narrow, well-trodden path on the edge of a stream. On one side, tall houses bordered the monastery. I crossed the stream and looked over the stone wall on the other side. The whole valley came into view! Patches of fertile emerald farmland transformed the barren brown landscape into a lush Himalayan scene. It was like looking at the amazing murals on the walls of the shrines.

Karsha was a bigger village than we'd been used to and it felt strange to enter a much busier world and to hear the noise of vehicles and machinery. I was happy to be in 'civilisation', but already missed the intimate, intense energy of the mountains and the solitude of the remote wilderness. I knew I needed to stay focused and present, and this allowed me to enjoy the ancient cultural heritage, the farming and the playfulness of the children.

The camp was right in the middle of the village and so there was a lot going on nearby. It was still early in the day when we arrived so I had time to relax, explore the monastery and watch the harvesting.

I put my tent up. Then found myself a place to sit near a haystack. It was a small space right next to the camp. The sun was warm and I sank into the earth. I breathed deeply and noticed that the younger women were watching me. A tiny older woman dressed in a mauve velvet cardigan lined with wool looked stern but brisk. A string of prayer beads hung around her neck outside her cardigan. I could see that she was also wearing a necklace of coral stones.

A whitish ragged woollen yak skin with long hair hung from her shoulders. She also wore the same strings of pearl earrings, made into a loop, as the hardworking woman I had met in the fields of Hanupatta. I noticed that she didn't like me watching her. But it was something about her ancient features and characteristics that intrigued me. Maybe those missing teeth symbolised the impermanence of life.

I also watched the young men as they threshed the barley with the help of six *dzo* walking around in circles, so the crop flew up into the air. The women's responsibility was to sift the grain.

My mind started to drift and I thought of the intriguing pyramid formation that reminded me of the idea of Mother Nature's womb. The ruby opening with its triangular downward pointing shape reflected the upward pointing shape of the pyramid. I thought of *shakti,* the feminine power, and I got my journal from the tent and started writing.

'The divine consciousness dwells within our essence and holds the ancient codes of our natural intelligence. The secret energy of nature is formed like layers of sacred geometry in the form of a pyramid, diamond, womb, serpent and many other shapes and patterns. These forms represent the male and female vibrational forces and they are manifested on earth. By connecting to the places in nature that draw us, our core vibration awakens and prepares us for the ultimate union with the male and female forces that leads to oneness. These centres are gateways and portals to the archetypal essence of our spirit selves, through the interplay of nature and consciousness.'

I stopped writing and looked up into the clear sky. It reminded me of the higher self, just like the upward pointing triangle.

Within a short time I started to get restless and decided to explore the Karsha Monastery—the largest in Zanskar and a home to 150 monks. On my way, I met four children coming home from school and a little girl who was carrying water. I took some pictures and they greeted me with innocent laughter and love. An old man carrying a baby on his back was turning a decorated prayer wheel at the base of the stairs to the monastery. The faster the wheel turned, the stronger and more frequent the sound of the bells attached to the painted cylinder filled inside with mantras became.

The sound of the bells echoed in my mind as I climbed the many stairs up the steep hillside. Buildings clung to the cliffs like mental thoughts hanging on to material attachments. The architectural design of these monasteries reminded me of a mandala and the urge to climb into higher consciousness, where I could be free and access divine wisdom.

And there she was, like the scent of rose incense. This time Mother Nature spoke directly to me.

By walking the steps, shedding layer upon layer, the innermost subtle layers are awakened by sounds of mantra, where the essence of inner self resides. As you move from the outer to the innermost layer, your awareness gradually shifts and perception changes to view the world from within rather than from without.

What I had learned through *kundalini* meditation quite a few years ago started to make sense. I stopped and looked at the marvellous view of the broad valley and the surrounding mountains. I got my recorder and continued to reflect.

'Maybe it is the case. Perhaps the primordial life force energy coiled like a serpent at the base of my spine is actually awakening and transporting me along the way with every breath and every step.'

It is believed that the serpent energy rises up through the body, opening the energy centres (*chakras*), piercing upwards until it reaches the seventh chakra of the 'thousand petal lotus flower'. Located just above the head, this is where the union of the masculine and feminine takes place. When these two energies (respectively believed to be the solar and lunar energy currents) are balanced within us, we dance with eternal bliss, in oneness with who we are, beyond the duality of the mind.

Still talking into the recorder, I continued to climb the steep stairs. I was playing with the idea that this may be what happens when I experience the flow of intimacy with Mother Nature. In those moments my body releases sensations I can only explain as an intangible orgasmic bliss with a feeling of being fully immersed in a shower of infinite wisdom and divine love.

I stopped to catch my breath and drink some water. By tilting my head back I saw the white buildings seemingly hanging in the air. Not too much farther to go. From here the view over the Zanskar Valley was glorious with the yellow and green cultivated fields inserted into the mountainous picture frame. The young and old monks dressed in red were part of the architectural design. The intensely royal blue sky seemed to reflect the monks' nature, shimmering with clarity and delight.

I took one step and one breath, panting my way up the long flight of stairs through a maze of buildings. I eventually reached the main courtyard of the monastery. There, I spent some time looking around, gently breathing in the energy of the amazing art, murals and *thangkas*.

Suddenly the image of a breathtakingly beautiful and delicate deity caught my attention. I looked at her and she was still intact, oozing a sense of heroic integrity and eloquent beauty even with the deep cracks in the wall around her. Despite a huge, central crack that divided her in two, she seemed incredibly whole. As I watched her closely, her eyes started to radiate a golden, white and silver light. She exuded a living presence. Enchanted, a light flashed in my mind and I saw into her third eye and entered a world of light. It was not just something I felt and intuited, but something I could see through my inner eye.

I walked closer and positioned myself so I could move my right hand over the mural, without touching it. Spontaneously, I rested my forehead on the wall just where her feet would be. As I prayed for freedom to just be, I was filled with deep gratitude. 'Where have you been?' I mumbled. 'I have missed you so much. By being separate from you, I have not been myself. Yet, looking back, your presence has always been with me, guiding me.'

Words appeared in my mind like a gentle wind sweeping through the valley.

> *I am your divine consciousness. Surrender to infinity and find the reality of your divine essence hidden in the perfection of wholeness and eternity. By shedding the old paradigm and moving into the new is a transition that expands consciousness. The reality of silence opens you up to the innermost secret wisdom and vast energy of your soul.*

I didn't know what to think. Stunned, I reminded myself that I didn't need to analyse this. The crystal-clear eye that spontaneously appeared took me far beyond my thoughts and the world I could see with my two ordinary eyes. It took me into an open landscape that felt like pure light energy without form or shape. I remembered

I had been musing about finding the invisible divinity in a tangible form, or a living, physical representation of the Mother. Here it was.

Moving along, another ancient faded image of a Buddha made its deep impression, together with the nearly thousand-year-old murals and frescoes that adorned the walls. The predominant deep red in the art comforted me. I turned around again to glance one more time at the esoteric deity. Softness came over me and it felt like I melted into fluid gold.

Chirpy and joyful, I made my way back to the camp situated on a small patch of grass in the middle of the village. In a harmonious state of mind, I found a place to sit in the warm sun to admire the monumental snow-capped mountains bathing in the light of dusk. 'Unbelievable,' I thought. In the same breath, I had an epiphany. I got my journal from my backpack and scribbled:

'The deity felt like the essence of Mother Nature. Had I connected with Mother Nature's cosmic consciousness? Maybe this is what Mother Nature really looks like. Maybe she looks like pure eternal light, only visible to the inner eye—the soul. By seeing beyond the mural painting, perhaps she reflected the unconscious in the same way as she did in nature.'

It was getting cold and the last I wrote was: 'Maybe I am just imagining it all anyway, although I intuitively know that it is showing me something. Perhaps I am feeling and seeing the essence of true love from within. When I am thinking this, it feels in resonance with my deeper angelic self.'

I got up and started to prepare for the next day. It didn't take long before I noticed Mother Nature's voice saying:

Trust your voice. Have faith in the invisible that you can see.

Observe your doubting dualistic mind as if you are looking through a lens—until it becomes empty of thoughts and you are fully present in a natural state of pure awareness.

Reassured, I knew the next day was going to be different. My restless energy told me so. I was on the threshold of something.

DAY 10
Padum—Halfway
3610 metres/11,843 feet

As soon as I woke up, I went outside. The air was cold and crisp, and I stretched my arms in the air and jumped up and down, welcoming whatever might come today. The vast scenery never failed to open me and make me feel that there was more space inside me. I stood still, eyes closed, and I could see visions of light. With one palm on my chest, I connected with the heart of nature.

I heard the sound of laughing children and readied myself enthusiastically for the day. We started walking immediately after breakfast. Today, it was only a two-hour stroll to Padum. By the time I reached the river, I was on my own again. I crossed the calm water and entered this hub of the Zanskar Valley. Being at the halfway point gave me a strong sense of freedom. It was as if I had topped the last major hurdle and it was all downhill from here. Even though we had crossed eight of the nine passes, I knew there was much more to come. I thought about my birth time, perhaps because I was truly beginning to integrate the reality of becoming new again.

As I moved through town on my way to the hotel, I immediately felt a change of atmosphere. It felt stark and alien. The majority of the population was Muslim, and I noticed that there were no streamers of prayer flags flapping from the rooftops. The streets were bland, lined with concrete buildings of no distinction or beauty. And the hotel was not much different. I had expected the capital of Zanskar to have better facilities but I was not surprised.

After ten days without a shower, the scruffy hotel without a shower, hot water and electricity disappointed me. Nevertheless, the cold bucket shower kept my vibration from plummeting. On a positive note, we were very close to the snow-capped peaks, and I could easily tune in to the vibration of *Jooley* (hello/welcome) from children's happy voices. This was also a place for the trekking team to get food supplies for the remainder of the journey.

The cook moved into the open courtyard just outside my room. I found this hilarious. Maybe the banging of cooking pots would save me from the strangeness I felt being there. In India anything could happen! I reminded myself to stay open to new experiences and continue to be in the flow.

Later, as a group, we walked to the different monasteries around Padum before driving to Sani Monastery. It was the oldest Buddhist worship centre in the area. Here I met a little girl who touched me deeply. I have thought of her ever since. We couldn't take our eyes off each other and she followed me around. Her smile melted my heart and her eyes sparkled with the radiant beauty of unconditional love. She reminded me of the pure innocence I felt in connection with Mother Nature. She exuded presence and self-acceptance. Without words she made me think of the spark of self-worth ignited by the sun that can transform any wound or pain into wholeness.

Day 10

We returned to the dusty grey streets of Padum where there was an odd mix between the new and the old. Though I wanted to run away from the ugliness, I stayed focused in the vibration of unconditional love, and it helped me allow the intrusion of the noisy, smelly cars and trucks. Thankfully there was one street populated largely by monks, who brightened my experience with the passionate red that symbolised the life force energy of Mother Nature. Their soft, flowing movement gave me a sense of Tibet.

From the next day on, I was going to continue totally on my own with just the trekking team. Even though I had walked on my own most of the time, and had become accustomed to the way it was, I was now looking forward to really being alone; the French woman and the Austrian man would leave the trek at this point. At dinner we were surprised with a special meal and a cake to celebrate their last night.

The cook and his assistant made another delicious meal. It was amazing what they could do with what they carried with them. As I enjoyed the feast, it struck me how strange it was to sit on a chair! I had not even thought about that before, and I missed the rough wilderness and my intimate connection with the earth. I had discovered, though, that by just thinking about Mother Nature, the sensation of sweet loving warmth would flow through me. And when I was in that state, everything I encountered felt sacred. Even a chair!

After ten days of walking, I was looking forward to a day's rest before moving on for another ten days. And I was wondering what it would be like to sleep in a bed that night.

DAY 11
A Rest Day in Padum

I woke at sunrise, long before I could hear the gas fire from the kitchen outside my room, where the cook, his assistant and the horseman slept. Although hard as the floor and not particularly comfortable, the bed I had slept in gave me a weird sense of familiarity, as though I had come from the past and was just discovering civilised life.

I had my last breakfast with the Austrian man and the French woman. They were taking a jeep back to Leh. Prepared to start my day of relaxation, I said goodbye and wished them well on their journey. I found a place to sit in the sun and made some notes in my journal.

This capital town was unlike most others I have experienced. It was remote and the single road in and out added to the otherworldly feeling, which was further emphasised by the unreliable electricity and lack of water supply. I could see there was a gradual process underway here though, by which modernisation from the west was changing the nature and culture of the people. 'I am not sure if it is for better or worse,' I scribbled in my notebook.

Both the harshness of the life that surrounds poverty or the comfortable life that makes the heart long for simplicity have their own challenges. Who am I to judge them?

Perhaps wherever we are we are tested to maintain our integrity and be the best we can be, no matter how much or how little we have. And for countries that have come further along the road of materialism and technology, which role do we play? Where are we in terms of our own being, and are we living in balance and harmony? No matter where we are, we need to be connected deeply with nature. Like individuals, countries and certain parts of the world face different challenges. Maybe it is about what approach and attitude we choose to solve these challenges. Perhaps the more we have, the greater the need to stay present—because we are so easily seduced by the many temptations external to ourselves.

Blind Faith

Sonam, a short, physically strong Tibetan man who I had met earlier that day offered to take me to a place by the river to show me a special rock.

We crossed the field and as soon I saw the rock, it inspired me. The huge rock was engraved with five sitting Buddhas and one future Buddha in a standing position. I listened to the sound of the flowing turquoise river as I studied the rock. Even though it was lovely, I was aware that it was different from the 'real' mountain spirits. It was manmade. Nevertheless, it made me reflect.

'We are impermanent beings and nothing is perfect other than perfection itself. The Buddhas reminded me to be grateful for what life is all about without losing myself in the worldly mind of illusions. And isn't that what we are here for—to become free from the limitations of the mind? That's the true meaning of enlightenment, the definition of nirvana."

We found a place to sit, and after a long pause Sonam said: 'It is still a lot of blind faith, and people believe that by giving offerings, building *mani* walls, doing ceremonies and getting blessings, things will come to them. I don't believe so. We cannot depend on anyone; we must truly practice. It depends on the seeds we put into the fields. If we put rice into the field, it is not going to change into wheat by getting someone's blessing.'

I could relate to what he was saying and replied: 'It is my heartfelt belief that the utmost truth is manifested by the practice of pure speech and correct action. I can't start to flow with nature's balance and harmony, and walk the path of being true to myself, until I trust my own inner guidance, from a divine mind and a pure heart, without relying on others. For our external circumstances to change, we must have a sincere and strong intent, rooted in our divine will. The power of thought must come from our heart and not from the worldly mind based on greed, insecurity or fear.'

Sonam kept talking but I had stopped listening. I was looking into the turquoise river. Although I had switched off, I was aware that I felt uneasy around him. I got up and told him I wanted to go back into town. On the walk back, he became increasingly 'too friendly'. When he asked me to meet him for dinner that night, I felt uncomfortable. I didn't want to meet him alone after dark. Without rejecting him, I tried to be kind and considerate. Instead, I asked him to come to the hotel after dinner so we could sit in the open courtyard where I had the 'young boys' from the trekking team around me.

Day 11

When he came to the hotel, I was relieved I had not met him elsewhere. As soon as we finished our tea, I politely said I was going to pack my bag and get ready for the next day. As he left, he tried to kiss me and I heard him whisper, 'I love you.' I turned my face away and the smell of alcohol from his breath made me even more uncomfortable. With a smile, I said good-bye and wished him well.

As I got ready for bed that night, I thought about why I'd felt the need to be considerate in a situation that made me so uncomfortable; it would have been better to just say I couldn't do anything. This was definitely a life issue and here I was facing it in the middle of the Himalayas!

I turned my attention to the next day. 'Where will my journey take me now?' So much had happened and I was looking forward to being enchanted by the mountain spirits again. As I drifted in and out of sleep, I prayed to Mother Nature for a safe journey ahead.

DAY 12
RARU VILLAGE
3850 METRES/12,631 FEET

I had finished packing my bag when I heard a knock on my door. In his gentle voice, the cook told me, 'Tea is ready.' The voices of the trekking team gave me a sense of comfort.

The porridge filled the rest of my little void of anticipation. With the warmth of the sun shining on my back, I wrote in my journal: 'The sun soothes the anticipation of something new to be revealed. May I walk lightly, so I can flow like a river without identifying myself with the grasping mind. May the power of pure awareness melt the shadow of fear into joy.'

I paused and looked at my hands. My nails were clean after washing my clothes but my hands were dry. I hadn't brought any hand lotion and such things were not available here.

I was happy to move along, now only with the trekking team. But I was less impressed walking along the relatively boring, dusty jeep road. I hid under my cashmere shawl to protect myself from the burning asphalt fumes and what seemed like hundreds of eyes staring at me. Some of these eyes were friendly and smiling, saying

Day 12

Jooley, while other eyes made my heart pound. It reminded me of a disco scene. The road workers were dressed in pink, purple and bright blue shirts, with trousers and shoes to match. Some were just sitting there while others moved rocks. I clung to my camera and walked faster. The guide was already far out of sight.

His behaviour irritated me and I was having prejudiced thoughts. Many emotions were bubbling within me. My inner voice told me to observe it and let it go. I noticed how sensitive I was to the environment around me, how my inner reality matched the outer—this time instead of it bringing out my visionary nature, it worried me. I looked past the disturbed energy of the road to the deep canyon beyond that was shimmering with a beautiful contrast between the turquoise river set against the stark grey and brown land.

In that moment, I saw how I could walk back and forth over the bridge between my worldly and divine mind, which had two different realities—the shallower and the deeper. My worldly mind reflected what I saw with my eyes. It was up to me to choose what I let myself be carried away with. I was not going to let a guide or some road workers interfere with my communion with the pristine, joyous landscape. I was going to have to make sure I kept my focus.

By choosing the reality I truly valued I was able to watch the negative thoughts arise and dissolve away again. Each step, each breath, was an opportunity to refocus my mind. By doing this, I slowly faced and accepted more of my inner truth. Engrossed by the stunning view, I relaxed and allowed the moments to be as they wanted to be.

Ahead, I could see Bardan Monastery perched dramatically on top of a large needle-shaped cliff spur, right by the deep winding canyon with the river flowing far below. It was an incredible sight that became even more stunning as I walked closer and closer. The guide was waiting for me there with a monk, but the rooms were closed. He went with the monk into one of the ancient protective deities' temples, but I was not allowed to enter.

I immediately turned the huge and beautifully engraved prayer wheels in the courtyard before I sat down and had a snack. After a short rest, I continued on, this time walking with the guide. I had tried several times to tell him that he should keep a shorter distance between us so I could see him. However, he became offended and I didn't want to rock the boat.

We reached Mune after a couple hours, and stopped to rest by the entrance to the tiny village with only a few white, flat roofed houses. I sat on the ground under a tree, next to two white square and dome shaped stupas, a mani wall and a flagpole. From there, I admired the quiet village life and the picturesque scenery that oozed with Tibetan symbolism. The atmosphere was totally different from that which I had felt in Padum with its mixed cultural influence. By now, I was hungry and enjoyed my lunch and something to drink while the guide talked with a local from the village.

Raru Village

I was happy and relaxed as we resumed the walk. In an hour, I was pleasantly surprised to reach the campsite, particularly given that I had missed the turnoff. As usual, the guide had disappeared into the blue horizon. I had concluded that he was like a goat, and I simply walked too slowly for him. Even though I found his behaviour irritating and irresponsible, I did enjoy walking on my own.

I walked down to the camp through the rocky land and as soon as I got there I spontaneously connected to the earth's harmonious resonance. The emerald green grassland made me feel totally relaxed and the still lake filled me with peace. The many colours in the sandy mountainside glittered and I felt the same way. I dropped my bag and quickly organised my tent.

Lured by the majestic snow-capped peaks, I felt drawn toward the very edge of the rocks. Raru Village and a huge oval field came into sight. And there was a stunning white *stupa* on a hill at the end of the oval. I felt hypnotically affected by what I was seeing. It reminded me of the faces of gods and goddesses I had seen in other places.

Soothed by the sun, I felt relieved to be away from the craziness in Padum. Here there were no boundaries or limitations imposed by my mind trying to conceptualise every little thing. My mind was as open and still as the pure sky. I allowed myself to be caressed by what felt like the earth's caring and passionate embrace.

Then, something happened. The sound of the rustling wind and the bells on the ponies faded. I could see a pregnant woman in the rocky mountainside. Green in parts, she was in a birthing position, giving birth. I felt spellbound by an all-encompassing experience of nature's fertility. My body felt like it was swelling with love and compassion that flowed into and out of me with shivers of the secret earth energy.

I allowed myself to be enchanted by merging with the mountains in my imagination. Mother Nature was there, crystal clear in the open space in my mind and heart. The dance of images, visions, colours, waves of fluid energy and translucent light rose spontaneously, as if reflected by another sphere of existence—and seemingly totally real.

I sat there on the rocks in a meditative state. The visionary perceptions and sensations of pregnancy, birth and the womb that Mother Nature was symbolising told me that a new and unknown reality was being revealed. I was crossing a threshold from one state of consciousness to another, from one stage of life to another. To this day, I still think it is incredible that the divine reality could be revealed to me by faces in the mountains that resonated directly with matching energetic experiences inside me. And all this was because I formed an intimate connection with Mother Nature.

Above the woman giving birth, I could see two faces on top of one another. They took shape as mother and child. Then I saw ancient elders gathered around them. There were three prominent elders to the left, just above a green village. The child and mother became very clear and had a powerful presence, surrounded by silver and gold light. Then, an eagle—a real, physical eagle—flew over me and sent chills down my spine!

My gaze shifted direction. As I looked straight ahead into a sandy landslide with colours of silver, iron and copper, a silhouette of a beautiful young girl's face appeared. Her long hair flowed down her shoulders. She had prominent eyes and nose but she seemed veiled. She was surrounded by green light—giving a strong feeling of vitality.

When I turned my attention to the snow-capped mountains, I spontaneously saw another impressive face on the side of the ridge! It was a young man, almost clown-like. I sat, staring in a relaxed and trancelike manner, and my eyelids started to flutter. In an instant, a small ancient man's face with thick hair and a beard showed up just above the young man's face. It didn't stop.

Above this one, half of a bald man's face appeared, revealing eyes and forehead clearly. I thought, 'This is incredible beyond belief!' The top of the mountain reminded me of a castle. Still not disturbed by

Day 12

my reasoning mind, to the left of these images I saw a big, almost flat face that looked like a Knight Templar with a cross on his forehead. I recognised it from a painting I had seen when I stayed in Mandarin, on the Camino de Santiago.

A Knight Templar is a member of an order of knights founded in southern France in 1118 to protect pilgrims in the Holy Land during the second Crusade. The knights had a strong presence when I walked across Spain. Maybe they were still protecting pilgrims on a quest for truth. Perhaps it explains the protective deities I connected with here in the Himalayas. To my amazement they were now making themselves visible in nature and the mountains. Maybe this is their home, where they can lift their veil and reveal themselves. Could this then be the power of nature that protects people and the land?

I concluded that I had simply walked into their kingdom and they have made themselves visible. No wonder I had intuitively asked for permission to enter.

Suddenly I snapped out of it, thinking: 'I don't get this. This is too much.' Whatever it is or isn't, real or unreal, my head was now spinning with an intense pressure. The sun had gone and it was cold. I moved inside and closed the tent. I focused on my breathing and simultaneously organised the tent and wrapped myself in layers of clothing.

The intense vibrational energy and the sensation of the physical pressure penetrated my body. A current of the intense fire, like a serpent energy force, was rising up through my body again. My heart rate increased and I started to shake uncontrollably. I dropped everything and just sat with my head in the palms of my hands, breathing deeply and slowly. The energy was familiar and by trusting my inner knowing, I surrendered more easily and naturally to the innate intelligence of nature and sacred knowledge rippling through me. Even though my body was now cold, my head was on fire, ready to explode into fireworks.

I lay down, and the images were still flicking through my mind. It felt like I had been struck by lightning. I observed what was going on, and I was aware that I was also freezing cold. There was no peace. The boys outside were chatting nonstop and their voices were making my head spin even faster. I was irritated and impatient at the constant spray of a language I couldn't understand. It sounded like garble. I needed food to physically ground my body and I was just waiting for the call. Finally, I heard, 'Can you come for dinner?'

'Yes, thank you,' I replied. I opened the tent and looked straight at the mountain. Formed like a mask, another human face, large, square and uneven, fitted into the frame of the mountain! Almost dark, I shook my head in disbelief and quickly gathered my things. I needed something to eat!

I staggered over to the dining tent. The food helped me calm down and soon I felt much better. I went back in my tent and tucked myself inside my sleeping bag. I listened to the silence of nature flowing through me. My mind was calm with quiet anticipation.

DAY 13
Pepula Camp
3750 metres/12,303 feet

Still in my woollen underwear, I opened the tent zip and greeted the dawn. To my private amusement all the mountain faces were still there. Despite the cold, I immediately jumped out of the tent. I stood there in the sun, and then, I heard myself say: 'Blow me down!' The human mask had now changed into a huge elephant face with a trunk, big ears and human-looking eyes. The face seemed half human and half elephant. On the ridge next to this was a woman's face, as if lying down, facing the sky. Her hands were folded on her chest. She reminded me of a goddess. Below her, I could see many faces of warriors. 'What an incredible mountain,' I muttered.

I performed my morning ritual and had breakfast. We had been blessed with another deep azure sky. Ready to leave, I said to myself: 'I have no idea what this means.' Nevertheless it didn't bother me; I was feeling fully alive and energised. As I walked down to the village, with the guide leading the way, I chanted the village name, 'Raru'. It had a nice vibrational tone that resonated with my inner self. Just before entering the village, we passed long rows of white *stupas*. A more antique single *stupa* with strings of prayer flags stood between the houses. As I turned the corner of a house, a goat admired the view through a single window.

Already awake and working on the daily chores and farming activities, the local children greeted us with curious eyes. Some were carrying water and a man was climbing a ladder with a load of dried wheat on his back, up to the flat roof.

Just after leaving the village, we met a man herding a large flock of goats. Although easier than the previous day, it was a relief to get off the dusty jeep road and away from the roadwork at Ichar Village. From here on there was no road. Today, we walked up and down on the narrow trail in the mountainside slope, above and along the stunning turquoise river that had carved out the craggy gorge. Now and then I could catch glimpses of charming farmsteads across the river.

With the warmth of the sun, there was no need to wear my woollen sweater and down jacket. But I still had the shawl wrapped around my face and head. I walked effortlessly through the enormous, sweeping landscape, and I could smell the fragrance of bliss in the air. There was only one more pass to cross in a few more days.

We reached the Pepula campsite much earlier than expected. It was surrounded by wilderness and at first it felt a little disappointing to be down in a valley, closed in by a gorge. Then the faint inner voice reminded me, 'I guess it is a matter of flowing with it.'

We were camping right next to the river. I got organised and found a place on one of the big rocks. It was wonderful to take my boots off and wash my feet in the soothing, cool water. I bathed in the warmth of the sunlight on my body and reflected on the day. Today my mind had been focused on the graceful river and I had

Day 13

only occasionally thought of my relationship. I also noticed that I felt some insecurity that was related to not working. But now I relaxed into the flow of the rushing, transparent river and watched the glittering reflections of the sun on the water.

And as I absorbed the strength from the spiritual essence of the sun, rays of love radiated out from within me, giving light and air to the roots of my being that had been either squashed and suppressed into a bundle or bent out of shape during certain times in my life. Even though I didn't think I had any luck with love in my life, my perception of what love was all about was subtly shifting.

Tea was ready, so I went to sit by my tent. I slowly sipped the tea and wrote in my journal. The cook had again made me a table and gave me some biscuits. I paused and looked up at the snow-capped peaks in the distance. I heard myself say: 'You've got to be kidding.' Another face appeared—a distinct, large face, similar to the multiple faces; it was as though it was magnified in a mirror. 'It is a warrior,' I scribbled in my journal.

After some time, the face of a small, old, wise-looking man appeared. He had a cloth wrapped around his head, like a snake. A cloud of dust on the path at the top of the gorge distracted me. The sound of the horse bells grew louder and I could see lots of horses and ponies approaching. A gang of young men stopped at the teahouse a local monk was minding.

My tent was not far away. I noticed that I didn't trust the gang and guarded my things. It was 3:30 p.m. and the sun was going down, shining its golden red light on the peaks. The horsemen finally left. Another face revealed itself, overlooking the others; a little less distinct, but ancient. 'It may belong to the Knights Templar,' I wrote.

I started to get restless, so I walked over to get some washing water. Again, I looked up at the valley in the east, and said to myself, 'Oh, now another one. What is this?' The answer was spontaneous. It was another distinct warrior face on the snow-capped mountain. By seeing it from the side, 'he' was looking north.

As I left Raru that morning, I felt relaxed about the mask images, the half human and half elephant face, the goddess and all the other impressions I had seen. But I had not expected to see more and now I felt quietly baffled by the mysterious surroundings. Then, I became aware of the inner voice.

Relax, let it be, whatever it is will lead you to whatever needs to be known through this connection.

'This must have something to do with my changing perception,' I thought. I continued to write. 'What can I do anyway? What can I say? Nothing. I have learned that everything will unfold and reveal itself at the right time. I just want to be free, like the flowing water.'

It didn't take long before I looked up at the mountain again. I noticed that the large face on the top had closed its eyes, as if 'he' were sleeping. 'He' looked rather serious, with a sombre expression. I wondered whether the series of faces I'd seen was a representation of several generations of gods. Deep in thought, I drank my tea, which had now grown cold.

Even though I was impatient to know what this was all about, there was no logical answer. I could now accept that it could only be revealed by nature's intelligence. I knew, though, that there was a deeper symbolic meaning. 'Whatever is meant to be will be,' I reassured myself. Again, I closed my eyes and let go as the sound of the rushing river calmed my mind and filled me with lightness.

I waited for the dinner call and wrapped myself up in my purple down jacket, the cashmere shawl and put my headband on. It was getting cold and dark, and I needed to go to the toilet again. With my eyes focused on the peaks, another face appeared on the side of the mountain. I noticed that the ancient, small face at the front had faded.

I stood there until I heard the guide's voice calling me for dinner. It was not far to the dining tent. I removed my boots and left them outside. Inside, I made myself comfortable on the floor and reached for my vegetable soup, which I ate while watching the candle flame on the table. The sound of the rushing river supported and nourished me as much as the food. In perfect stillness, I set my focus to walk with my feet firmly planted on the earth.

Satisfied, I returned to my tent. I wiggled into my sleeping bag that night and felt as though I went into the heart of the cave in nature. What I had previously experienced as Mother Nature's womb now also existed within my own heart. The hard shell had melted and I was as naked and vulnerable as a new-born baby.

Pleasantly lulled toward sleep, my sleeping bag transformed into a luminous blanket. Despite my clothes and the usual constriction of my sleeping bag I felt weightless, as if I was floating in the air. In that moment, rays of ecstasy surged through me. I was grateful and joyous for being in my body as I watched a vision of a deep red flower opening before my inner eye. It pulsated with vibrant and passionate life force energy and sprouted seeds of joy within me.

DAY 14
PURNE VILLAGE
3775 METRES/12,385 FEET

'Good morning!' I heard the guide's voice outside the tent. Morning tea had just arrived and I was dressed. It must have been 6:30 a.m. Half awake, I put sun cream on my face and reflected on my strange dream, related to pregnancy and something about the earth being pregnant with so much power and energy.

I stretched my body, and slowly woke up to a new day. I saw my boots in the corner of the tent and thought about how comfortable they were. The movement of walking was going to soften my body into a relaxing flow.

These thoughts gave me the push to pack up my things before I went to eat breakfast. There was always plenty of food and I ate well. It tasted especially good trekking in the mountains. After finishing my porridge and several *chapattis*, I was ready to start walking.

With yet another day of the comforting royal blue sky, it was surprisingly easy to walk. We continued up and down on the sometimes thrilling path that snaked through a deep rust-coloured valley with stunning pinnacle formations. The magical river was flowing

Day 14

elegantly below. And I was still flowing with it as I watched the lovely, tiny isolated hamlets on the other side of the river that seemed to reflect a rustic way of life. The laughter of children danced in the air with waves of love and pure innocence.

Apart from this, I was alone with nature and its seductive power. At one point, a flock of ponies passed me on the mountainside with large and heavy loads on their back. Soon after, I came to a pass with a large white *stupa*. I automatically asked for protection and left some of my beads.

I got my recorder and continued to walk as I started talking. 'Something was different this morning. I felt more anchored within myself, more accepting of the visions, the gods and goddesses that I see hidden in the spirit of the mountains. I became aware this morning that instead of questioning or doubting what I see or what it is, I pray to accept the faces that show me a new reality. By doing so, I honour the spirit of this land.

'And as I continue to walk with my eyes on the path, above the river, I think of the elder I saw yesterday above all the other faces. The captivating image gives me peace in my heart. Perhaps by accepting my surroundings and what I see, I can accept more of who I am. And as I walk, one step at a time, I feel an odd strangeness in coming home to myself. It feels like I am getting ready to deliver something.'

The guide was waiting for me a little further ahead, so I put away the recorder. After a hike of five hours we turned off the path and crossed the meandering river, walking over a hanging bridge made of wooden planks. With shaking feet, I slowly moved across, suspended in space. I walked the next ascent and passed a *mani* wall, a *stupa* and a flagpole at the entrance to tiny Purne Village, which consisted of two stone buildings and twenty people. Chickens were running around and women were doing chores. One woman dressed in bright yellow walked toward me. She carried a huge load of hay on her back. I immediately felt at home and comfortable.

The whole village was situated on the edge of a large canyon but the campground was on a pleasant grassy area among the locals. After setting up the tent with the boys, I sat in the sun. I took off my boots and socks, but we were far from the deep canyon with the turquoise water. I rubbed my feet on the grass, and felt a lovely tickling sensation. A sense of deep relaxation came over me.

It was a long time since I had eaten and I was hungry. As if reading my mind, the cook came with biscuits and a mandarin. As he did, another woman came by with a load of hay. I got up and shared what I had with her before she walked off. The surrounding scene was pretty and colourful. The shimmering hues of yellow, pink, purple and green reminded me of the powerful energy patterns I had connected with on this journey. Inner visions started to appear wherever I looked.

Then my inner knowing whispered a prayer. 'Just take me to where I belong—in the land of freedom.'

In the distance, in the dazzling light, toward Phuktal Monastery, I could see another open womb in the great copper mountain formation. I got my recorder and started speaking. 'Nature's pregnancy is reflected all around me, or perhaps within me. With what? True nature? Am I pregnant with Mother Nature's power? I can see her in a birthing position and the opening to her womb is pulsating with a strong surge of energy. I understand that this is not a sexual energy. It symbolises nature's creation and fertility.'

My focus changed and I continued to speak into the recorder, without expecting an answer. 'Walking is my salvation. When I flow with what is, I become more present in the moment. Here I am walking the path. I should stop saying I don't understand what is going on because the intuitive part of me knows. If only I could trust more. But trying too hard and thinking too much only binds me and creates resistance. I have learned that expectations only make it more difficult and frustrating, and prolong my suffering.'

I felt restless, and stopped the recorder. As I glanced up into the heavenly blue sky, my intentions for freedom fluttered like my eyes. I wanted to get up and dance. In the next moment, I stood up and faced the mountain where I could see the womb. I held my hands in a prayer position against my chest, and silently aligned myself with the four directions—North, South, East and West, by turning and bowing in honour to the mountain in each direction. The dancing play of hues became part of me and I felt a tingling sensation of being transformed. I started to hum the *Om Mani Padme Hum* mantra, which changed into a song.

'Where ever I am—I am in the womb of Mother Nature, embraced by her endless eternity and maternal mystery.'

Suddenly I stopped, as Mother Nature began to speak.

Take a deep breath and listen closely. I am truth speaking to you. Ask your mind, 'Who am I' and you will never know, because it will just seduce you with illusions and attachments.

Only the sacred essence of your true nature knows 'who I am'. So, therefore, ask your inner knowing to guide you.

Ask and then listen. Stay open for the unexpected and you will do things or find things you never expected. The answers you seek lie in the moment-to-moment experiential awareness.

And when you receive the answers—trust and believe in me. You are beginning to understand this now.

I put the recorder on the ground and knelt down with my knees and hands touching the grass. My body went naturally into a resting position with my legs bent. I kissed the earth and was filled with a surge of pulsating life force energy. Overflowing with unconditional love and gratitude I stayed there for some time, then sat up and started speaking into the recorder again.

'In presence of your divinity I feel love, tenderness and compassion rising from the earth in patterns and codes interwoven into my being. By singing tones of pure love, I humbly observe how the vibration moves around in my body, endlessly flowing, and so my body, mind and spirit enlightens. When I stand on top of the mountain, I breathe the air of light. I know it is you—the divine light of consciousness. With the sword of light in my hand, I am fearless. I know it is your protection. In love and devotion I surrender to you.'

I sat there for a while rocking back and forth before I got up. Before doing my usual washing ritual, I walked around the tiny village. I admired the locals and how they lived. The row of six *stupas* was painted in white, gold and silver. They reflected the spiritual significance of this cherished land.

At dinner the guide told me about our day excursion to Phuktal Monastery the next day. This was a special monastery built inside a cave in the mountain. We were coming back to the campsite so I didn't have to pack my things. For a change it was nice to stay in one place more than one night.

DAY 15
Phuktal Monastery
3900 metres/12,795 feet

I woke that morning feeling suffocated. I had dreamed about my relationship again, and I was irritated. And it was not just my mood; my glasses were fogging and my pen was not working. The dream showed me what I had suspected—my ex-boyfriend was involved with another woman. The habitual part of me was bound in destructive knots. I heard myself saying: 'Yes, I know all this and I know it is working through me for a reason. I am sick and tired of carrying around this part that doesn't feel loved.'

My hands felt cold, but as I rubbed them together I ignited a fire within me, and I thought of my beloved father who had warmed my icy hands under his armpits after ice-skating when I was 12 years old. My mood instantly changed, as I felt the presence of his unconditional love. I was ready to move around. My inner voice started to repeat words like a mantra. 'Just take me to where I belong—in the land of freedom.'

After breakfast, the guide and I were walking to Phuktal Monastery and then back again. The path was easy so I told the guide that I was happy for him to run ahead. As soon as he did, I was inspired to get my recorder and start talking.

'I am aware that the feelings I woke with this morning are from a part of me that resists walking the path. It was the part of me feeling irritable, grumpy and impatient at not getting what it wants. But as soon as I started walking, I realised that I am on the path, and that's where I belong—in the present moment of flow. Frustration and suffering keeps me off the path. That is the old part, the worldly ego mind.

'I have learned that this part needs to be watched so I can have faith in the intuitive process more easily. And not only that, every time I struggle up a steep mountain and remember to pray, everything becomes easy and graceful. I am beginning to realise that this is part of Mother Nature's experiential teaching.

'The experience this morning showed me how fast the mind can go into those darker places. And if I am not aware, I get caught in the darkness. By not being afraid of those darker places that suppress my spark of divinity, the path is illuminated.'

As I continued to talk into the recorder and walked along the perilous path, I looked down in to the river and pondered. 'The river of life is flowing through every one of us with different shades and shadows of light and dark, constantly changing. On a pilgrimage into ourselves, we walk closer and closer to our true being and receive the blessings of truth and clarity to stay even more present on the path.'

When I stopped talking, I saw how effortlessly I was flowing through the landscape. Even though it looked like the heavily eroded path could collapse at any time, it didn't worry me. Again, I got the recorder and spoke. 'Whatever happens, it doesn't matter, because this is the path. Whatever comes, it is okay. Even if it is the old stuff, it is part of it. The lesson is to embrace the grumpy and irritable part with loving kindness and forgiveness. When I remember to pray and be in the flow, I can just be with what is, because whatever it is, it is in this moment of truth. And right now, this moment is about being with the rushing river, just flowing with it, on the rocky path to Phuktal Monastery. The ancient path, along the turquoise river of life.'

I put the recorder away. After two hours of walking, I crossed the river. As I rounded the mountainside and walked under the strings of prayer flags, the scene that met my eyes was spectacular. Many whitewashed buildings cascaded out of a huge cave in the rocky cliffside. I stood there by the entrance, next to the *stupas, mani* walls, and prayer wheels, and admired this stunning architectural wonder.

Together with the guide, I climbed the steep hill before reaching the gate. From there, I was guided through narrow doors and up dark stairs to a large outdoor balcony. Despite the maze of rooms, the magnificent cave with all the small temples and the monastery itself that felt like an antique fortress was just another place to me.

Even though there was a slight hope I would find something in the monasteries, deep down, I knew I would not. But having said that, as I looked into the eyes of the young boy monks dressed in their red robes, I saw that they radiated joy and compassion. Their smiles and laughter filled me with playfulness in the midst of the serious atmosphere.

I listened to my intuition that told me not to leave my silver bangle as an offering at the monastery. It symbolised my past. Was I not ready to let go of my past? Or was it simply not the right time or place? I let it go, and as I mused over the view and wild nakedness beyond the rocks, the soft silent voice of Mother Nature surprised me.

Your connection is with nature and the spirit of the mountains. True nature is the only truth. And like everyone—even like Buddha, he also needed to be realised. There is so much more beyond the dogma and paradigms of the teachings, easily polluted by the ones who carry them. Although it shows you 'what has been done' you must walk beyond others' paradigms and concepts and go even deeper into your own essence to tap your own life force energy—pure and simple, in nature. If not, you walk into the trap of blind faith—no matter who you are—others, whoever they are, can only take you so far. By standing in your own wisdom and the power of your own faith, you don't rely on others to make you feel good. When you walk your own way, where no one else has trodden, you are walking the sacred path of truth.

Contemplating the Rocks

We stayed at the monastery for a while, but as we walked back to the campsite in the afternoon, I contemplated what Mother Nature had said. The rocks, the river, the bare mountainside and the reddish sandstone were coming alive in what felt like a gallery of sculptures. The unusual pillar formations of golden pebbles were sculpted into various forms. One of the pillars looked like a huge mushroom and had a distinct masculine energy. I wondered how it had been shaped by nature's elements—just like we are all shaped into being. I knew that the male focus in the visual scenery was still just part of Mother Nature's work. And there she suddenly was with her clear voice.

By walking the truth, life reveals itself, beyond your thoughts and emotions of everyday shallowness—and you surrender to the bare nakedness of the pulsating earth. As you drink from the pure sky of awareness, a flowing river, rocks, mountains and the impulse of light and colours, you are nurtured with purity and strength from nature's true wisdom and natural rhythm.

I continued to move along through a landscape that shimmered with soft shaded colours and light. My mind was curious. 'Maybe it is the elements of earth, water, fire, air and ether that connects me with nature's divine energy impulse.'

I could feel nature's passion moving through me. It felt like a raw nakedness that held nothing back. When I asked the naked emptiness what I was here for, it begged me to just be with it, in my purest form without preconceived ideas. I experienced a great silence and then I heard her voice again.

If you don't know—just be. If you don't know how—embrace me and just listen, see, hear, touch, feel, witness, acknowledge and register. Just do this as long as you have to. Still your mind; watch your eagerness, desire, restlessness, impatience, frustration, joy, peace, sadness—rise and fall, fall and rise—over and over— moments of blissful energy—momentary and transient. Give these emotions room to express themselves. That is the way to freedom; that is how you surrender to the naked emptiness beyond who you have become—beyond who you think you are—by being present with the flowing essence of who you are in truth—whatever happens is a step on the spiritual path.

I almost knocked my head on a rock as the path cut through the cliffside like a tunnel. It helped me slow down and reminded me to stay present on a path that kept changing and at times was totally eroded. I took my time and enjoyed the careful walk back to camp.

A Night in the Dark Womb

After a short nap in the late afternoon sun, I walked around the village again and interacted with the locals. I was tired and soon returned to my tent to do my usual rituals before dinner.

That night it was not easy to fall asleep. Although the noise and the mixture of music, voices and laughter had stopped, the confused, doubting voices I'd experienced before were still alive inside me. It was as if every time I made progress toward becoming clear, it magnetised more of my fear to the surface.

There was a disturbance inside me and tears welled up. Despite trying to swallow, there was a lump in my throat and I felt like I was choking. Rivers of water ran into my ears and the tissue paper dissolved in my hand. My hair was sticky; I tossed and turned. I thought about my ex-boyfriend and his touch. His tender sensitivity rolled me into waves of grief. It took me deep into the sadness of what was the naked and bare reality of feeling totally alone. I wanted to be stroked and held. But there was no one. In that moment, I was totally alone. The pain in my diaphragm felt like a big black hole.

I breathed deeply into my stomach, and the sensation of heat suddenly started to move up my spine. The energy vibrated through my body with surges of electrical currents, awakening consciousness within my body and being at the same time. I immediately thought about the white luminous serpent and I entered another reality.

Visions of serpents came into my mind. They were hissing at each other. There were two big ones, and many small ones dancing to the hissing, vibrating sounds they created. It felt like the powerful and pervasive *OM* sound of universal consciousness was moving through my veins, kissing every cell in my body. I understood that the visions of the serpents I saw were symbolic of the heat I experienced rising

Day 15

upward like two energy forces entwined. I was on fire. My mouth was hot and dry, and my head was like an electric light bulb.

I surrendered and heard Mother Nature's silent voice.

Become aware of any resistance in your body and let it go. Allow yourself to feel the physical sensation of energy vibration. Let your body register the experience. It knows what it is doing, without you having to control it. Trust the innate intelligence of your body so the energy of higher consciousness can align the masculine and feminine forces within you.

Allow yourself to surrender so you can go beyond the mind, where true intelligence resides. Have faith and let it happen naturally.

Aware of any tightness in your body, hold your hand on the area of tension and feel the contraction. Draw the energy of high vibration into that area and breathe softness with awareness of unconditional love… and let it go. Relax and feel the difference between tightness and relaxation.

Be aware of your breath. Feel and become aware if you are holding your breath. Feel the power of will that moves you, compared to forcing it or holding back. Feel the powerful energy that moves you and let yourself be nurtured by divine consciousness. By connecting to nature you are in alignment with what gives you the power to heal and transform.

I listened and breathed into the heat rising in my body. At the same time, I relaxed and could see my fear of nature's strength. With the power of the serpent fire, I took a deep breath and blew the fire onto the fear hidden beyond my sadness and grief. When I allowed myself to let go, I watched the deep fear of being born into this world, being extinguished by a deep red and black, fierce volcanic fire.

In the same instant, I scattered into a million stars of light. And I looked into the eternal eye of Mother Nature. An abundance of light was created. My cells were dancing ecstatically and I saw and felt intricate patterns of golden flowers that pulsated in my body.

In this moment of vulnerability, sadness and grief, I realised how many times I had been fooled into a false sense of hope and security when I had people around me who I thought made me feel safe—only to discover that I was clinging to dreams and ideas that were not real.

I felt totally naked in the womb of Mother Nature, and opened up to fearlessness and emptiness. Nurtured and held with unconditional loving kindness by Mother Nature, I was not alone in the womb of nature's essence. She whispered:

By understanding the power that drives you, mountains can be moved, when you trust the natural flow of nature's intelligence. This life force energy is the divine power of higher consciousness within you.

Consciously aware or not, you influence everything around you charged with nature's vibration. Feel the fire of this energy inside you. Use it wisely and move with it. Get to know it and you shall know yourself through the experience of this vibration.

I tossed and turned and tried to settle into the silence. The night was long and the crescent moon told me this was a new beginning. I asked for guidance. Like a new-born baby I was finally free to sleep with the *Om Mani Padme Hum* mantra kissing me with the vibration of a gentle mother.

DAY 16
SKING CAMP
4000 METRES/13,123 FEET

The following morning I woke up with an inner knowing that told me this:

*Sadness cries in longing for the meaningful—
Joy is found in connection with our true nature.*

'How nice,' I thought. Filled with gratitude, I started my morning ritual and packed everything before breakfast. Words were flowing effortlessly so I found my recorder and said: 'I watch the nature of my emotions, dancing with thoughts of a similar nature. Happy thoughts flow in harmony and balance, with joy and lightness. Sad thoughts filled with darkness are transformed and harmonised in rhythm with being at peace.' I didn't think much more about it. Only in hindsight did I realise that it was an observation from the detached, higher mind.

Today was a longer walk of seven hours. I had a sense of 'nowhere to go, but everywhere to be.' It was something about the barrenness that helped me feel freedom in the nothingness. Walking through the grand landscape of villages, fertile farmland

and plateaus framed by the snowy mountains continued to emanate divine meaning.

As I passed through a village, laughing children filled me with the joyful vibration of *Jooley* as they greeted me. The locals, working hard in the large fields harvesting their crops for winter, were part of the landscape and the art of nature. I stopped to say hello and took some pictures.

Walking on with lightness, I reflected on the experience from the night. I recognised that the sorrow of lost love needed to be acknowledged and passed on to the earth for transformation. The pain was something that needed to be held like a baby and loved until there was no more suffering.

As I kept walking, the sound of my breath sang a song to set me free. Charmed by this wide-open desert land and the many spiritual monuments dotted everywhere on the path, I could smell the sandalwood fragrance of earth. I prayed that we could all live and face the truth in every moment.

I looked into the greatness of the sky and was soothed by the soft music of the riverbed that was now almost level with the plateau. Touched by the gentle wind, I asked the gods and goddesses, the sun and moon, the stars, the gorgeous clear blue sky and Mother Nature for oneness within. With the feeling of being swept along the path, I chanted the *Om Mani Padme Hum* mantra. My awareness heightened and I heard the whispers from Mother Nature.

When you accept your true nature, you accept the creation of earth you are walking on. Until then, you do not believe fully in yourself.

Day 16

Still walking along the windswept plain, I mumbled: 'When I walk with ease and grace, I become the vastness that I am, I become the nothingness the sacred land emits.' Then, seemingly out of nowhere, a woman appeared. She was carrying an old straw bucket full of dried dung on her back. Her shoes were full of holes. 'If only I had socks and shoes to give her,' I thought.

After many hours, I began the gradual ascent to the edge of Sking Village. I rounded a mountainside and another wide plateau opened up, marked by rows of large, white *stupas* and long *mani* walls. The divine symbolism connected me to the enchanting land. I felt spacious.

Then, from a mighty mountain in the far distance, an enormous rock face appeared. It intrigued me. What looked like a remarkable natural statue was immersed, triumphantly in the noble sky. I was filled with shivers and felt like bowing in reverence. I continued to walk along the flat ground.

As usual, the guide was miles ahead, and I nearly missed the campsite; I was far from Sking Village on the other side of the river! When I did see him, I again mentioned that he was walking too fast and it would have been good for him to wait. I felt tired of his behaviour and being 'nice'. He gave me a dark look and simply withdrew. He continued to sulk until the next day.

I let it go, carried on and unpacked my bag. It occurred to me that the campsite was much more exposed than on previous nights, which had felt much more protected and warm. I organised the mat and my sleeping bag on the hard, rocky ground by the bank of the river.

After a long day of walking and many days, weeks even, without a proper shower, I performed my usual washing ritual by the very inviting river. The cold water drained away any remaining tension I was holding about the guide. I went to sit outside my tent and, feeling comfortable, wrote in my journal. Once again, a mountain face appeared. The mountain was black and I could see a huge being superimposed over it. Further below I saw a shape that looked like a large, round rock. It was divided in two and out of the open crack, a face with a serene expression appeared. It reminded me of the circular black rock and the face that had come to me in a vision during the powerful night that occurred at the end of day four. Was it the same face? What was it telling me? An answer came to me. 'Out of separation and fear, we come into union with the universe, with the greater self.'

I could see faces and feel their presence wherever I looked. I was learning to experience the faces outside and inside myself as matching states of consciousness. It was getting cold and it was time to wrap up before the usual dinner at 7 p.m. When I rested briefly on my sleeping bag, Mother Nature gave me a question to focus on.

What gives you peace?

She continued.

Whatever it is, it touches your inner being, tickling you with experiences and tingling sensations, in its purest form, without demands or expectations, unadorned, without illusions attached to it.

Take a moment to relax. How might you find the source of peace, you may ask?

Feel your skin. Touch your lips. Stroke your hair. Feel the sensation of your breath, through your nose. Put a hand on your stomach and one on your chest.

Rest here—and notice what you feel, as you allow yourself to be nurtured. As you are connected, your true nature stimulates your awareness through nature's own rhythm and flow. Simply master your mind.

How can that happen, you may ask?

It is through willingness to sacrifice anything that will set you free, to simply be yourself. Then, you will learn to know and understand yourself and the nature of your mind.

Practice patient awareness and turn the mind inward; look deeply at yourself in the mirror of divine consciousness and ask these questions:

Who have I become? Who am I?

These are questions to dwell upon. Ask and you shall receive.

'Who have I become?' I wondered. 'Who am I? Who are you?' I asked Mother Nature out loud as if she was right there with me. These questions were not new. She didn't answer back straight away this time. Instead, I felt a wave of relaxing energy wash over me, like the current of the river next to me. The only difference was that the sensations were warm and loving. Then, she did answer.

The answers you seek are wrapped in the mystery of who you are. Not knowing protects the mystery. Thinking you know only sabotages being who you really are, in the presence of your core vibration. You need certain experiences to open up to the wisdom of higher consciousness. The mind simply does not understand the essence of love and therefore you live a separate life, disconnected from the very essence of your true nature. Unconditional love must be nurtured by connecting to the source of self.

I listened carefully and in those brief moments, I saw that the intellect was a veil to be lifted. And when I rested in the seat of my inner self, I found the answers hidden in my unconscious.

DAY 17
LHAKHANG CAMP
4470 METRES/14,665 FEET

I was still asleep when my morning tea arrived. I rose, accompanied by the sound of the rushing river. Outside my tent, I stretched up as far as I could, into the crystal blue sky, and again Mother Nature spoke to remind me of her words from the day before.

> *Beyond the veil of what you can see there is a reality beyond the unreal—hidden in the secret energy of nature—only revealed when the veil of ignorance dissolves.*
>
> *I am revealed by the perfection of divine intelligence—*
>
> *To those who know me deep within.*

I went to wash in the ice-cold water and instantly woke up fully. It was still early and I packed my things. Satisfied after a hearty breakfast, I was eager to get going. When I started to walk that morning, words danced on my lips. 'Every time I have faith in my inner knowing, my trust strengthens.'

'Yes,' I thought. 'I can receive what I need right now.' It occurred to me that Mother Nature always gave me what I most needed, whether it was from an external vision or a new perspective arising from within.

It was good to be moving again. As I breathed in the fresh crisp morning air, I had a weird sense that the plateau was vibrating more strongly than before. It felt as though I were merging with the pulsing land. 'Maybe the earth itself is waking up,' I mused. 'Well Borghild, that's an odd thought,' I giggled.

Happily, I walked into the golden dawn along the rocky path toward the Kargyak Village, which at 4050 metres (13,287 feet) is the highest permanent settlement in the Zanskar region. The immensity of the plateau and the gentle breeze filled me with a surge of excitement and butterflies in my stomach. Mystical smoke from the rooftops created an auspicious atmosphere for nurturing. It reminded me of a life force rising into thin air.

It was still early when I walked into the primitive village. I stopped by a tiny bridge to let some little children who carried water and some villagers with bundles of hay on their back pass by. They all seemed shy and when I said hello, they looked down and didn't reply.

After a while, I passed the Kargyak River, and on a ridge, a majestic rock face shot up into the air. It was the same one I had seen glimpses of yesterday. My heart was a drumbeat as if celebrating something special. The hefty rock face kept changing in a diversity of hues, and I wondered if this was the place with the cave I had heard about. I asked the guide if it were possible to climb up to a cave or small temple.

He said, 'It's nothing there; only some people with very good *karma* can see gods.' Then he added, 'They say there are seventy gods in this rock known as Gonpo Rangjung.'

Day 17

The Mysterious Universe

I was aware of the spaciousness of the Himalayan plain. And I wanted to slow down a bit and proceed on my own to see if something might come to me from this awesome holy rock. I automatically started to sing out loud. 'Om Mother, come to me, be with me, colours of the mountains, colours of the naked land, colours of the soul, infinite blue sky, come to me, I am here.'

Then it happened. As I looked at the rock face, the whole thing came alive with an amazing array of forms, shapes and visual images: a castle, some faces with different personality characteristics, some animals and many eyes. 'My God!' I exclaimed. 'How many dimensions are there?'

I could feel the earth shaking. Something was becoming totally real that I hadn't seen as totally real before. Although I was walking on the ground beneath me, I felt I was not on an earthly plane at all. Was I having some sort of 'out of body experience'? I wasn't too sure what was making my limbs move.

I felt baffled and reached for my recorder. This was something I had to capture, but before I could speak, it happened again. What I thought of as Mother Nature, the almighty power of cosmos, appeared as a huge rock and looked like a roaring lion with her mouth open, as if she were receiving something from the sky.

When I gazed longer, I could see the breath of fire from her mouth. I moved closer and closer. Then I felt the heart flame of that fire. The weird thing was that it wasn't just external—my flesh wasn't burning. It was more that her pulsating energy was rising within me. My hands trembled and tremors filled my whole body. It immediately occurred to me that it was, indeed, a sacred temple. Maybe there really was a cave inside this temple, perhaps even in her mouth!

The whole of my insides were shaking like a rattle. I noticed that when I saw heat in her, I felt it in me, or was it vice versa? I experienced electrical nerve impulses firing in all directions like a harmonic symphony. I understood that I was in fact living inside a burst of the earth's own *kundalini* energy.

The sacred rock face projected a huge, sitting lion. It looked like Mother Nature was sitting there waiting for me. She had the cutest face of a baby puma in the area of her throat. With her neck tilted back, and her huge lion's mouth wide open, she called out with a fiery roar, into the vast sky and space around her.

I spoke into the recorder. 'Mother Nature is breathing in the universe through her mouth. She breathes with the powerful frequency vibration of creation. It looks like she can swallow the sun. I am witnessing scenes within a mysterious 'other' realm—one that exists beyond fear. Along the length of her lion-like body, I can see a library, held within the frame of a skull, which holds ancient records, sacred scriptures and codes. I get the feeling that I am watching the extraordinary reality of the unknown self—hidden in the universe, within the soul's temple, which holds the memory of universal consciousness.'

I continued to speak. 'Mother Nature is inviting me into her temple where I can see a projection of nature's hidden, creative energy grid. It has wavy lines with codes and patterns imprinted on them.'

Every nerve ending in my body was vibrating with presence; I was united with the environment around me, the sun's energy, the combinations of colours, the earth, the stones and the water. She was in everything, lifting the frequency of my own energy higher. 'I am part of her, I am part of nature,' I softly whispered.

Day 17

I put the recorder in my pocket and understood something quite profound. Total purity exists within the awareness of life force energy. This was an ancient secret of nature's perfection, expressed by a deity disguised in an animal form (in this case a lion). I asked a question. 'Could it be that the animal rock face is a manifestation of a deity—a disguise of Mother Nature?'

Later, the animal in the rock face and the fire became recurring symbols. As I stabilised my higher state of being, the visionary experiences became part of a new reality—and way of being—as I accepted my connection to the divine.

The Rock Faces

My ability to see faces in the mountains and rocks became a teaching vehicle for me. The longer I held my attention quietly on a mountain, the more easily the faces appeared. I saw a heroic king's face, wearing a hat with a feather, floating inside a castle or a fortress. I refocused on the lion's head and saw it more now as a puma, which morphed into a beautiful young girl, just like the girl I'd seen and loved a few days ago. The images of the puma and the girl alternated continually back and forth. I had learned from Andean traditions that the puma represents the centre of our being and symbolises self-realisation. And I couldn't help but wonder if the girl represented my own inner, innocent self. As I continued to watch and walk closer, the girl shifted to the image of an older woman; was I bringing my innocence up to date into my present self? And was my essence similar to the courageous lion's?

When I shifted back to look at the king, I saw a large crown on top of his head. His eyes became large and deep, full of ancient wisdom. And he now seemed to be living inside a pyramid. Was he a protector or teacher for me? The images were changing to elicit ideas from my deeper self, which were perfectly in tune with where the flow wanted my mind to go next.

I would have these intense periods of visionary immersion, then come back to 'ordinary' reality. I'd notice for example that I was suddenly ravenously hungry and thirsty. I'd reconnect with the beauty of crossing the fertile pastureland where yaks were grazing on the mountain plateau. I'd think about how people could possibly live here. Then I'd be back, sitting in a sunny spot, eating my lunch.

So here I was again, in a new moment. I made myself comfortable and re-centred, as was my new habit, into the calming vibration of the earth, feeling somewhat magical. What I had seen only a short while ago was something I was enjoying tremendously. It was endlessly entertaining and meaningful. Looking around as I ate, I noticed the image of a handsome warrior wearing sunglasses; he had long, thin blonde hair and looked wicked; he made me think of a Norse god—the one who was linked to the underworld from Greek mythology.

I drank some water, still watching this 'movie' in the mountainside. Now an eagle appeared above the puma, with a snake and a horse in the background. What previously looked like a pyramid now looked like a male skull, resting his chin on his hand. A multitude of friendly faces with illuminating eyes appeared around the base of the mountain. I couldn't even count them. I felt they were welcoming me to this sacred land and without a doubt were watching my movements.

Soon, it was time to get going. As I left, a vision of a boy and an animal that looked like a dinosaur with deep hollow eyes became

Day 17

apparent, as if guarding an entrance at the base of the mountain. I walked over to the yak settlement where the guide had finished his lunch. I thought this as though talking to Mother Nature: 'I thank you. I greet you. Incredible faces. I can see your face in multiple forms, but I can only feel your essence. Are you showing me that the mountains are the power of a divine reality in tangible form? Yet the visions keep changing. It makes me think that my essence or energy vibration has no form; no face. Nor does fearlessness or love. And perhaps that's why the visual perceptions keep changing.'

Walking on through the camp full of yaks, I met the local mountain tribe. When I saw the tents made out of yak wool, it occurred to me that this might even be a group of nomads or people who have devoted their lives solely to herding. I watched as the smiling women milked the cows.

Lhakhang Camp

With the guide ahead of me, we continued to the upper reaches of Kargyak River. I plodded along in a world of my own. As I crossed the riverbed I sang and chanted prayers out loud. I felt an immense gratitude for what now felt like a blessing of meeting the gods and goddesses. I crossed through more of the beautiful yak grazing pastureland of the Lhakhang area and the trail at this altitude (4470 metres/14,665 feet) was rocky. I needed to pick my way carefully.

It was getting late in the afternoon and the sun was going down. After many hours of walking, I reached the camp tucked right at the base of a striking mountain at the back of the rock face. Apart from our tents there was physically nothing else there—no village, no other people. I looked around and watched the fading golden light on the mountain peaks. Enchanted by the magic scenery, I could see more vivid faces with distinct features, in what I believed had to be a kingdom of gods and goddesses.

Today, I knew I had greeted and spoken to the deities, thanking them for my extraordinary experiences of expansion and transformation, for their blessings and a connection to intuitive wisdom. And the sculpted old man that I was now looking at made me think of my ancestors. I was aware of thinking: 'Maybe the seeing is part of awakening my memory of universal consciousness.' Mother Nature had told me this, but I had not really understood or believed how this could be possible.

It was getting cold. About to get into my tent, I paused and looked up at the snowy peaks. 'There is the elephant-headed god again,' I mumbled. And there is the female!' I went inside and warmed myself for a while in my sleeping bag. It was still an hour before dinner. I thought about what my guide had said. Was it good *karma* to be able to see the gods and goddesses in the mountains? Perhaps I had done something right to have my vision open this way.

I knew that in the language of psychology my visions would be labelled as illusions, hallucinations or even delusions; experiences of the unreal. However, I felt it was the other way around. What if the truth is that I can see the real beyond the illusions of what the mind thinks is real? I had not really believed this until now. Without seeing, we cannot really believe.

Part of my change in attitude was because I had so often spontaneously shifted into a higher state of consciousness where I could see into or through the physical world into the energy world. I now knew the energy world was absolutely real. And I had experienced

Day 17

how what I saw externally paralleled what was happening in my inner world, and vice versa.

Northern India was a place I had never known existed. And it was opening me to another realm, beyond the dualistic daily consciousness of my habitual reasoning mind. What I was experiencing felt like an on-going eternal state of bliss. When I acted on my intuition I was rewarded with the revelation of a dimension of divinity.

By walking in the mountains I was learning to accept every experience from nature as sacred and as a blessing. The sound of a bird, or the sight of a genuine smile made me glow. I could see the invisible; I could feel but not touch. And I was starting to believe in a world much deeper, richer and grander than I had ever thought possible.

Here in this pure land, I surrendered to the nothingness of everything and the emptiness of open space. I could smell the sweet fragrance of freedom. The closer I got to the ultimate beyond, where I sensed the source of knowledge existed, the sharper my mind became and the more vivid the pictures. My heart opened ever wider.

I let my musings go for a moment as I got ready for dinner. Right outside my tent, I turned around and looked at the mountain. In the same instant, Mother Nature returned.

Veiled by illusions of untruth, you know me not—
Until you see the truth,
I will only unveil to those who see me clearly.
By knowing within who I am, you will come to me—
As your secret energy of nature awakens—
I shall reveal myself to you.

What did she mean? Surprisingly an answer came immediately.

True nature can only reside in the abodes of pure consciousness— therefore you can only discover your secret energy of nature as you purify and cleanse. By purifying you will initially see glimpses of who you are. As you become more and more aware of your inner knowing and where I reside in your essence as a secret formula of true nature, my guidance will become more obvious. It will be gently revealed as you learn to worship the essence of your inner self. As you harness the divine within self, unity is experienced directly through experiential awareness and contemplative natural art.

In the middle of this I was abruptly called for dinner. I felt disturbed, but Mother Nature persisted.

When you see me without a veil, you have discovered the secret energy of your inner essence—the core of your being. You then remember the ancient wisdom of the whole that I awaken in your cells, which hold cellular memory of the sacred places you have come from.

Her words were quite something. I pondered what she said. It was already dark and I was fumbling around trying to find my torch. Also, I was getting flustered with all this information. 'Breathe deeply and lie down,' she said. And so I did, holding the recorder up to my mouth. Dinner could wait a minute. She continued.

When the memory of where you came from is awakened, you access the path and remember your core vibration hidden in the secret energy of nature. This moves through you with nature's perfection and intelligence. I am the seed within you that contains your unique DNA script and formula that transforms

Day 17

everything into perfection and restores equilibrium to its original form and shape.

Without realising, I had fallen asleep! I woke suddenly when one of the boys rustled the tent and called, 'Ma'am, can you come?' I didn't want to move, but I eventually stepped out into the cold night and rushed over to the dining tent.

And as I enjoyed eating the delicious warm meal of soup, rice, spicy vegetables and *chapattis,* I reflected on my experiences and trusted the full understanding would come later. Could it be that only someone with some spiritual awareness and a desire to understand life at a deeper level could have these experiences? I thought of everything I had done over the last few years. Perhaps the one-time meditation retreat I attended years ago in Mumbai, India, could have been a seed that was now sprouting and had something to do with this.

I had also done many spiritual practices and rituals, including chanting the 108 names of different gods and goddesses. One of them being the 108 names of the elephant-headed Hindu god, Ganesha; and subsequently I had integrated this practice into my life.

Ganesha has the body of a man with a huge belly. His elephant head symbolises wisdom and is identified with the *OM* (universal consciousness) mantra sound. It is believed that he removes obstacles and gives blessings on the path to success. According to the Vedic literature he represents the primordial vibration that created the universe, composed of the letters (sounds) A, U and M, and each letter represents a state of consciousness.

I wondered whether, since I had been worshipping Ganesha through meditation and chanting, he now manifested as the elephant-headed god in the mountains. Even though I had read about the powerful impact of yoga and embodiment of deities, I had never thought it would be possible, nor in what way it could happen.

Since my marriage breakup many years ago, I had been searching for something more. Most of all I desperately wanted to find true love. By accepting that I could not find this outside myself, I finally started to look inside. As part of my quest for true love and something more, I had worked my way through myriad psychology methods to the more ancient secret practices of yoga, meditation and rituals.

I also practiced eating strict diets over long periods during times of solitude that helped me clean and purify myself. The practices came spontaneously as I surrendered more to the mystery of my intuition. If I tried to force something I thought I should do, it didn't lead anywhere. I gradually and subtly became the guide of my own spontaneous nature and wisdom—and learned to stay in the flow.

In hindsight I can see that it was my courage and devotion to follow my intuition to walk and face the unknown that led to these experiences in the mountains. I was actively integrating my spiritual practices, included breathing, mantra chanting, yoga and meditation as I trekked. I have come to the conclusion that the type of mystical connection I had been experiencing could only occur through real, physical activity.

I returned to my tent and wrote about my reflections. In the divine presence of all the gods and goddesses it felt like I was surrounded by the magical essence of nature's alchemy. I put away my journal and, wrapped up in all my clothes inside my sleeping bag, I fell asleep thinking about the eternal mystery of Ganesha. As I felt

Day 17

the warmth of protection and serenity from his presence, one of his mantras made its way back into my consciousness.

With the left palm on my stomach and the right on my chest, I felt the internal humming on my long out-breath as if it were riding on a rhythmic sound wave in the mountains—*Om Gong Gana Pataye Namah.*

DAY 18
SHINGOLA PASS
5096 METRES/16,719 FEET

As dawn broke I woke with the Ganesha mantra still in my mind. Had it been repeating through my head all night? *Om Gong Gana Pataye Namah.*

I continued to recite the mantra internally while I performed my usual rituals to get ready for the day.

I noticed that it was particularly cold so I didn't wash in the cold water. Instead I put plenty of sunscreen on my face. My lips were by now very dry from the high altitude and whenever I moved my mouth, they felt sore. I moved fast, got dressed and went outside; I spent half a minute jumping up and down to warm myself. My hot tea had been placed just outside the tent as usual, but my hands were almost too chilled to hold the cup. So I drank the tea very quickly, because the heat wasn't staying in my body. I knew it wouldn't be long, though, before we were fully on the move and the walking would warm me up properly.

Today we were crossing the last and highest mountain pass on the border between the states of Jammu and Kashmir, and Himachal

Day 18

Pradesh. It was another clear beautiful day and we started early, right after breakfast. We ascended a rise of over one hundred metres (three hundred feet) to the first viewpoint overlooking Lhakhang and the impressive valley we had come from.

After an hour of this slow, tedious ascent, putting one foot in front of the other, I finally felt the warmth of sunrise shining on the mountains. Half way up, I stopped to remove a couple of layers of clothing. The sun was a blessing and the panoramic scenery was astonishing. It filled me with an immense lightness and gratitude. No matter where I looked—sideways, forward, backward and up—more faces were there to be seen. I never tired of the shifting patterns of shadow and light, changing the colours like a kaleidoscope.

At the flat, wide-open viewpoint, I paused to admire the valley. Far in the distance was the tiny village called Kargyak that we had passed early in the morning the day before. It was as remote as it could be, and the only way to get to and from there was by foot.

I continued to walk, and when I glanced back at the view more faces appeared. One reminded me of a Greek god. Surrounded by crystalline snow-clad mountains, I felt as though I were walking in the heart of the world with Ganesha, the spiritual healing goddess and all the other gods and goddesses.

The path was now flat and gradually rising. Ahead of me was a tall, pyramid-shaped mountain. As I watched, it morphed into Ganesha, with a goddess lying on the ridge above, facing up. I took it as a confirmation that the male and female appeared together as one. I was experiencing walking straight into Ganesha, who watched me with kindness. He melted my heart. I chanted his name out loud and wandered along happily. 'What a kingdom,' I smiled to myself.

ShingoLa Pass

I crossed the fledgling icy river, deep in snow. And as I did, I thanked the gods and goddesses for their blessings. Again I prayed for strength and protection and for any obstacles to be removed from my path. Although I had been warned that it was going to be the hardest day to walk, I found it easy. After climbing another three hundred metres (close to a thousand feet), we got to the top of another ridge with a small cairn. The pile of loose stones shaped like a cone told me we had reached another main marker point and were going in the right direction. The trail ran along the ridge with a gushing stream below, covered in most parts by ice and snow. There was a sound of thunder, which I fancifully thought might be a deity playing a musical piece for all the mountain spirits.

As I approached the pass, I could feel that familiar pulsating energy coming from the earth—and possibly also from the sky. I stopped frequently to breathe. When I did so, I could smell the fragrance of earthy incense in the cold air, like sandalwood, making me feel warm inside despite the low temperature. I felt I was walking inside a giant natural temple where huge canvases of sacred art were hanging everywhere. I thanked all the spirits, and with every step and breath, I prayed for divine truth.

When I walked the last few hundred metres toward the pass, the heat of excitement rose within me like a serpent. At the same time the wind on my face was cold and sent shivers down my spine. A healing wind swept through my body like tiny purifying ice crystals.

Finally, I reached the very top of ShingoLa Pass, and a whole new world opened up. I walked the last part slowly, on the edge of the ridge, to get to the summit, which was marked by a larger cairn and streamers of torn prayer flags. Smoke was coming from between all the loose, piled-up rocks. The scent welcomed me and I felt like celebrating. I noticed that the guide was burning special Tibetan juniper incense. It impressed me that he had carried the dry shrub with him all this way.

We had come to the highest pass and in the blowing, freezing wind, at an altitude of 5096 metres (16,719 feet) it was time to pay our respects to the earth.

I paused to look at the view. It was breathtakingly beautiful, with majestic mountains on all sides. Right in front of me, below and in the middle of this picturesque scene, was a large turquoise glacial lake partly covered by ice and snow. Here was another room in Mother Nature's temple.

I closed my eyes and took a deep, reverent breath. Then, something strange happened. I felt a gentle, literal yet intense sensation of a single large drop of water splashing onto my forehead between my eyebrows. I touched my forehead to see if I could feel anything, but also instantly understood that it was a special experience that I could only feel with my heart.

My mind was blank. Unconsciously I knew where it had come from. Just as a drop of water hits a lake in slow motion, so this energy water drop affected my consciousness. I awakened from a dream and I heard the faint voice of Mother Nature in the humming breeze.

> *When your heart is pure, purity fills you with the divine desire of love, beyond all obstructions of the ego worldly mind, there is nothing—only love.*

The guide interrupted me then and said I needed to hurry. He said it was too cold and windy. Humbled by what just happened, I quickly made my offerings and prayers by the landmark. I left some of my few remaining prayer beads and the silver bangle that represented my past in among all the rocks. I lit some incense sticks and, as I placed them among the rocks, I prayed for blessings and for peace in the world and for Mother Nature to take care of all her children.

With ShingoLa in my heart, in the midst of the celestial glacial lake and the mighty layers of the extravagant Himalayan peaks, I knelt down and bowed in honour and devotion to Mother Nature and all the other gods and goddesses. With my forehead touching the ground, I thanked my ex-boyfriend for helping me move forward. With one of my hands placed firmly on my heart, I said goodbye with the intention to release both of us from any further attachments. I prayed for my family and everyone I come in touch with. When I rose from the ground, I took a deep breath and felt nature's invisible heartbeat as a wind of compassion, sweeping integrity over the land. In that moment I saw Mother Nature as ShingoLa.

Located here on the roof of the world, I spontaneously started to sing, out loud, a song to her (with my recorder in my hand).

'I can feel you in the wind. I can breathe you in the heart of Himalayas. You are tall and strong, you are white and pure. I can smell you. I can touch you. You are in me. I am in you. You are everywhere. You are where I am. I am where you are.

'You speak the divine truth and the wind blows away any illusions. Solid as the naked mountains, only the essential truth speaks with the essence of who you are. How it is, is what I see.

'Blessed by the gifts of your dignified beauty, I bow to you in deepest gratitude. At one with you, I pray. You are my true love, without delusions and attachments. It is wild and pure. It is everything, it is mystical, and it is magical. It simply is; what I make it to be.'

The Descent

Intoxicated, I started the descent, slowly and carefully picking my way through the scree slope of loose rocks next to the icy riverbed and a mighty waterfall. The mountain faces continued to appear and accompany me as I walked. This was a steep and treacherous path and it was important that I keep my eyes focused.

Humming the mantra, *Om Gong Gana Pataye Namah*, I made it down the first part of the descent. The guide was waiting; he had found a place for lunch that was sheltered from the cold wind. We ate quickly and continued. It was not easy to walk at all. I let out a deep sigh of fatigue and disappointment when the campsite we reached was not ours. Apparently we had another forty minutes to walk.

Still watching the mesmerising 'movie' of mountain faces, I saw the shape of an eagle between two hovering peaks. Its great wings stretched out to either side of the mountains and it had a big face with distinct eyes and a beak. As I continued to descend, the image slowly disappeared behind the mountains. The vision of the eagle allowed me to feel that I was spreading my wings, preparing to take off. Maybe I was learning to fly, to see from a higher perspective. By now I was talking and praying to the mountain deities.

After a while I started to feel tired and it was a challenge to concentrate. When I reflected on the day, things seemed blurry and my 'pressure-cooker' head had manifested a rare headache. The external vibrations were strong and it felt like my whole mind was being rewired. Perhaps the lack of oxygen at high altitude was affecting my body and brain in such a way that it shifted my consciousness. I was certainly seeing with 'new' eyes and could see different perspectives. At the same time, I had started to notice that my lips felt very sore from the open cracks and my nose was running.

For the first time, I lost my motivation to hurry. The guide was once again way ahead and my irritation and 'stuff him' attitude started to arise. I walked up and down one hillside after another, but it seemed like I wasn't getting there. Forty minutes? I wondered if I had missed the campsite, like I had almost done a few times before. Worried, I entered a valley that first expanded and then grew narrower. Then there was another long ascent. At last I could see the guide waiting on the top, in the distance. Finally, after an hour, I too got to the top. I was not happy and neither was the guide. He reacted irritably and said I was walking slowly this afternoon.

'And so what?' I replied. 'That is an even better reason for you to not run ahead.' Agitated, he started to defend himself and I lost the little respect I had left for him. I told him to stop it and take me to the campsite about 20 minutes away. I knew he would not speak to me again until the next day. 'Irritability breeds irritability,' I thought.

Ramjak Campsite (4300 metres/14,107 feet)

The happy, friendly cook and his assistant (who was his brother) greeted me with a hot cup of tea and soup. What a relief, both physically and emotionally! Within minutes I was fine. The tent was already up, in amongst the rocks, close to the steep mountains—as were the tents of the trekking team. We were in a small, enclosed space that reminded me of the final passageway to 'the other side'. The path had become narrower and smaller that day, just like my frame of mind.

I sat outside the tent on a rock and watched the ponies that were grazing by the rushing river. The moving force of water relaxed me and carried my negativity away. There was a stark contrast between the

Day 18

snow-covered peaks and the bare mountains—and I was reminded of the opposites, dualities and complementarities of life.

A round face appeared in a nearby mountainside—that of a young boy wearing distinct expressions of both frustration and curiosity at the same time. Maybe my own frustration was being mirrored to me. On the ridge closest to me I could see a mask that reminded me of the protective deities. It was animal-like and would have been scary if I hadn't known what it represented. Above it, I could again see Ganesha's elephant-head. Next to him there was a man who reminded me of an explorer.

It was getting cold and the sun was going down. After the usual cool and refreshing wash, I thought of my irritation with the guide and wondered why it had been triggered so strongly today. I got organised in my tent and my thoughts turned to my relationship. The sadness I felt seemed to have transformed into loving kindness. I truly wished him well. I also noticed that the visions I'd been seeing were helping subdue the analytical and critical part of my mind.

I went to bed that night feeling embraced by the entire environment, both physically and non-physically. As I was about to fall asleep, words filtered in. I fumbled in the dark for my torch, so I could scribble down what spontaneously came.

Fear me not.

I am the power you possess in the essence of your true nature;

I am the one who sets you free from illusions.

I was exhausted and therefore glad that Mother Nature was brief this time. With a big sigh of relief, I pulled myself back into the sleeping bag. Only my nose was visible, free to breathe the cold, crisp air.

DAY 19
Pallamo Camp
3700 metres/12,139 feet

'**G**ood morning mountain spirits!' I murmured, as I glanced up at the mountains through the opening of my tent zip. I had slept off my headache and runny nose during the night. My sore lips were not so bad either. And, even better, all my insignificant thoughts and emotions had been washed away.

I looked into my new reality. The amazingly deep blue sky made everything seem so clear. Why worry? Everything was perfect. All I had to do was walk. I was aware of thinking: 'So just walk, let it happen and all shall unfold.' What a relief!

I felt ready to move on, physically, mentally and emotionally. With a sense of a new revelation, I could watch my thoughts to catch any worries or projections about what was going to happen and how. By staying in the present moment, I could catch my mind when it started to grasp for thoughts of the past or future. I could bring myself back to the simple now.

The guide came with my morning tea and I knew the quarrel we had had the day before had been forgotten. Still sitting in the tent

Day 19

opening, I sipped my tea and breathed gently. I thought of Ganesha and started to hum the mantra, *Om Gong Gana Patayé Namah*. By just thinking about my impressions of him, which had come alive in the mountains, I could connect with his presence. Obstacles were now fleeting. In a lightning flash, I could see that my path was straight, as long as I followed my own truth. Everything would play itself out, naturally and without force or will, if I let the spontaneous moments of intuitive wisdom guide me.

I finished my tea and stepped outside. Half dressed, I stretched my arms as far as I could. Then I let go and with a deep sigh of relief I let my arms drop. The essence of the air was as fresh and crisp as my thoughts and feelings of vitality and freedom. I quickly dressed and washed. I brushed my teeth by the river and contemplated the mountains.

I realised how, beyond the mundane life that was so easy to get caught in, the visions were showing me that there is greater significance to life. I glanced down into the river. The water reminded me of how quickly the insignificant thoughts and illusions could be washed away. It showed me how fluid my vibration was, how it could change from a lower energy to a higher state of being, very quickly. With this reflection in mind, I returned to my tent and packed my things before breakfast.

Today was the last part of the descent from the high mountain range. The trek was coming to an end. As I slowly ate the smooth, silky porridge, I was aware that I felt both excitement and sadness for the mysterious beauty of life here. Before leaving, I wrote in my journal.

'By walking through nature's sacred landscape and climbing mountains, I have entered into communion with the forces of Mother Nature, who has been guiding me. The immense symbolism projected by the mountains validates my visionary experiences of a divine dimension. Without them, I would not believe its magical and eternal existence. Nor would I understand the natural wisdom of consciousness and the dimensions of my soul.'

We started walking next to the river soon after breakfast. It was still early and cold. The guide kept a reasonable distance, so I continued to mull over my profound experience that morning.

'It really is something greater, and I don't have to worry about anything that happens 'down here' or 'up there' other than being the best I can be and flow with it. I know that the greater 'up there' knows the truth. And what goes on 'down here' is what I sometimes feel as the lower vibration of illusions, wants, jealousy, fear and ignorance. I can see how these structures of the mind also serve a function for me to understand the nature of mind and overcome any obstacles.'

Then the mountain range opening up before me caught my attention. Multiple peaks that seemed like temple pyramids stretched into the sky, just as I had done this morning. I felt reassured by their strength. The constantly changing elements around the river, the mountains, the light and me were all evolutionary symbols of healing and understanding.

At that moment I stumbled on a rock and I was made aware to stay present on the often perilous path. The trail had become narrower and it was now a long way down into the rushing river. Some inner force was indeed looking out for me!

As I continued walking, I reviewed my interaction with the guide. I saw how I could transform my irritation and frustration through forgiveness to find understanding. I saw that the teachings of true love could be as harsh and demanding as the climate and the

Day 19

primitive living conditions in the Himalayas. And at the same time, Mother Nature provided healing in the most challenging times, and even her fierce healing could be gentle and soft.

Still walking, I felt drawn into the lofty peaks hovering in the distance ahead of me. I wanted to pause, but thought: 'Maybe stopping to look will stop me from seeing. I have seen so much—is there more to see? But I must look, just in case.' I smiled as I saw two peaks forming into a large field with a staggering wall around it. Between these two mountains, there was something like an opening, with a stream flowing down.

Then I could see what looked like Jesus engraved into the top of the peak, in the part without snow. In front of him was a flat platform that looked like an altar. Even though he appeared as Jesus, he felt like a prominent older deity with long hair, beard, nose, saggy eyes and ears. The beautiful face held me spellbound. True love flowed through my veins like crystal pure water.

I continued to walk in silence. But it didn't stop. I could see a wall of protective deities with complex masks. There was a large round puma face with clear facial features. I concluded that it was the knowingness and faith I placed in something greater than 'me' that led to seeing the invisible.

Again I almost fell on the rocky path. I spotted the guide in the distance. He was sitting on a stone, waiting for me. When I got there, he said: 'Look up there, I can see something.' 'Great, what does it look like?' I asked. He said it looked like an animal. I gazed up and could see eyes and what looked like the faint face of Ganesha. Next to him was a large male skull. I was happy the guide had started to open up to seeing the invisible.

We walked down the long canyon until we reached the last

point, before starting the final steep descent to the river. The guide kept walking and said he would wait by the bridge.

Just before the last part of the descent, I looked up at the mountains from a different angle, and was astonished. I could see the mountain goddess of Stok Kangri, with her face up in the air and her hands in a prayer position. As I gazed straight ahead, I could see the head of a wolf and the elephant-headed god, Ganesha. They were superimposed on each other. As with Ganesha, I knew the reoccurring visions of the wolf were telling me something. Was I being reminded to keep my spirit alive and trust my instinct and intuition? Just thinking about the wolf, I could feel a supreme confidence and resilience to continue walking the path I was on. I felt protected and blessed as I ventured into the depths of the unknown here in the Himalayan mountains.

Down to Bassi River and Himachal Pradesh

I picked my way around the slippery scree slope, slowly making my way down to the river and the open plateau. Visions that connected me to a higher state of mind were everywhere. I felt I was flying like the soaring eagle, along the path to the Bassi River.

The guide was waiting for me. We were now in the state of Himachal Pradesh and we had to cross a manned pulley bridge to get to the other side of the valley. This was unexpected and not at all easy. As I stepped onto the bridge I started to shake like a leaf. For a moment it was quite impossible for me to cross the hanging bridge. But to reach my goal I had to cross this bridge.

I took a deep breath and told myself: 'In light of fearlessness, I walk through darkness, illuminated by higher consciousness. In the light, I am not afraid of the dark.' The guide walked in front of me and, after two attempts; I finally made it across the moving, swaying bridge. I decided it represented a part of me that was still afraid to let go. Was I still hanging on to something?

The experience of this shakiness was unusual. Perhaps I didn't really want to leave the mountain kingdom. Perhaps I didn't want to enter the wide valley on a rocky dusty trail that would lead to our last campsite, before reaching our final destination—Darcha. Was this land the only place I would be able to know the kind of love I'd been experiencing? My inner voice said: 'Pure love will always suffice. Anything else is an illusion, as with hanging on to the scree slope for the fear of falling into the abyss. The greater nature of love is the truth of surrendering to the state of being—eternal bliss. And it is always available.'

I started to ruminate over how easily I had, in the past, been fooled by the idea of worldly love. Blinded by illusions of what I had thought love was, I had needed to understand and face the seductive parts of the intellect. It was a bit like walking over the bridge and facing the fear inside. By facing the fear of not being loved, I had found true love within myself, and the truth of nature's love around me.

Walking over the hanging bridge with the rushing river beneath, symbolised how I was now able to place my trust in something greater than 'me'—divine love. Yet self-mastery of physical, mental and emotional endurance was part of the path. Walking!

Happily floating along, like the white fluffy clouds, I started singing. 'Who am I? I am love, just being without trying to be. I am free without the shackles of the mind. I am worthy and nurture myself with nature's truth. I am the flowing river. I am the rock solid mountain. I am the living plant that grows between the rocks. I am the naked landscape. I am the colour, I see. I am the purity of the mountain plains. I am the crystal snow. I am earth. I am dust. I am here with every step I take. I am that I am, everywhere.'

Without rushing, we stopped to eat lunch by an old ruin. I found a spot on the short grass and lay flat on my back so I could admire the vibrant blue sky that looked like a big lake of calm water. The warmth of the sun filled me and I sank deeper and deeper into the breathing earth. Before I knew it, I had nodded off.

Pallamo Campsite

After our rest, we continued to walk beside the river on the dusty road. I could hear the sound of water in the riverbed and felt soothed by its music. I got my recorder, always close at hand.

'I walk and continue to move and act in accordance with who I am. And I know that love breaks the shackles of the mind and the illusions of the intellect. And that is perfect, because it is the way it is supposed to be—simply because the intellectual mind is not the truth of divine love.'

My fascination with the kingdom of the gods and goddesses was still with me. The mountain goddess of Stok Kangri appeared on top of the mountain. Ganesha was also there. So was the eagle I had seen yesterday. I also saw a mandala that looked like the sun. It dawned on me that all this must be within me, otherwise how could I see it? It must be a part of who I am.

I reminded myself to just keep walking and more of the mystery would reveal itself. I knew that whatever happened, there was a greater meaning to life that would eventually unfold, if I had

Day 19

enough self-compassion to let it happen. And if I allowed it to just be, 'the way it is'.

I soon started to see road workers. I felt disappointed and noticed that my energy level and mood had started to drop, just as it had when we had reached the halfway mark at Padum. I remembered my profound experience that morning and by listening to the rushing river, I could shift my vibration back to the state I preferred.

I kept walking, and now I saw the image of a big temple and a huge king with open arms. Faces were everywhere. Some turned their heads and looked at me. I felt they were welcoming me home. Then I felt an energy jolt. The mountain goddess of Stok Kangri was now sitting up, like a lion. She kept changing between a woman and a lion. It was bizarre and spooky at the same time. Even though I was startled, I kept walking. The faces continued to look at me.

To my surprise, we reached the Pallamo campsite much earlier than expected. Despite the loveliness of the open grassland, the camp was uncomfortably close to the road workers. I was still in the mountain spirit and walking back into civilisation was happening too fast.

However, with a cup of tea and some biscuits, I settled down with my journal by the shallow stream that flowed right next to my tent. Local women, dressed in colourful clothing, were working in the distant fields. It looked like they were carrying something on their heads. Alongside this, or within it, I continued to observe the divine reality of another dimension. I had expected that it would end when I came down from the higher mountains, but it didn't. Instead it intensified. I could still see faces. And every time I looked away and then returned my gaze, something else was there.

My mystical, intuitive connection to these visions and trancelike experiences was giving me complex, subtle messages. For example, I could only see one eye of the eagle. I wondered if the message was that I was only seeing with my one, inner, third eye. What did the eagle's other eye see? Was it looking into the non-physical worlds? I looked down and wrote in my journal: 'I am invited into nature's magical alchemy. The visions really do show me that there is a greater meaning to life and that everything is transitory. Yet my essence is as real as the flowing stream.'

I continued to write. 'Knowing the answer might be difficult, without some clear sense of anything greater than 'me' or 'I'. And I am aware that, as a human on this earth, I can attach my sense of identity to material wealth and other physical attributes and accumulations. Yet when I am attached to these things, I can close down my awareness and this may even lead to a suppression of what I think of as my 'life force energy'. I believe that this kind of energy—this inner, vital force of passion and electrical energy—requires nurturing, loving kindness and goodness in order to blossom. We literally 'come to life' when the heart opens and the source of purity flows through us. Here we are entwined with nature's own rhythm. Without it, the experience is of a different order or existence, almost. We may feel suddenly a little lost, away from our inner 'home'. We can have a sense of detachment from our true, personal nature and natural sense of being.'

I felt exhausted, and wanted to put down my journal to give myself a break. The whole valley was shimmering in the golden light of dusk. I leaned over to the side, and I could see all the visions, just like in a theatre play. I was intuitively attracted to look at a particular peak, where a small, very cute, baby puma appeared to be playing in the changing light. What was it showing me? The puma symbolised the centre of the

Day 19

self, and of the divine feminine. Was I like that puma, new to this sense of real self and the provision granted by the goddess?

The visions kept changing, like the evolution of consciousness in a multidimensional reality. I felt lifted into an immense open space of light-heartedness, where nothing mattered. All I had to do was to walk in rhythm and harmony with nature.

An Ancient God

Still captivated by the visionary play, I turned to my left, and looked to the other side of the river; the bare, ragged mountain was scattered with short, green grass. A large area covered in white and gold rock formations caught my attention. There he was! A Greek god, or maybe it was Aristotle. I could see many eyes around him; they made me think of disciples. 'Maybe I am one of them,' I pondered. The Greek god seemed to signify the transformation of the self and my absolute connection to the divine.

I made some notes in my journal. 'Mother Nature is my higher consciousness. Nature's reflection is a mirror that projects a message to me. It tells me something fundamental about myself, simply because I am the one who perceives it.'

When I looked up, I noticed that the visions had changed again. Although surprisingly unfazed by all this, I felt tired. I lay down, so I could listen to the sound of water flowing past me. I could hear the soft tones from a Tibetan singing bowl. I observed different thoughts and feelings that came and went peacefully, ebbing and flowing like a tide. I sensed how water holds the secret to flow and harmonious life force energy.

I sat up and hugged my knees. Then, with my elbows on my

knees, I rested my head in the palms of my hands. Absorbed in feelings of tranquillity, I massaged the area between my eyebrows—the third eye—with my index and middle finger in a circular motion. At the same time, I looked over again at the Greek god, and I suddenly knew that my third eye was opening and that by following my intuition, I had been initiated into the mystery of inner vision.

'There is no veil of illusion! It has been lifted,' my awareness told me. Then, I had a separate thought: 'Is it really possible?' And there she was.

> *Obviously. I unveil myself to you…seeing me…feeling me… you can now believe deeply in the heart of your essence—you never have to feel alone again. With your intuitive insight, you can see as though you are looking through someone else's eyes, looking at you. You can observe and sense.*

Mother Nature had spoken. In the same moment, I realised that I needed to wash before it got too cold and dark. As I got up and performed my washing ritual, I mused as to the next application or development of my intuition.

It was all making sense. The third eye is the sixth chakra (the energy wheel between our two physical eyes) and the centre of our intuition. It symbolises seeing with one eye. I could no longer deny my strong, intuitive sense, particularly my foresight. Yet, all along it had been a challenge for me to trust these things and be patient.

I felt excited as if a spark of energy had been ignited within me. I knelt down and kissed the solid earth. Then I moved behind my tent in hopes that no one would see me. I felt a strong desire to dance in honour of Mother Nature's life force that I felt rising within.

In my light clothing, I surrendered to the movement of celebrating

Day 19

what now felt like serpent energy. I was shedding the skin of my past. As I danced, I entered deep inside myself, visualising the mountain goddess in her beautiful, silky dress. I could see the fire of her life force in her eyes. Her essence flowed into my heart and became fully alive within me. I knew as I danced that I had forgotten to live this way for a long time.

Soon, though, I was called for dinner. I shook myself out of my trance by washing my face in the cold river water again. Then I changed into my woollen clothing for the night. My tent was already organised. When I was eating, I thought of Ganesha and all the visions I had seen: the puma, the eagle and the serpent, as well as the lion, the Buddha faces and the Greek god. I acknowledged that the visions were inside the essence of my being.

After dinner and before going to bed I stood outside my tent. The crescent moon gave me a sense of a new beginning. I thought of Mother Nature and felt the presence of her natural intelligence. The guidance I had received day-by-day, step-by-step, was astonishing. Perhaps that was why the earthly trekking guide had so often been unavailable—I was learning to focus on the inner guide.

I moved into the tent and slipped easily into my sleeping bag. To my surprise it seemed more spacious! That night I entered quickly into a dreamy state. But then, just as suddenly, I woke up gasping for air. I re-centred into my connection with the land, my deep self and Mother Nature, and was immediately soothed for the rest of the night.

DAY 20
Darcha
3300 metres/10,827 feet
to Mt. Mulkila
6517 metres/21,381 feet

When I woke, I greeted the sun and felt instantly thrilled—I was free from my mind's usual dialogue! My new reality was occupying the space my old reality normally claimed. Words were humming in my head. 'You are in my breath, breathing through me, you are within everything. I am guided by your spontaneous will of perfection into the land of pure heart.' Mother Nature seemed to have left a footprint inside me from my experience last night.

It seemed hard to believe I was completing the 21-day trek across the Himalayas, and I had experienced so much! I realised I no longer needed to question my soul's will. My inner self—me, really—knew what it was doing! Just thinking about it filled me with a sense of liberation.

As I got ready for the day and had breakfast, it seemed unreal that this could be the last day. Just four more hours of walking ahead of me! I only had to look at my surroundings to be reminded of the visions I had seen—and that made me feel I could relax. The Greek god was still there reflecting my divinity.

I felt fortunate and grateful as I helped pack up the camp. The boys gave me my packed lunch, as usual. We got on the trail that was now more like a dusty road. Within a short time, I was walking alone, through little villages. The outer landscape now reflected civilisation, but I was still inside Mother Nature's temple.

The hovering eagle in the distance gave me the freedom to fly with a new perspective. Ganesha (the elephant-headed Hindu god) blessed me with strength on my path and removed obstacles from my mind. I was grounded in the present moment. An intense feeling of gratitude made me feel that I could just be at peace, in the kingdom of pure love, without any strings of attachments or limitations.

It occurred to me that the hanging bridge I had crossed yesterday symbolised the bridge between the divine kingdom and the mundane world. It was now up to me how I would walk between the two realities. How could the divine and the mundane meld together in harmony so I could embrace both worlds?

It was not clear to me if I would continue to have visions and if they would merge seamlessly with my new 'ordinary life' to come. Just thinking about it concerned me, to be honest. I knew then that I had to let it go and come back to this moment. I noticed I was now walking through a village where they were harvesting potatoes. And it seemed so sweet and real. The simplicity of life spoke to my heart. It made me think of the gifts nature had given me when I grew up on a farm.

I also noticed that I had started the last part of the descent into Darcha. The mountains looked different but I soon realised that it was me—I was different! I started to wonder where the guide had gone. He then appeared out of the blue and showed me a shortcut through some trees, down a slope, into the village. I experienced a flood of vague emotions and thoughts—both of relief and disappointment—as I reached Darcha.

'Is this it?' I thought. My last night of camping and the end of my glorious journey was a dusty place with debris scattered everywhere! I could see tin roof shacks, an ugly road, trucks and cars. There were no signs of Buddhism, no spiritual symbols. Where were the monasteries and houses with colourful, flapping prayer flags? Where was the musky smell of Tibetan incense or the sound of the chanting monks and nuns? By thinking of them, though, I started to hum the *Om Mani Padme Hum* mantra. I could feel my mouth forming into a smile. Again, I was connected to the sacredness of the divine land, even without the external reinforcement.

Darcha, the end point of the trek, reminded me of what the material world is like. Despite its noise and busyness, I was thankful to still be in a remote and desolate place. The mountain peaks of higher consciousness were still with me.

We quickly found the place where the evening's final camp would be. It was on the banks of the river, behind a row of roadside stalls or what looked like tin shacks that sold basic food. In fact, only the stalls separated the campground from the Manali-Leh Highway that would take me to Manali, a large town in the Himalayas and a popular tourist spot for Indians, the following morning. From there I would catch an overnight bus to Dharamsala.

The boys were busy erecting the tents so they had a place to cook and sleep. My tent was still not up. The place didn't excite me so I wandered off and found a spot on the grass among the trees.

DAY 20

I removed my boots and got my lunch pack. I had been lost in thought and had forgotten to eat my lunch.

The rushing river fed into a large plain formed mainly of rocks and sand. Then, my gaze lifted and I noticed the mountain peaks in the distance that reminded me of the big picture beyond what was right in front of me. Mother Nature was still here and she whispered, in the gentle, warm breeze.

Stay open and flexible and be aware of the obstacles—thoughts and emotions, telling you how it has to be. Don't let them cause frustration or hinder you.

I felt like I was watching the streamers of prayer flags, hearing their flapping and snapping. Mother Nature had made herself as real as the sound of those flags, or of the prayer wheels turning. I could now more fully appreciate why the Hindu and Tibetan Buddhist traditions worshipped the earth with such devotion.

I stretched my legs and went over to help the boys who were putting up my tent. For the last time! It didn't take long before it was up and I was organised.

Standing by the River, Watching Mount Mulkila (6517 metres/21,381 feet)

I felt restless and went over to the rippling, fast-moving river. It seemed peaceful and wrathful at the same time. I stood on a large rock and watched the sun shining on Mount Mulkila in the distance. Shadows and a spectrum of colours played across the surface. I whispered: 'There she is. Wow! She is beautiful.'

Engrossed in the tangible experience I was having, I began to see the image of a woman with her hair blowing straight back. She rode a lion and moved forward very quickly. There was a puma with her. I recognised her immediately. It was the mountain goddess of Stok Kangri in Leh, who had unveiled her face and guided me across the Himalayan kingdom into the unknown recesses of my psyche. I knew she represented Mother Nature. She was my companion and inner guide; the one who revealed the mystery of my own divinity, hidden within the power of the *kundalini* energy force.

I realised then how my steady and repetitive walk through the ancient land, imbued as it was with divine energy, had awakened my sleeping life force—my *kundalini*. Singing my mantras also activated this universal energy coiled dormant within me. The energy had risen like a serpent many times on the journey, opening my pathways through the *chakras*. As a result, my internal vision—my third eye—had been stimulated to see beyond what I normally could see with my physical eyes. I had been given a true glimpse of my inner world of being. It was a dimension of my soul that was in many ways new, but also oddly familiar.

For this moment, though, I was absorbed in the snow-capped beauty of Mount Mulkila. The white snow, flowing down the mountainside, reminded me of the silky dress worn by Mother Nature, which I had seen so clearly in my vision the evening before. I took a deep breath and felt the sensation of the soft fabric swishing against my skin. It made me feel warm, even though the mountain was covered with ice and snow. It was the same feeling I had when I drank a hot cup of tea.

The image of this dress, and the sense of Mother Nature's presence, made me want to dance again. But I didn't. Instead, I stood still on the rock, gazing ahead as the presence of the serpent energy flowed through me like the fast-moving river.

All that she offered was what I had longed for; the feeling of unconditional love. Mother Nature felt like something ultimate and perfect. She still does. But this is something I continue to find hard to put into words. How it works is that even when she is in the far distant horizon, on a mountaintop, I can feel, touch, hear and see her; this knowing comes from my heart.

I took another deep breath, and as I listened to the sound of the river right next to me the warm, liquid, tingling sensations continued to rush through me like a current. As the river water spiralled along gracefully, it mirrored my inner fluidity passionately and endlessly. The intensity of the serpent energy got stronger—like a spiritual ecstasy.

'Please enlighten my mind, so I can understand the essence of who you are,' I muttered. I closed my eyes and taking a deep breath felt a wonderful satisfaction as the sensations around filled me with an experience of what is greater than me. Mother Nature started to flow fast, like the enchanting river. She sang a melody that emanated from the mountains.

> *When you admire the mountain spirits, you are looking at me. When you gaze into the blue sky, there is no sky, only me, looking at you. I show you how the faces of nature's reality can unveil the wisdom of higher consciousness.*
>
> *Since you see me in many forms, you will see me everywhere. You know, I am everywhere without; as well as within. I am the new perception of reality you see in the mountains, beyond the physical world, I am your own divinity.*

Soon it started to get cold, so I went to my tent, got my jacket and sat down cross-legged with my feet resting on my thighs—the yoga 'Lotus' position. Mother Nature continued.

> *Believe in me and I am with you. When you move with the secret energy force, you learn to know and understand me deeply. Continue to worship me and I will come to you, in the spirit of nature. I am subtle, without form, and speak the language of spiritual inspiration.*

I closed my eyes and sat with it. Even though the mystical soul of nature has no form, I could at times capture the changing perceptual visions with my internal eye and through my camera. By the direct and immediate experience of this intuitive and sublime connection with Mother Nature, she came alive. As a symbol of primordial energy, she now had a face and a body.

Relaxed and utterly calm, I looked up into the intense sky, and Mother Nature continued to drift into my awareness.

> *If you think you are good enough, then you are worthy.*
> *If you honour your worthiness, you are respected.*
> *If you connect to your true nature, you are a living goddess.*
> *If you lovingly feel the essence of who you are as goddess nature,*
> *then you are worship able as a goddess.*

Without words I could only bow in honour and devotion as I surrendered to the divine will that had taken me to this destination. In that moment Mother Nature's loving, secret energy physically circulated down and up through my body like a loop. I knew that she resides in everyone's true nature. She whispered:

Day 20

Come to me with selfless ness and you shall find shakti (the power of female energy). Come to me without fear, doubt, anger or shame and I shall bless you with 'Shri'—the grace of everything desired by the perfection of your divine will.

Embraced in Mother Nature's loving arms, I was unable to move. The intimacy of the moment melted every cell in my body, as love flowed into my veins from the milky source of higher consciousness. Words came effortlessly from the moment-to-moment awareness of her presence and floated up onto the surface of my mind.

Nurture is a softness that can be felt in hearts of infinite love.

Still on my mat outside my tent, I was lulled into a nap; suddenly, I was jolted awake by the sound of barking, fighting dogs. I felt hungry. As I got up to move around, my body felt soft and flexible, with no aches or pains. The Camino had prepared me for this. And in fact, giggling to myself, I had not only fallen in love with nature, I had also become infatuated with my mountain boots. The freedom to just walk and let everything unfold as my feet carried me was both revealing and healing.

Deep in reflection, I started my usual washing ritual before dinner. I thought of the chuckling smile of the monk I had met at Lamayuru (at the beginning of the 21-day trek). Just thinking about him, I could feel my heart widen into a pool of compassion for myself and others. My mind was empty, and humility washed over me along with a string of mantras. I concluded that there was no end and no beginning to the powerful mystery that had been revealed through the faces of truth looking at me with benevolent eyes from the mountain rocks.

I needed to get some food to ground myself. It occurred to me that I had not seen the guide all afternoon. Yet in a few minutes he magically appeared, as happy as ever. The timing was perfect. 'I have been and had a haircut,' he said.

The cook had prepared a lovely farewell dinner and even managed to make a cake. It was amazing what they did in their portable kitchen. The time had come to say goodbye to the team who had supported me across the Himalayas. The food had been excellent and I was so deeply grateful for their hard work. Also I was thankful that I had not had any health challenges in this land of high altitude. My medicine bag had remained untouched.

Back in my tent I got excited about the six-hour four-wheel drive route to Manali that I would be facing the next day. That in itself was going to be an adventure. But more so, I was thrilled that I was continuing on my own. While the trek had come to an end, I was excited about embracing new possibilities that would emerge from the unknown. I thought: 'I am free to flow and be like the eternal river of life.'

With my remarkable experiences safely tucked inside my heart, I felt serene and slept well that night.

DAY 21
MANALI
2050 METRES/6398 FEET

Like music playing in my ears, I woke up with words impressing my consciousness, beckoning me to sit up. Still half asleep, I found my recorder and Mother Nature started to express herself.

> *My name is Mother Kundalini. I am your divine breath. I am the language of cosmic love.*
>
> *With every experience you learn to trust more and more how I move through you. By connecting with me, you embody the secret energy and we flow together, spontaneously in the sacredness of truth and, in the consciousness of oneness.*

I wanted to cry, but no tears came. Instead, I put down my recorder and chanted *OM*, as I stretched to wake my sleepy body. The humming waves brought words to my mind. 'Nature is my ashram and she is my perfect teacher.' Again, the *OM* filled me with an awareness of being connected to everything. My body danced with joyful tingling sensations. I felt a powerful sensation of being alive.

Still chanting, I opened the tent zip and glanced up at Mount

Mulkila. It immediately struck me that the element of Mother Nature, or *Mother Kundalini*, as she described herself, my teacher and inspiration, was hidden in another dimension. More words came. 'By being true to myself, I go where I am, and find the infinite beauty of creation.'

It was now perfectly clear to me that the deepest mysteries of this ancient land had been revealed to me through the astonishing faces of deities, animals and humans I had seen in the mountains. The often, animated nature of what I had witnessed was like a moving revelation, showing me layer after layer of meaning.

The extraordinary manifestations of Mother Nature's beauty and presence had transformed something within me. I had come home to a special temple, untouched by the material world that was always seeped in serenity and bliss. I could be myself fully here and breathe freely—and I could now feel the earth's heartbeat anywhere. Although there was no incense rising from the rooftops, I could smell the rose fragrance. As I performed my usual morning ritual wash, Mother Nature gently continued.

> *I only become mystical and mysterious when I am separate from you, and when you are not aware of the power that lies within. When you connect to my life force, you interconnect with a matrix of consciousness, opening up to super consciousness, which then becomes your reality. Yet, it is the intuitive part of you that has always been there. When your conscious mind weaves with the unconscious, your true nature is no longer a mystery because you are in a rhythmic dance between the inner and outer worlds of the light and dark. Constantly balancing these energies, you navigate between the male and female*

aspects of your energy without and within—and you experience the freedom and harmony of oneness.

Nature is a reflection of your reality, mirroring what you see. At different times and place, the images and the visionary perceptions change according to the evolution of your consciousness. You are the walking mystery of creation—an art of evolution, reflected by the outer landscape.

With a grateful sigh, I started packing. I could no longer suppress my own spark of divinity. Mother Nature had lifted my veil and she looked like a stunning, powerful mountain goddess. And, it was clear that the awakening of *kundalini* was the real beginning of my spiritual pilgrimage.

'What now?' I wondered. I remembered what Mother Nature had told me before, that there was only one thing to do. Surrender to the will of walking! Just walk! That was it—simple. And, so, walk I will, so that I can go with the flow. Her words echoed in my mind. *Remember me, and I am with you.*

I recognised that by understanding how I was affected and influenced by the energy around me, I had learned to work with and transform my own energy. Just by thinking about the mountain peaks I could shift into a state of higher consciousness from a lower vibration. This discovery truly intrigued me and I wondered how it would manifest in my life.

Suddenly I heard the guide calling, 'Breakfast is ready!' It was still early, but a private driver was picking me up at 8 a.m. to take me to Manali. I needed to hurry. I ate a hearty breakfast quickly, aware that my driver was already waiting. After packing up my tent, I thanked the team and gave them a tip.

Although the pressure was on to get into the car and get going, I paused to look at Mount Mulkila one more time. With my eyes closed and my hands folded before my face, I saw two separate streams of water flowing down the mountainsides until they joined into one big river. I knew the internal scene symbolised the mundane and divine worlds uniting in oneness. I felt gratified and, I was buzzing with what I can only describe as 'being in love'.

With a big smile on my face I waved goodbye to the team. I didn't have to say good-bye to Mother Nature. What I had originally come to get—the secret energy of nature, hidden in this kingdom of gods and goddesses—now came with me.

Just before jumping into the car, I paused, tilted my head backward and looked straight up into the sky. I took a deep breath and opened my mouth wide, just like the roaring-lion rock face. The mighty sky became a chalice that poured infinite light into my mouth. I drank it, just like water.

On my journey forward, I no longer felt alone. And I just kept walking. As I would discover later, the faces hidden in the rocky, snowy mountains spoke to my soul, and became my greatest source of creative inspiration.

Aum Surya
Sun with thousands of rays
Your true love is a mirror of who I am
Reflected by the mountains of deep compassion
I drink the pure water of truth
Embraced by your rays of life force energy

AFTERWORD

That final leg of the journey, the drive to Manali, took seven hours. It was certainly a different kind of day on the road and another enchanting continuation of my adventure. After walking for so long, it was a strange experience to drive in a car. The journey along the narrow, windy road (known as the Leh-to-Manali Highway) was incredible. I still had the reflex reaction of gasping in awe, as one vision after another came alive in those steep and mighty mountains. Fully entertained by nature's beautiful, colourful artwork, its intricacy and complex patterns, shapes and forms, Mother Nature continued to be wherever I was. Now I knew in my heart who she was and what she looked like. Yet, every time I saw, felt, heard and smelled her, I had to surrender to her intuitive intelligence.

We stopped in many places so I could take pictures before we finally descended to Manali in late afternoon. I was dropped off at a place where I could get a room. It was hot and sticky and there were lots of people, so I took the first room I got. Even though I had been looking forward to the luxury of a hot shower, I was happy to at least get a cold bucket shower. In one way I felt great, but I also felt very restless.

I was experiencing mixed emotions of vulnerability and strength. My encounters with Mother Nature and the new divine reality she had revealed made me feel the sheer nakedness of my newfound openness. Yet the mountains made me feel strong like a lion. And now I definitely sensed the atmosphere of India in the air. Instead of monks in red robes, the many streets lined with large buildings and stalls were filled with beautiful women wearing every variety of colourful sari. I no longer needed to watch where I put my feet on a narrow path, but instead, I had to watch for the fast moving rickshaws, bikes and other vehicles. Despite the loud noise, the green trees and wild, playful monkeys jumping around soothed me.

I treated myself to a nurturing massage. It was heavenly to feel at one with my body and complete within myself. Afterwards, I enjoyed exploring different Hindu temples and observing the people and the Indian culture. Even though I had found the real temple of Mother Nature in a cave within the heart of nature, I could still pay my respects to her in the long-standing stone and timber temples around me.

I stayed in Manali for a couple days before catching the night bus to Dharamsala and McLeod Ganj in the state of Himachal Pradesh, where I stayed for another month. That was an adventure of its own that ended with a visit to a Yogini (female meditator) at Rewalsar Lake (West of Mandi, Himachal Pradesh), before returning to Norway.

I told the Yogini about my recurring visions of Ganesha, the Hindu god believed to remove obstacles on the path to success. She looked deeply into my eyes and said:

'When you feel from the depth of your heart that you need a teacher, who can show you the real path—the straight way—then Ganesha will send him to you. Maybe you will meet with this person very easily and your heart will say, 'This is my teacher.' You will know and he will show the path to you. First, you have to trust deeply in your heart. Then you can get there pretty straight, without the need to zigzag; you don't have to go here, there and everywhere.'

I realised in retrospect that my practice of praying and chanting mantras focused and concentrated my attention onto another dimension. My mind was exploring a divine plane of consciousness as I walked across the plains of India. As a result, the spiritual reality that my heart already knew became real. I came to see this as a process of revelation and transformation, a technique that when applied as a consistent practice of reflection, allowed the essential self to be experienced in its purest form. From this, I developed a technique I now call Connect • Focus • Flow™.

It is fair to say that my prolonged and intense period of trekking—beginning with Spain and extending through India—had finished, but the pilgrimage continued. However, at that point I felt that I had found the teacher within. I didn't know exactly what the Yogini meant until a whole year later, when India called me to 'come' once again.

Meanwhile, I travelled to the Andes in Peru and returned to McLeod Ganj, India, for a couple of weeks before I continued on to Rishikesh (in Uttarakhand, also northern India). From there I completed a ten-day trek to Gaumukh, the source of the Ganges, and hiked further beyond to a peak called Topovan. The place where the Ganges rises is a major pilgrimage site, and is also known as 'The Mouth'. I finally reached Varanasi (known as The City of Light) in the state of Uttar Pradesh.

To my surprise, through some mysterious synchronicity, I came across my teacher, Guruji (an Indian master in *kundalini* meditation), on my second night there. This convenient meeting just happened, quite effortlessly, and as a result I lived for a while by the holy river of the Ganges (treated as the Mother of everyone by locals and pilgrims alike). There in Varanasi I practised meditation, mantras and rituals every day for six months, before continuing my journey to Nepal.

There is always more to discover in the never-ending, transitory, outer and inner worlds. One answer leads to another question, just like one step prepares for the next. Mystical and magical experiences have inspired me to look even deeper into the unknown. And so I carry on walking, as the many symbolic reminders so full of ancient faith and wisdom support me. It is a consciousness that comes from such a variety of sources: great masters, gods, goddesses, sacred chants, rituals, teachers, life within the monasteries and last but not least, nature itself.

If someone had told me then what was going to happen two years after I finished the trek across the Himalayas, I would not had believed them. Not in my wildest dreams could I have imagined that the impressions of the divine faces would appear through my fingertips and become alive and visible on canvas before me.

Although I had never painted before, I surrendered to the powerful energy of creative fire that arose within. And as I did, I went on to produce thirty-three paintings in six months. I have now collected them into a book, called *Fire of Creation*, which you can find on my website.

GANESHA

Blessings on Your Journey to Success

Painting by Borghild Bø

APPENDIX 1
Meditative Moments

You and I are made of a bundle of electrical currents called energy vibration. Walk with this vibration, experience it, listen to it, taste it, feel it, and drink it. Move with your life force energy, and Mother Nature will open you to higher wisdom and the intuitive process. Let her show you the way to the infinite possibilities that lie hidden and dormant in your core.

For each of my three journeys, I have created a variety of contemplations, called Meditative Moments. As you read each story, pause and contemplate the Meditative Moments that go with each segment. In Parts 2 and 3, I recommend you do these in order for each day, but you can use your intuition as well and let yourself be drawn to whichever one feels right.

You can repeat the words inwardly or say them out loud. Then connect your inner experience to what's going on in your life. I suggest you take some time to write about your experiences, thoughts and feelings. Journaling can help you become more aware of what your inner knowing is trying to say. Over time, you might also want to write about how your perception is changing and how this is affecting the shape and form of your life.

The Meditative Moments guide you to experience intuitive insight spontaneously, available at any time. They encourage you to practice awareness and stay present in the flow so that you can open more easily to new perspectives and possibilities. These exercises do not require any previous experience with meditation. Willingness to open to the new is the magic of transformation and creativity.

The practice requires patience and should be carried out with simplicity and peace. Just begin and let it unfold.

MEDITATIVE MOMENTS FOR PART 1

(You can do these in any order)

A Pilgrimage on El Camino de Santiago de Compostela

1
In the moment of looking for something, we disconnect, lose our focus and don't find what we are looking for.

Are you looking for something? When we are looking for something we already have a notion or idea of how it should or ought to be, we suffer when we don't find it. We become entrapped by the intellect and we think things are right, real and true. By being attached to things or the world being a certain way, we are in fact seduced by the intellect and the door to our heart is closed.

Say to yourself, either out loud or inside your mind: 'When I think I know, I listen to my intuitive mind and let the wisdom come from the source of the flow. This way, I am in my natural state of mind, and the answers come to me.'

2
In the moment of staying focused, we are present and create the future that is in alignment with the reality of our truth.

Take a moment to notice where your attention is right now. What are you thinking and how do you feel? Ask yourself, 'Where am I?' If you have lost your focus, simply refocus and ask, 'Where do I want to be? What do I want to experience right now?'

Say to yourself, either out loud or inside your mind: 'As I walk and take one step at a time, I become aware of what lifts my energy vibration up or down. What happens to my energy when I think of doing something that does not fulfil me? When I do what feels good, I nurture the core of my being with loving kindness and compassion.'

3
In the moment of acting spontaneously, an immediate experience is carved into our being.

Take a moment to feel and express how grateful you are for being able to see, feel, hear, smell, taste and touch the beauty of who you are reflected by the magnificence of your surroundings, whatever they may be.

Say to yourself, either out loud or inside your mind: 'I am grateful for the truth revealed to me in the moment of awareness. I have faith in my heart and follow my intuitive wisdom that comes spontaneously by just being, when I naturally let it happen and go with the flow.'

4
In the moment of making a decision, clouds lift and we move with the energy of transformation.

Take a moment to acknowledge the truth of your reality. Ask yourself, 'Am I willing to take the path of least resistance and move forward?'

Say to yourself, either out loud or inside your mind: 'When I focus on and visualise what is best for my highest good in this moment, I can make a decision and move forward. I observe my thoughts and notice that my rational mind can take me in all kinds of directions and talk me out of going where I want to go (either mentally, emotionally or physically). In that moment I focus and ask, 'What is best for my highest good, right now?'

5
In the moment of listening to our inner knowing or gut feeling, we open to the unknown that becomes visible to our mind.

Walk, move or sit still, and let nature's reflections open you to the inner fields of awareness—a space where you can just be, watch and explore with detachment what appears on the still lake of consciousness.

Say to yourself, either out loud or inside your mind: 'As a witness to what I see and experience there is no right and wrong other than my own truth of being present in this moment of contemplation.'

6
In the moment of being present we connect to the source of our inner self.

Find a seed of any kind and imagine this as the core of your essence and who you are. What does this seed need in order to grow? How can you take care of this seed so it can reach its ultimate potential?

Say to yourself, either out loud or inside your mind: 'My being is a seed of love and I choose to nurture and honour this seed by saying 'I am love' so it can blossom with joy, beauty and strength. By doing so, I am willing to participate in the creation of my authentic life. I let go of struggle and step into my heart and smell the fragrance of love, freedom and wisdom.'

7
In the moment of accepting who we are, we surrender to our inner knowing and our intuition illuminates the way.

Get an apple. It may be red, green or yellow. Contemplate the apple. What does it tell you? You know when the fruit is ready to be picked. You know when the right moment comes to do what your intuition tells you. TRUST!

Say to yourself, either out loud or inside your mind: 'When I surrender to what is, I accept and let go of attachments to elements of my life that no longer work. Ready to move forward, my mind walks hand in hand with my heart into the sea of courage and determination. With my eyes open, I listen to the melody of water, I see and understand any disillusions. I pray for purification and strength to carry on and that the natural power of intention takes me where my heart wants to go.'

MEDITATIVE MOMENTS FOR PART 2

A Six-Day Journey through the Mountains and Valleys of Leh in Ladakh, Northern India

DAY 1
In the moment of surrendering to what is, we welcome peace into our life.

Take a moment to become aware of the rhythm of your breath. Is it slow, fast or steady? Any time throughout the day, or before going to sleep, relax your body and slowly breathe in and out, without trying to force it. When you rest, put your right hand on your stomach and the left one on your chest. Focus on peace, as you inhale, and then breathe out any tension and stress. Notice how you feel and allow feelings of relaxation, peace and harmony to come to you. Let a beautiful scene in nature be a mirror for calm and tranquillity to flow through your whole being with blissful joy and peace.

Say to yourself, either out loud or inside your mind: 'I practice trust and cultivate peace. I walk in peace, I sit in peace, I eat in peace, I fly in peace, I am peace whenever I choose to be peace. When I trust my inner knowing or intuition, I am breathing peace, always available.'

DAY 2
In the moment of trust we can open up more to the guidance of inner knowing.

Take a moment to contemplate the mystery of inner knowing. Breathe into your stomach and as you feel it rise, let your mind expand beyond the physical reality and into a new realm of possibilities. What is your inner knowing telling you about this? What message is being shown to you? What is that message showing you about your life?

Say to yourself, either out loud or inside your mind: 'When I drift off to sleep I allow myself to be caressed by the light of higher consciousness illuminated by Mother Moon. In the morning, when I wake up, I trust what my inner knowing tells me to do in this moment to follow my heart's desire. I can observe what my reasoning mind may talk me out of.'

DAY 3
In the moment of relaxing and letting go, wisdom rises like transparent mist from within the unconscious.

Tonight, or one evening soon, look up at the moon in the sky and ask:

Who are you?

Who am I?

Where do we come from?

Say to yourself, either out loud or inside your mind: 'When I look into the face of the moon, I let the unconscious rise into the conscious part of my consciousness. By listening with calm, I can receive the knowledge mirrored to me by the moonlight.'

DAY 4
In the moment of self-compassion, we become at one with who we truly are.

In a quiet moment, imagine that you are stepping into the innermost sacred garden in your heart. Inside, the delicate and eloquent flower of life opens up to the sunrays and receives the golden light of self-compassion.

Say to yourself, either out loud or inside your mind: 'Every time I smell the sweet fragrance of a rose in my heart, or any flower—I can feel, touch and look into my pure heart. When I allow myself to be embraced by the loving arms of Mother Nature my heart opens up wider and wider. She is the perfume of love in my heart. At one with my divine essence, I see myself in the colour of the rose. By breathing into this divine essence, I nurture every cell in my body with unconditional love.'

DAY 5
In the moment of clarity, the mind is open and flexible to contemplate the unknown.

Allow yourself to breathe in the silver light and open up your 'inner eye' to see the invisible, unconscious reality of the unknown universe. Let the full moon illuminate the path of truth for you. No mistakes exist in the perfectly imperfect circle of life.

Say to yourself, either out loud or inside your mind: 'Through the act of seeking, my mind opens to see the invisible. In truth, all possibilities lie in what I see beyond the worldly mind of the mundane. With an inner knowing and deep feeling of trust, my mind shines with crystal, luminous clarity. With an awakened heart and mind, I look into the 'eternal eye' of inner knowing'.

DAY 6
In the moment of letting go of what no longer serves us, we suddenly see through the veil of illusion—and watch the view with our luminous 'inner eye'.

First thing in the morning, right now or any time during the day, take a deep breath, stretch your arms up into the blue sky and on your out-breath, let out a big sigh of relief as your arms fall down to the side and you feel relaxed. In this moment, allow yourself to release and let go of what has become a burden and too heavy to carry, so that you can walk lightly into a new reality of being. Breathe naturally and let everything just be the way it is. Smile and relax.

Say to yourself, either out loud or inside your mind: 'I feel safe and protected to let go of anything that I am holding on to that no longer serves me. I choose not to analyse or judge. By thinking of Mother Nature, I release the limitations of my mind. When I let go, I step into my heart's desire with lightness of trust and flow. I am fearless.'

MEDITATIVE MOMENTS FOR PART 3

A 21-Day Journey through the Himalayan Kingdom of Ladakh and Zanskar

DAY 1
In the moment by the riverside we relax and flow with the energy of what is already perfect.

Take a moment to be by the riverside—or imagine a place where you can immerse yourself in a flowing stream of clear water. Simply watch the flow of life—a river of evolution in constant change and motion.

Say to yourself, either out loud or inside your mind: 'Watching the river, I am flowing with the inevitable current of natural intelligence. I drink water to allow my energy system to be cleansed, open and flowing. As I allow myself to relax and slow down, I flow freely and effortlessly like the water to be more of who I truly am. By flowing with nature's rhythm I am in harmony and balance with the power of being present in the moment. In union with the stream of consciousness, I open up more to the subtle messages of nature. When I flow with Mother Nature's energy of truth, she gives me what my heart desires.'

DAY 2
In the moment by the cave, we harness the power of Mother Earth within us.

Find a quiet place and visualise that you are walking up a mountain to a cave.

Whatever that is for you is perfect. When you see or feel the cave you find a comfortable place to sit at the base of the cave or by the opening. Here, sit in stillness and watch the door as it opens up to your higher consciousness. Let yourself be guided into the cave of your heart. Notice what happens and how you feel. Whatever happens is fine. Flow with whatever comes or does not come. Let it be a moment by the cave where you don't think about anything or expect an outcome.

Say to yourself, either out loud or inside your mind: 'I allow my body, mind and spirit to wake up to the sacred energy innate within me. Mother Nature, please take me to higher consciousness.'

DAY 3
In the moment inside the cave we deepen our connection to nature; we can feel the strength of a mountain and get the courage to walk the path of truth.

Make your way up the mountain and find a place inside the cave. Sit in stillness with your eyes closed. As you listen with a deep focus, you may start to hear the movement of a hissing serpent. Allow yourself to feel the sacred energy vibration of the earth coiled within you and move with the energy. Have faith in her, and she will unite you with the essence of your inner self.

Say to yourself, either out loud or inside your mind: 'I move with the secret energy of my inner self, and the sacred fire is ignited.

The essence of my true nature knows exactly where it is going and I trust where it leads me. Wherever I am drawn to go, the deeper understanding of the unconscious reveals insights as conscious awareness.'

DAY 4
In the moment, inside the darkness of the night, we transform in the light of the stars and the moon.

In the stillness and silence of the night, imagine that you sit or lie down under the stars and contemplate the universe. Focus on the point of light and let it come closer and closer to you. Suddenly you are looking at a shining, crystal-white diamond star, right in front of you. When you look closely, it glows in darkness with the essence of your secret energy. Invite the energy of transformation inside you and visualise a white luminous glowing serpent. Imagine that it ignites the spark of your life force energy and activates your higher consciousness. Ask for it to align and balance your mind, body and spirit self.

Say to yourself, either out loud or inside your mind: 'I trust deeply in my heart. I am the light shining like a star in the darkness of the night. I am the universe of consciousness within my body. With the sword of white golden light, I can cut through any illusions and be who I am.

'Please take me to super consciousness. In love and devotion, I surrender to Mother Nature and become whole.'

DAY 5
In the moment of laughter and joy we can enjoy everything we do.

Open your arms. Open your heart. Open every part of your being. Laugh and smile. Let the earth nourish you with her beauty so your vibration can be lifted by a compassionate touch and a warm smile. With every act of loving compassion, nature sends currents of calmness through you.

Say to yourself, either out loud or inside your mind: 'Filled with laughter and joy, I become more and more aware of the beauty around me. As I open up even more to everything around me, my senses are stronger and I can see, touch, hear, smell and feel the amazing energy of nature in the depth of people's being and the astonishing bounty of the earth I step on. It makes me tingle with sensual excitement and aliveness to touch the essence of who I truly am.'

DAY 6
In a moment of breathing consciousness, we can simply be everything we are.

By breathing deeply into your belly, flow with whatever comes without judgment.

Be aware of the worldly mind that may want to talk you out of something because it may seem unreal or illogical. This moment-to-moment awareness will help you to break away from the shackles of the mind so that you no longer imprison yourself with intellectual chains. Free from the mind, you can breathe the sweet fragrance of a divine reality.

Say to yourself, either out loud or inside your mind: 'I take this opportunity to move past any obstacles and ideas of my mind that may think that this is strange. By feeling the power of my secret energy vibration hissing like a snake at the base of my spine, I let myself be embraced by the freedom and happiness of my heart's desire. I allow myself to step into and honour the healing power that lies within me.'

DAY 7
In the moment of purification, we are healed and rejuvenated.

Allow yourself a moment to relax and imagine how the water purifies your whole being. Let the waves of water wash over you and drain away any stress and tension. Impurities can easily dissolve and flow away.

Say to yourself, either out loud or inside your mind: 'I allow the water to wash away any blocked energy and dissolve any judgment or unnecessary worry so I can move forward. I let the water naturally balance and harmonise my mind, body and heart. It energises me and lifts my vibration. When I surrender, I flow more with the energy of who I truly am. With awareness of moving with whatever is—I am present—and I move with the fast rushing water of how it is right now, until it becomes calm and still.'

DAY 8
In the moment inside the protective womb of Mother Nature we surrender to nature's power of healing love.

Choose a day when you are relaxed. As you drift in and out of sleep, imagine that you are held in the safe warm womb of Mother Nature. At the same time, visualise yourself surrounded by the presence of protection. Ask Mother Nature to heal you and give you exactly what you need in this present moment. Let whatever arises flow through you. Trust her!

To do this, you may not be aware of what this means in the present moment. By allowing yourself to do this without expectations or judgment you open up to the unknown that will reveal itself to you when you connect to the secret energy of nature. In this spaciousness, you can let the subtle energy vibration of nature's intelligence come to you with transformative power. Remember that it will naturally unfold without trying to find 'it' or forcing 'it' through the means of the intellectual, reasoning mind.

Say to yourself, either out loud or inside your mind: 'I open the door to my soul and allow myself to surrender to the energy vibration. As I do, I reconnect with Mother Nature. Through letting this happen, nature's intelligence reveals itself and activates the vitality of my life force energy.'

DAY 9
In the moment of looking into the clear blue sky, we open up to visions of infinite self and perceive the invisible.

Find a comfortable place to sit and look into the intensely blue sky. Close your eyes and look into the open spacious vastness. Breathe in the vibrant blue sky and let the universe open up within you. Let it fill your heart with infinite possibilities. Taste the drops of potent nectar on your tongue and let them slowly and gently stimulate your divine imagination and intelligence.

Say to yourself, either out loud or inside your mind: 'When I focus and breathe the fullness of air a new level of perception awakens and I connect with infinity. I invite the unknown into my life and fill my lungs with infinite bliss—to be more of who I am.'

DAY 10
In the moment of unconditional love flowing through us, we experience the essence of our life force energy.

Let the thousand sunrays fill your heart with a warm glow of playful innocence. Allow the energy to come inside of you. And the more you get inside the energy, feeling it, seeing it, working with it—the more it shifts and the more you flow with the motion and fluidity by just being in a natural state of calm.

Say to yourself, either out loud or inside your mind: 'When I look into the eyes of my soul essence, I see the eloquence and beauty reflected by the nature of who I am. I experience the sensation of unconditional love flowing gently through me. Filled with peace and blissful joy, the flame of life is the mystery force smiling with the truth of natural intelligence. Immersed in the conscious light of the sun, I walk in lightness, as I let the innocence of wisdom and love illuminate the way.'

DAY 11
In the moment of complete rhythm and harmony with nature, we connect to the presence of being.

I invite you to set aside some time to physically take a walk in a nearby forest, lake, park or mountain to harness the power of nature. Or you can imagine taking a walk. Either way, relax and gently breathe. Allow the elements of the earth you step on to harmonise the light and dark aspects of your being with visions of colours and electrical currents of divine energy flowing through you.

Say to yourself, either out loud or inside your mind: 'By walking, I constantly change in rhythm with nature. As I keep on walking and trust each step of inner knowing, forever in motion, faith leads the way.'

DAY 12
In the moment of silence, we rest in the seat of spaciousness and discover our natural state of mind and way of just being.

Take a moment to come into the awareness of sitting in silence. Light a candle and focus on the flame. Or find a picture of a tranquil scene in nature or anything that soothes you. Focus on the flame or the picture for a minute or two and allow yourself to retreat to a quiet place within. Repeat silently: 'Love, wisdom, light.' Notice what happens and stay open for any reflections that appear. If you are expecting anything in particular to happen or if you are trying to force it, nothing is likely to happen, until you let go. Don't think about it. Let the innate intelligence of your mind, body and spirit naturally reveal itself to you.

Say to yourself, either out loud or inside your mind: 'Nature is a reflection of who I am.'

DAY 13
In the moment of just being, our body rests like a mountain and our mind is calm like a lake of awareness.

Meditate or pray, in your own natural way, to Mother Nature for clarity and discernment, to be content in your body and to fully accept any thoughts and emotions. By feeling safe and secure, allow any outer masks of illusion to dissolve. With a blanket of protection and permission to be yourself, feel the freedom to be fully in your body, connected to your breath and earth and at the same time dance with the flowing essence of who you are.

Say to yourself, either out loud or inside your mind: 'Without waiting for something to happen, doubting it will happen, or expecting anything to happen in a particular way, I can see and feel the essence of who I am, beyond the veil of the intellectual mind. When I live in harmony with my inner self, I am free to flow with playfulness and innocence between the inner self and the outer world.'

DAY 14
In the moment of surrendering to nature, we empty the mind and become at one with our own true nature and everything around us.

Take a moment to imagine what Mother Nature looks like to you. Without trying to see what you think she looks like or not, allow her to spontaneously reveal herself as you breathe and walk in harmony with the rhythm of nature. Look at the mountains, water, fire, air, sky and ether as Mother Nature. Then she will reveal herself in subtle forms in your 'eternal eye'. She gives you glimpses of signs and clues and teaches you to trust your inner knowing.

Say to yourself, either out loud or inside your mind: 'Nature is the source of manifestation; nature without connects me to the essence of true nature within the source of my being. True nature is what I see beyond my mundane eyes. By looking into my internal cosmic eye, I can see the reality of true nature.'

DAY 15
In a moment of chanting *Om Mani Padme Hum,* our mind calms, and we awaken and open to higher wisdom and compassion for self and others.

Sit in a comfortable place. Rest your hands on you lap or hold the palms together against your chest. Gently close your eyes and focus on breathing in and out. Then, as you breathe out say the mantra below silently to yourself or out loud. Recite this any time, as often as you like in your daily life. Trust the wisdom given to you in ways beyond what you may expect.

Say to yourself, either out loud or inside your mind: '*Om Mani Padme Hum.* I breathe the air of compassion and discover the world of truth. I let it guide me into the light of faith and trust.'

Say each syllable slowly and feel the action it catalyses.

Om (purifies ignorance);

Ma (purifies anger);

Ni (purifies the miser);

Ped (purifies attachment);

Me (illuminates hatred);

Hung (purifies arrogance).

DAY 16
In the moment of relaxation, we find inner peace and experience the natural spark of unconditional love.

Take a deep breath and rest within yourself. Feel what it would be like to nurture yourself with unconditional self-love, and for your soul worthiness to be honoured for who you truly are.

Say to yourself, either out loud or inside your mind: 'By loving myself with peace, joy and truth, I nurture the essence of my true nature in every moment that I open to the presence of Mother Nature. Presence is my guide in the moment.'

DAY 17
In the moment of chanting *Om Gong Gana Pataye Namah*, we remove obstacles from the mind and we are blessed with success in our practice and all undertakings on our path to be all that we are.

Create a moment to sit in silence. Focus on an obstacle that you would like to let go of. At the same time bring your attention to the point of white light and let any worry or tension dissolve in the luminous light. Allow yourself to merge and become at one with the light. Let the feeling of fearlessness grant you the freedom to act in harmony with your inner self.

Close your eyes and breathe your body into the presence of total relaxation and awareness. As you breathe in and out, chant internally or out loud—*Om Gong Gana Pataye Namah*—on your out-breath. You can do this any time, for a short time or as long as you like.

Say to yourself, either out loud or inside your mind: 'I am free from all distractions. I am willing to overcome any obstacles so I can move along the path with success and integrity.'

DAY 18
In the moment of breathing the essence of air, obstacles dissolve as we gaze into the infinite sky and become at one with all that is.

Look up into the spacious blue sky and feel how it expands your mind and fills your heart with purity and freshness. Let the clear, fresh air awaken you. Ask Mother Nature to grant you the wisdom to honour and respect your own inner darkness, with forgiveness and self-compassion. Watch the shadow side of nature evaporate as you open up to a new reality, beyond the rational mind.

Say to yourself, either out loud or inside your mind: 'In the silence of the night, I sink deep down into the solid earth. I am surrounded by protection and safety to face reality the way it is. Beyond the polluted clouds of the mind, beyond the two eyes of the worldly mind, I go beyond, into the blue sky of awareness. I surrender and enter the internal eye (the third eye) and the realm of pure consciousness opens up. Here, I find comfort in the infinite light of the moon energy that illuminates the unconscious world, stimulates my intuition and lifts the silky veil.'

DAY 19
In the moment of watching the mountains in the horizon, we open our arms and invite freedom into our life, to walk forward.

Take a moment to do something different. Nature is our greatest source of energy. Smell, taste, feel, and touch its beauty and magic, and see and hear the wonder of it. By opening yourself to the elements of the earth, water, fire, air and ether, sensations of aliveness and vitality can awaken within you and expand your vision. As the veil lifts from your eyes, you can start to see beyond the world of limitations and into the unknown land of inner knowing.

Say to yourself, either out loud or inside your mind: 'As new levels of perception awaken, my consciousness expands. I can watch the visions of new horizons. I open my arms to welcome freedom to surface within my open heart and flexible mind. The stream of harmony flows into my life. I soar like an eagle.'

DAY 20
**In the moment of connecting to Mother Nature,
we awaken and ignite the fire of life force energy within.**

With an open heart and mind, take a moment to feel that you are connected with Mother Nature on a deeper level. Allow your mind to merge with the essence of your true nature and receive what is best for your highest good, right now. Let your heart be filled with rainbow-coloured light. Smell the perfumed roses of love, dance and celebrate, knowing that everything is better than you could ever imagine.

Say to yourself, either out loud or inside your mind: 'I breathe peace into my body. I breathe silence into my mind. I breathe love into my heart. I receive the energy of nature's elements, colours and light. I walk in confidence and my thoughts, beliefs, emotions and actions greatly enhance my miraculous life.'

DAY 21
**In the moment of chanting—OM—our mind is free from
chatter and we allow ourselves to surrender to the
cosmic sound of universal consciousness.**

Chanting opens the mind to higher wisdom. It helps to maintain presence and awareness so you can understand your mind and feel the essence of who you are more easily. Take a moment to relax and focus on breathing in and out. Concentrate on the space between your eyebrows and let your mind be calm. When you are ready, with your mouth closed, take a deep breath in, fill your lungs and then recite *OM* internally or out loud on the long out-breath. When you say it out loud, on your out-breath, slightly open your mouth and let it form an 'O' as you feel the vibration of the *OM* sound on your lips.

After a short time, gently close your mouth and let the sound vibrate down your throat and into your heart. Feel and listen to the pulsating sound waves as they fill every cell of your body, mind and heart with the vibration of creation, until it naturally fades. Focus on the vibration of *OM* in your heart, carry it with you and repeat *OM* with the feeling that you are infinite, all-pervading, free, eternal and perfect. Feel that you are absolute consciousness. You can repeat this three times, or as many times you like. But one time is enough.

Say to yourself, either out loud or inside your mind: 'I accept the precious worthiness of my soul, shining like a sparkling diamond star. I am the flame of life force energy smiling with truth of what is. I am love made visible. I allow myself to step into the beauty of my true nature. I am grateful for who I am in the arms of Mother Nature. By remembering who I am, I explore the world without and discover who I am within—and let the wind of faith carry me forth into the light of pure awareness.'

APPENDIX 2
Glossary

Chakras — subtle energy centres in the body and energy body.

Chang — a traditional butter tea made by churning butter in a long wooden churn, with milk, tea and salt.

Chapatti — a flat round bread originating in northern India, made of wheat flour, water and salt.

Ganesha — the elephant-headed Hindu god, believed to remove obstacles and give blessings on a path to success.

Gompa — the Tibetan name for a monastery, a solitary place of retreat for peace and constructive reflection.

Ghanta (handbell) and *vajra* (known as thunderbolt, symbolising the absolute) — essential objects of wisdom and compassion used together in prayers and rituals of worship to uphold harmony.

Japa — a Sanskrit name used for the practice of reciting mantras using a *mala*.

Karma — a philosophy in which every act of body, mind and speech has a cause and effect. It is believed that by doing a good deed or engaging in a spiritual practice such as walking the *kora* and repeating prayers, one can purify past life misdeeds and earn merits to live a good life in the future—or be reborn into higher realms—which leads to ultimate liberation from attachments and ignorance.

Khata — a white or cream silk scarf used for offering and blessings.

Knights Templar — an order of knights founded in southern France around 1118 to protect pilgrims in the Holy Land during the second Crusade. The order was disbanded in the early 14th century.

Kora — to move in circumambulation, clockwise around any sacred monument, deity image or temple to accrue spiritual merit (*karma*) for others and ourselves.

Kundalini — the Sanskrit name for the innate life force energy believed to be dormant and coiled at the base of the spine, like a serpent. When the subtle energy system of the mind, body and spirit is in harmony, *kundalini* can awaken and rise up the spine, resulting in the state of *yoga,* or divine union with higher consciousness and enlightenment, or *nirvana.*

Lama —a respected monk or spiritual teacher.

Mala — a string of 108 prayer beads, in a necklace, commonly used by Hindus and Buddhists to focus attention on the meaning and sound of a mantra while chanting the names of a particular deity or prayer. The beads are made from different seeds, including those of the rudraksha tree or lotus plant, the wood of the tulsi plant, animal bone, or different gems and crystals. The seeds are used for different traditions. For example, devotees of Shiva use a rudraksha *mala*.

Mani wall — a row of stone plates, slabs or rocks inscribed with Sanskrit texts of mantras or other holy images. They are typically carved with the six-syllable mantra *Om Mani Padme Hum*.

Nirvana — liberated from the limitations of the mind, *nirvana* is a natural and blissful state of mind (associated with ultimate stillness and peace).

Om Mani Padme Hum — a six-syllable mantra associated with the four-armed deity *Avalokiteshwara*. It is a practice of wisdom and method used to transform and purify one's impure body, speech and mind, and especially pride.

OM — a significant Hindu symbol and a mantra for universal consciousness believed to be the sacred vibrational sound of the absolute source of all existence.

Perak — a woman's traditional headdress worn for special occasions such as rituals, weddings and festivals.

Puja — a ritual of prayer, worship and offerings conducted by a *lama*.

Shakti — the Sanskrit name for the power of female energy.

Shrine — a Tibetan name for a temple dedicated to or dominated by a particular deity or deities.

Stupa (also called *chorten* in the Tibetan language) — a spiritual monument to symbolically help support devotees with their spiritual practice and in the making of offerings to become liberated from suffering. Some are more elaborate than others and can signify different ideas.

Thangka — Tibetan painting on cotton or silk, usually depicting a Buddhist deity, famous scene or mandala.

Third eye — the sixth chakra; the energy wheel between and just above our two physical eyes; the centre of intuition.

Yoga — physical, mental and spiritual practices to transform the body and mind; and harness the ability to direct the mind without distraction or interruption. The ultimate goal of yoga is to achieve liberation from the mind and attain a divine union with consciousness of higher self (enlightenment, or *nirvana).*

Yogi — a male practitioner adept at meditative yoga.

Yogini — a female practitioner adept at meditative yoga.

APPENDIX 3
Maps

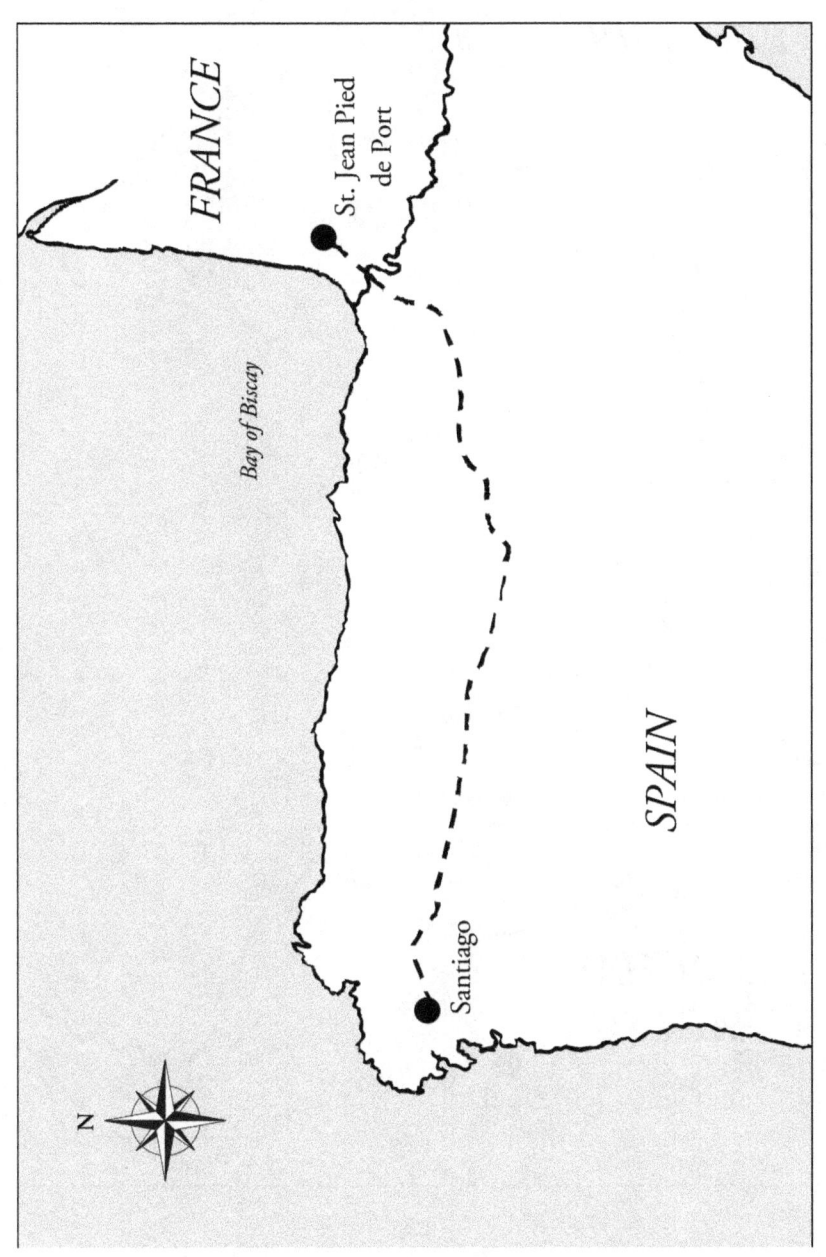

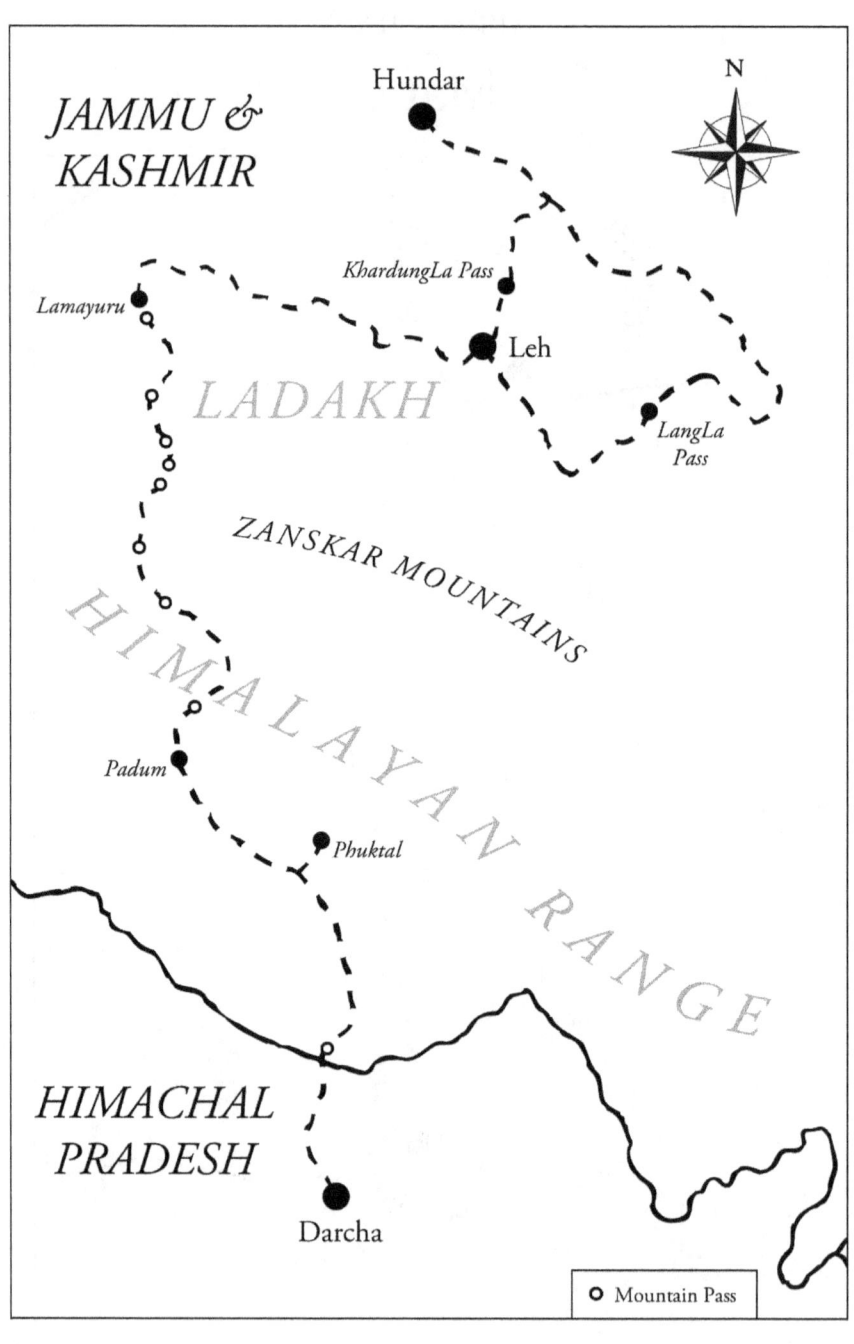

ABOUT THE AUTHOR

Borghild Bø is a clinical psychologist and life adventurer, who over the past twenty-five years has been deeply immersed in the inner workings of the mind and heart, both professionally and personally.

As a psychologist who specialises in stress, trauma, and critical crisis intervention, Borghild Bø helps people transform and create what they want in life. She combines the philosophies and practices of East and West with her intuitive, experiential approach to facilitating self-awareness.

Based in Bergen, Norway, Borghild consults for individuals and organisations and is in demand internationally as a workshop speaker, leader and facilitator.

OTHER BOOKS AND OFFERINGS FROM BORGHILD BØ

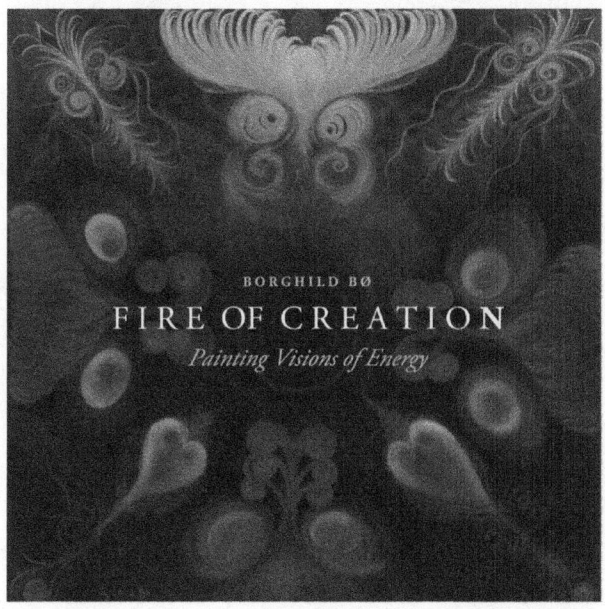

Fire of Creation: Painting Visions of Energy

Fire of Creation includes 24 large images of Borghild's visionary paintings, catalysed by her mystical opening during the pilgrimages described in *Walking Into It*. The book is available at www.borghildbo.com.

The Voice of Nature is a downloadable recording with four tracks. Borghild recorded this when she spontaneously connected with her inner voice. The voice speaks to the soul and offers inspiration to connect more deeply with nature. By listening to our inner knowing, we can find more peace and be more of who we truly are in a state of natural flow.

SACRED JOURNEYS WITH BORGHILD BØ

The story shared in this book is from the first of my many pilgrimages to various countries and sacred sites around the world. As I continue to travel, I discover new knowledge and connect more and more deeply to Mother Nature's secrets, wisdom, and intuitive mystery.

To fully appreciate and take in the boundlessness of nature's beauty and mystical land, you must have your own unique experience. Only then, with heightened awareness and consciousness, can you find what you are searching for—or what you need—within.

You may not consciously know what you're looking for, but I am convinced that your soul knows, and knows how to reveal it to you. As you heed the call and go where your inner knowing beckons, the enchanted land gives you exactly what you need. Ultimately, the mysteries of Mother Nature awaken latent energy and welcome you to a new reality.

The impact of my journey across the Himalayas changed my life in a positive and profound way. Are the wonders of the great mountains beckoning you? Are you ready to go on a sacred journey to the heart of nature? If so, a pilgrimage can connect you to your deepest self, and you can return a changed person.

I take women on remarkable journeys to sacred sites and retreats in Norway and around the world. I combine the philosophies of the East and West with a practical and experiential approach to learning and healing—what I call the Connect • Focus • Flow™ self-awareness practice.

When you walk with me, I guide you on an inward journey to gain a better understanding of yourself through focused awareness. You learn to connect more deeply with nature and fully experience your own unique energy and the power that resides in the present moment. This opens you to new perspectives and possibilities. It allows you the freedom and joy to flow with a life of vitality that resonates with what you truly want to create.

I wish you an auspicious journey to the heart of true nature!

For photographs of the adventure in this book—and other pilgrimages—to contact me or see where I am journeying next, please visit: **www.borghildbo.com**

SPEAKING, TEACHING, COUNSELLING AND CONSULTING

Borghild is passionate about helping others transform and connect more deeply with who they truly are (and with the world) through focused self-awareness. This allows people accelerated clarity, confidence and freedom to create the experience they want from life. You can work with her individually or in groups.

Learn more about the principles of meditation and the Connect • Focus • Flow™ self-awareness practice that Borghild developed based on her intuitive and mystical experience combined with her psychological training. This is an experiential and practical approach to transformation.

Borghild speaks and teaches worldwide on a range of topics, including stress as positive productivity. She teaches how to be more present in the moment to create focus, and how to listen to and trust our 'gut feeling' to experience vitality and flow. With her solution-oriented approach and methods, she inspires and empowers others to be their own heroine/hero, step into any situation, and create a fulfilling life that energises them.

www.ingramcontent.com/pod-product-compliance
Lightning Source LLC
Chambersburg PA
CBHW022104150426
43195CB00008B/266